Raves for Bob Dancer and
Million Dollar Video Poker

"Bob Dancer makes me sick. Here I am, telling everyone they have to scout the casinos, trick the floormen, and endlessly badger bosses and hosts for comps, and all he does is show up and play a lousy machine and he's outcomped me three years running. Dancer talks the talk and walks the walk and now anyone who plays video poker can walk with him—right to the bank."

> **—Max Rubin, author of** *Comp City: A Guide to Free Casino Vacations*

"Bob has written a book that every video poker player will love. It's not only a close-up look at the daily life of a working video poker pro, but also as close as most of us will ever get to the big leagues of video poker play. Bob Dancer is a pat hand, a one-of-a-kind whose book pays off 100%."

> **—Skip Hughes, publisher of** *Video Poker Player* **and host of www.vphomepage. com**

"A surprisingly candid look at the ups and downs, successes and failures, of a professional video poker player. Bob reveals both the mistakes he made and the mistakes the casinos made."

> **—John Robison, author of** *The Slot Expert's Guide to Playing Slots*

"A fascinating glimpse into the high-roller video poker world, with useful information even a low-roller can use."

> **—Jean Scott, author of** *The Frugal Gambler* **and** *More Frugal Gambling*

> *more ...*

"While primarily informative, this is a fun read. It's easy to see why our readers voted Dancer 'Favorite Gaming Personality' for both 2001 and 2002. "

—**Glenn Fine, publisher,** *Casino Player* **magazine**

"If genius is where inspiration meets perspiration, Bob Dancer is a video poker genius. His million-dollar saga is not so much one of luck as of recognizing opportunity and working hard to take advantage."

—**John Grochowski, gambling columnist,** *Chicago Sun-Times*

"An intriguing behind-the-scenes look at the life of a professional gambler. From the lows of hustling $2 coupons to the highs of hitting a $400,000 royal flush, Dancer reveals what it took to make him the winningest video poker player in the world."

—**Steve Bourie, author of** *American Casino Guide*

"Bob Dancer's adventures of an 'edge-hunter' make for fascinating reading. His observations are right on target. Peppered with profiles of characters, filled with advice and anecdotes about what every player seeks—how to get the money."

—**Howard Schwartz, Gambler's Book Shop**

"It's exciting to read about someone winning six-figure jackpots. It's exciting to read about the huge ups and downs along the way and the emotional reactions of the player whose money is being won or lost. Bob Dancer, a video poker pro, shares all this, and more, in his book *Million Dollar Video Poker*."

—**Stanford Wong, author of** *Professional Video Poker*

Million Dollar Video Poker

Million Dollar Video Poker

Bob Dancer

HUNTINGTON PRESS
LAS VEGAS, NEVADA

Million Dollar Video Poker

Published by
Huntington Press
3665 South Procyon Avenue
Las Vegas, Nevada 89103
telephone: (702) 252-0655
facsimile: (702) 252-0675
email: books@huntingtonpress.com

ISBN: 0-929712-11-0

Print History: December 2002, December 2003, November 2006

Cover design by: Laurie Shaw
Cover photo by: Jeff Scheid
Interior design & production: Laurie Shaw

Special thanks to Mike Fields and IGT.

This book is dedicated to everyone who has ever tried to beat a casino and didn't know how. Today the knowledge is readily available, but it's not easy to apply. How badly do you want to win?

Acknowledgments

Any mistakes found in this work are the fault of others. The fact that so much good solid information appears here is testament to how I have persevered in the face of great odds.

I'm pleased to announce that by including the previous paragraph I've just won a sizable bet. Now that that's taken care of, let me retract those two sentences and start over again.

This book is about success over a seven-year period of time. To a large degree, the associations I've made since 1994 have allowed my skills and success to blossom. I want to mention the most important of these people, each of whom you'll read more about later.

Jeffrey Compton is my friend and business partner. He's invested in my success in a way few people would. Jeffrey works 50 hours or so on our business every week. I work 30 hours or so writing and consulting and another 30 hours or so gambling. And we split the proceeds of the business fifty-fifty. I *like* this arrangement. Jeffrey realized that I needed to spend a large amount of time playing in casinos to give me the experience and depth to continually write about what I do. Jeffrey will earn as much from this book as I will, which is perfectly fine with me. I'm delighted to be able to reward the faith he's shown in my abilities.

Liam W. Daily is the smartest man I know, and he's interested in a variety of things. When he applies his efforts to video poker, we all benefit. Liam and I have co-authored strategy cards and *Winner's Guides*, with him producing the majority of the breakthrough discoveries. These products put learning the intricacies of video poker within the grasp of a large number of people. In addition to the work we've published jointly, he has peppered me with dozens of valuable suggestions about subjects to write about or ways to look at particular things. An indispensable key to gambling success is the mastery of the underlying game. For me to be able to share with others what I know, I needed to learn it first myself. Liam has been extremely generous with his insights.

Dean Zamzow is an extremely gifted computer programmer and the man behind *Bob Dancer Presents WinPoker*. Being the spokesman for the best computer trainer on the market has its financial advantages, to be sure, but more than that the program itself is a critical everyday tool for me. My success, as a player and as a writer, would be significantly less were it not for this program.

Anthony Curtis is a publisher who has collected within Huntington Press a formidable stable of gambling writers—including Jeffrey Compton, Max Rubin, Jean Scott, Michael Shackleford, Olaf Vancura, and many others—and he has allowed me to be the "video poker guy" in this sterling collection. There are big advantages to being a writer at a company that understands the genre and is committed to having its writers succeed. My closest associations at Huntington Press have been with Deke Castleman, Len Cipkins, and Bethany Coffey, but there have been many others as well—even occasionally some whose last names don't begin with the letter "C."

And, most importantly, there's my wife Shirley, who organizes my life so I can go do my thing. Allowing me to write about her and her "imperfections" demonstrates a huge degree of trust and love. You'll meet her as you go through the book, and you'll soon know why she's my favorite Dancer.

Table of Contents

Part One

The Ins and Outs
of Video Poker

Gamblers are always dreaming about hitting it big. My version of that dream came true during a six-month period between September 2000 and March 2001. It was that to-die-for time where all lights are green, chocolate doesn't have calories, and there are never lines at the supermarket.

It was a wonderful six months, but the real story is how I got ready for that period. Seven years earlier I had a very small bankroll and knew nothing about video poker. This book is about the seven-year journey to achieve the six-month dream come true.

The Easy Part of Video Poker

What's hard and what's easy is a matter of perspective. For example, if you ask Los Angeles Laker star Shaquille O'Neal whether it's hard or easy to dunk a basketball, his answer would be different from mine. For me, there was a brief period 40 years ago when I could jump high enough to touch the basketball rim, but I could never get any higher. Shaq can dunk the ball flat-footed.

Even with such an obvious comparison, some people will take issue with the proposition I am about to advance.

From my perspective, the easy part about playing successful video poker is learning to play the hands essentially perfectly. Knowing enough to distinguish in 9/6 Jacks or Better between K♠J♥T♥7♠5♣ and K♠J♥T♥6♠5♥ is the easy part of the game.

And I say this knowing full well that probably 95% of all players play these two hands identically, even though JT is the proper play in the first case and KJ is the proper play in the second.

So how can that be the easy part if so few people can do it? Because the information on how to play video poker without error is widely available, and computer programs will correct you whenever you're wrong, so most people willing to put in the hours can learn this game perfectly. It may take you 10 hours, 100 hours, or 1,000 hours, but it can be done. The reason why most people don't play that hand correctly is because they simply haven't put in those hours—or they *have* put them in, but they studied material from authors who do not believe that the difference between these hands is important. For whatever reason, these players don't see the value of learning the game perfectly. The players who really want to succeed, however, do the work that has to be done. For them, these hands, and most others as well, are not particularly difficult.

So if that's the easy part of the game, what's the hard part? Let me suggest some of the things that are difficult.

The Hard Part of Video Poker

Sometimes while playing quarter video poker, you'll lose $500 a day for three days straight. Or when playing for dollars, you'll lose $2,000 a day for three days straight. How does that affect your well being? And if you're married, how do you convince your wife that it's just a normal swing of the game and that she doesn't have to worry about it?

Some people are always in debt. These people, for whatever reason, can't get a bankroll to gamble with. And even if they somehow did, they couldn't hang onto it. Are you one of these people?

A casino is full of distractions. Every casino has an advantage on perhaps 99% of all bets available. Do you have the discipline to limit yourself completely to the remaining 1%?

The casino will ply you with free booze served by attractive provocatively dressed young ladies. The casino doesn't care whether it's the liquor or the ladies that ruins your concentration. Either way you fail is fine with them. Can you run that gauntlet and still concentrate on the game?

The casinos hire talented marketing people who dream up incentives for you to come and visit. Some incentives are extremely valuable and some are not. Can you distinguish between them?

On those rare nights when you win win win, can you keep your perspective and not go out and blow it? On those not-so-rare nights when you lose lose lose, can you deal with the actual loss of your bankroll, plus that ugly sickening feeling too? When it takes three years to build a bankroll and you lose half of it in a week, can you still function?

Playing in smoky casinos, sitting under air-conditioning vents on uncomfortable stools, and using the same muscles over and over and over again lead to a variety of ailments. Eating free food in a casino night after night has caused many of us to gain far more weight than is desirable. But to play the game you have to survive all of this. Can you?

Is it a problem when people look down on you, because they feel that being a gambler is an unproductive way to lead a life? And if you become real good, can you keep that fact a secret from the casinos so you can continue to play?

If you believe that telling the truth is always the best policy, then you probably don't have sufficient guile to succeed at this sport. Things are not always black and white here. Sometimes the pressures to push the envelope are enormous. The low road is sometimes more lucrative than the high road, but the risks are enormous if you don't succeed. Do you look good in stripes?

Can you deal with the repetition? Video poker is a very boring game when you play it 40 hours a week. Playing perfectly at home for 10 minutes at a time is a lot different from playing hour after hour after hour in a casino. Jeffrey Compton, my friend and business partner, has learned Jacks or Better perfectly and can play it well for an hour or two at a time. But if he has to sit at a machine for longer than that, he starts to make a large number of errors. So even though he has learned the game perfectly, he's unlikely ever to become a successful professional player.

Slot clubs provide lots of benefits to players. The most successful players study these slot clubs two ways from Tuesday until they know exactly how to extract the most from them. Can you do this?

The game is getting more difficult. When I started my video poker career in 1994, players told me about the "good old days" five years earlier when full-pay dollar Deuces Wild could be found all over town. Today, the games are not nearly as lucrative as they were when I started. It's reasonable to assume that in two years there will be fewer profitable opportunities yet. Can you keep current enough to stay ahead of the game?

You get my point. Mastering the correct way to play the hands just gets you to first base. This is absolutely necessary for success, but you still have a lot of work to do once you reach that point. Playing the hands is definitely a worthy subject for a book on video poker; indeed, the *Winner's Guide* series that I've co-written with Liam W. Daily deals with this subject, but this book doesn't.

Thousands of people have reached first base in video poker, but haven't done so well after getting there. This book briefly describes how I did it, but mostly dwells on how I hit subsequent doubles and triples, then finally my million-dollar home run.

Many of the specifics I write about here are one-of-a-kind and probably won't come around again in exactly the same way. But the same *types* of choices will arise and the tools I used to deal with them in the past will be the same ones I'll use in the future. Whether these are useful tools for you to use, you'll have to decide for yourself.

A large part of my success was a winning attitude—knowing when to hold 'em and when to fold 'em, as it were. This I can share with you, but my philosophy won't work for you until you modify it to fit your own strengths and weaknesses.

A lot of luck was involved in the million-dollar success that my wife Shirley and I achieved, especially one extremely lucky half-hour period where we earned a half-million in two big jackpots. That may or may not ever happen again for us—or for you. But having the bankroll, skill, and courage to even be in position to recognize the opportunity, and receive that good fortune, required a lot more than luck. It took years of study and play. It took surviving some very long and ugly losing streaks. To stay in the game, you must learn to cope with terrible losses. I'll tell you about all of that.

And there were benefits along the way. We stayed in gorgeous hotel suites and ate in the fanciest restaurants in Las Vegas. We could get up to eight free tickets to any event in town. And there are *a lot* of events in Las Vegas that will satisfy virtually anyone's taste. I'll tell you about that too.

It was an extremely stimulating and professionally gratifying, albeit bumpy, ride. I'll recreate it for you in the pages that follow. So fasten your seatbelt and let's get started.

How Good Am I?

I'm a solid professional player and I limit myself to the few games that I know well. There are probably 50 other pros that play every bit as well as I do. Maybe more. There are far better video poker mathematicians and theoreticians than I. Many are quite a bit smarter. I'm not a computer programmer, even though the top-selling video poker computer trainer, *Video Poker for Winners!*, has my name attached to it.

My claim to fame, I suppose, is that I'm the top professional player that writes about the game. My columns in *Casino Player, Strictly Slots, Jackpot,* and other periodicals have made me the best-known professional video poker player ever. A major reason for this is that most of the other top players shy away from the spotlight. It's not such a hard task, perhaps, to be the best-known if you're standing up and announcing yourself, while everyone else is ducking down!

That said, a "solid professional" is head and shoulders above the general public in terms of ability. To use an analogy from baseball, I would be a typical major league player—only occasionally making the all-star team. But even getting to the major leagues is more difficult than most people could manage. I get e-mails all the time from readers saying things like, "After a lot of work practicing Double Bonus on *Video Poker for Winners!*, I can now usually play at the 98% level. Is that good enough?"

My answer is always something like, "If you're interested in playing at a competent recreational level and want to enjoy casino vacations less expensively than most people can, you're doing just fine. Keep up the good work! If you want to be a net winner at the game, you're not even close."

Many people reading this book are doing so because they'd like to win a million dollars, too. Who wouldn't? But as I've mentioned, a professional gambler is worlds apart from the minor leaguers. By describing myself here, you'll have some familiarity with my background. Although no two professionals have the identical resumé, we all have certain things in common. This will give you an idea of what it takes.

First of all, every successful professional player I know is quite bright. Some of us are very nerdy and social misfits, but the brainpower is there.

Second, I've been playing games at a pretty high level all my life. As a boy I could beat everyone at Scrabble, chess, checkers, and other games. In college I learned poker, bridge, and pinochle. In the mid-'70s, I learned backgammon; I played it for money for almost 20 years. In the mid-'80s I taught myself to count cards at blackjack and became reasonably good at that game. By the time I came to video poker in 1994, I was highly experienced both game-wise and gambling-wise.

Third, strategic thinking dominates most of what I do. In college, my bachelors, masters, and Ph.D. work was in economics, which is basically applied logic. When I read novels, they're frequently about lawyers or politicians or spies. Most of these books present problems that are solved only through logical thinking. Even though I haven't played bridge or live poker for more than 20 years, I still read the bridge column in the newspaper and the poker magazines regularly. Why? Because every now and then I learn another key to strategic thinking. And sometimes I can use that key to unlock a secret to winning at video poker.

Fourth, I'm someone who can accumulate and keep a bankroll. I'm a good "saver," and the fact that Shirley is too was an important decision variable (among many others) that led to our marriage in 1997.

Fifth, I can maintain concentration on one task for a long time. One difference between Shirley and me is that she can do 17 things at once, all of them at a fairly high level. I can do one thing at a time at a *very* high level. In life as a whole, Shirley's way is better. In playing professional video poker, my way is better.

Sixth, I can deal with bankroll ups and downs. For whatever reason, losing bothers me less than most other people. By the same token, winning excites me less than most others too. This allows me to stay focused on the goals at hand without the big emotional swings that some other people go through. Trust me, bankroll swings happen to every player. Guaranteed!

Seventh, I'm willing and able to practice long hours on a computer until I have a game mastered. I don't need to venture into the casino until I'm at my best. Thirty-some years ago my memory was considerably better than it is today. (I'd tell you exactly when that was, but I can't remember!) I have to work longer than I used to in order to retain things, but I'm willing to do that.

Eighth, solving puzzles is fun for me and I'm good at it. If it's a crossword puzzle, I go for the ones marked "Expert" or "Challenger." If it's a cryptogram, I skip the first three-fourths of them as being too easy. Remember, every video poker hand presents a puzzle. There are 32 different ways to solve each puzzle and, almost always, only one of those ways is the best.

Ninth, I'm pretty good at math, at least through high school algebra and college probability and statistics. It's easy for me to add 348 and 793 in my head. This is a very useful skill if you want to calculate what double points would be worth on a particular machine at a particular casino.

Tenth, in recent years anyway, I've had friends around me to turn to when I didn't know which way to go. Most recently, these have included Shirley, Jeffrey Compton, and Liam W. Daily. Anthony Curtis has thrown some valuable tips my way, too, as have numerous other people.

Eleventh, for reasons I discuss later in the book, I've been a video poker writer and teacher since 1997. In these capacities, people ask me all sorts of questions, so I'm forced to keep doing research and making sure I know the subject inside and out. As Dr. William Allen, a professor of economics I greatly admired when I was a graduate student at UCLA, said, "Research is to teaching as sin is to confession. Without the first, you have nothing to say in the second."

Twelfth, I'm a pretty good negotiator. This might not seem to fit into the skills necessary to be a successful gambler, but it does. All kinds of situations, some dealing with lots of money, arise in which you and someone else have to decide on how to handle them. You'll see several stories in this book about how I was able to talk someone into something that was good for me. There's an art to that, and being good at it pays dividends.

Those are the dozen skills that I bring to every video poker machine in every casino. Now, no other pro has quite the same mix of skills that I have. Some are better at math or are proficient at more video poker games. Others are weaker at some of the things where I excel. No matter what skills any of us have, the test as to whether someone is a top pro or not is simple: If you can make considerable money at this game year in and year out, you're a top pro. If you can't, you're not. How much is "considerable money?" That's debatable. And many pros have had losing years now and then. But overall, this test is fairly straightforward.

So if I'm not head and shoulders above the other pros, how did I happen to win a million dollars while no one else did? For one thing, other pros did too. I know five different players who've had $500,000+ years, and there are likely more that I don't know about. And as I've said, a large part of it is that we just got plain lucky. Shirley hit a $400,000 royal flush after only 6,000 or so hands on a $100 machine. On average, royals come every 40,000 hands, so it could be said that we got the royal 34,000 hands early.

Another reason is that when the "casino opportunity to die for" came along, we had the bankroll, knowledge, and willingness to go for it with considerably more gusto than anyone else. For whatever reason, during this special six-month period, the video poker gods smiled on us and granted us royals every 25,000-30,000 hands on average, instead of the usual 40,000. And all 100 or so royals that we hit during that period were for $20,000 or more. Who knows why? Skill was a factor, to be sure, but other factors were just as important. It happened, nonetheless. And someday it will happen to someone else.

How Much in This Book is True?

Most of it, actually, but not all. Most of my professional-level colleagues would be horror-stricken at the thought of being identified in a book. So whenever I felt the need to speak about them, I changed their names and some of their characteristics. But the gist of who they are and what happened is factual.

The numbers I cite as to how much I won or lost at a particular time are reasonably accurate. But some of these events took place seven years ago and I just don't remember completely.

The names of the following people are real (or in many cases are the pseudonyms these people use). They're all described fairly, if at times flatteringly: Jeffrey Compton, Anthony Curtis, Liam W. and Katherine Daily, Tom and Margaret Elardi, Adam Fine, Glenn Fine, Lenny Frome, Paul Henderson, Skip Hughes, Dan Paymar, Lawrence Revere, Jean Scott, Shirley and her family, Arnold Snyder, TomSki, Stanford Wong, Dean and Sara Zamzow.

All other names in the book are fictitious and are used to represent people I've known.

Of necessity, a lot of what happened to me over the past seven years has been omitted. Some of it is repetitious, some has little to do with video poker, and some secrets are better left untold. The central story of the book, however—that I started with a $6,000 bankroll in 1994 and my wife Shirley and I together netted more than $1 million by playing video poker between September 1, 2000, and March 15, 2001—is absolutely true.

What You Need to Know About Video Poker to Understand this Book

Video poker is, at its core, an easy game to understand. You bet your coins and the machine deals five cards. You select the cards you want to keep, if any, and the machine replaces the cards you didn't keep, if any. If you make a winning hand on the play, you're paid according to a pay schedule usually displayed on the front of the machine. And then the game is over. The average video poker hand lasts about six seconds for a moderately fast player. If you want to play again, you can. If not, you don't have to. That's video poker in a nutshell.

For knowledgeable players, however, there are a lot of combinations, permutations, and related considerations involved. To aid in discussions and analyses, video poker regulars have developed a shorthand terminology to refer to different machines. The remainder of this section explains much of that terminology.

Winning players must first select the type of game to play. In this book, I concentrate on only a few games—Jacks or Better, Deuces Wild, Double Bonus, and Joker Poker. Dozens of other video poker games are found in casinos, but there's no reason to list them here, because they're barely mentioned in this book. Even among the good games, there are lots of variations in pay schedules. I pay close attention to the numbers on a pay schedule, because even a 1-unit reduction in the return for a full house or flush lowers the return by 1%, in addition to often making considerable differences in the correct strategy. How much is 1%? On a dollar machine, a 1% reduction costs $30 per hour, and during this time I was playing 60 or more hours per weeks. Giving up an unnecessary $1,800 per week is no way to build a bankroll!

Jacks or Better is the game of choice for high-stakes players in Las Vegas. The best commonly found schedule returns 9 times your bet for a full house and 6 times your bet for a flush (there are some rare games with better pays). This schedule is referred to simply as 9/6 Jacks or Better, or sometimes 9/6 Jacks. The game returns 99.5439% with perfect play, which means that for every $1 million you play perfectly, the machine pays you $995,439 and keeps $4,561 for itself. Players with a drive to succeed never make a bet unless it returns more than 100%, so this game is avoided by smart players unless the slot club or one or more casino promotions kick in enough to make the game positive (i.e., raise the return to more than $1 million for each $1 million played).

Deuces Wild is the most popular game for quarter players in Las Vegas. The full-pay version pays 15 for 5-of-a-kind and 5 for 4-of-a-kind. Playing it well yields a return of 100.76%. This game does not exist for dollars in Vegas today, although it did until 1999 or so. The NSU version (which stands for "not so ugly") returns 16 for 5-of-a-kind and 10 for a straight flush. It returns only 99.73% when played perfectly, but can be a good game with the right slot club.

A version of Deuces Wild called Loose Deuces reduces the pay for 4-of-a-kind from 5 to 4 and increases the pay for 4 deuces from 200 to 500. There are several Loose Deuces pay schedules out there, but the one discussed in this book pays 15 for 5-of-a-kind and 10 for a straight flush for a return percentage of 101%.

Double Bonus is a game similar to Jacks or Better, only 4-of-a-kinds pay a lot more in Double Bonus (and full houses, flushes, and straights pay a little more). The downside to Double Bonus is that two pair returns even money, whereas you get double your money back in Jacks or Better. The best version of the game pays 10 for a full house and 7 for a flush. It's called, not surprisingly, 10/7 Double Bonus, and returns 100.17%. It's also very difficult to play well.

International Game Technology (IGT) is the world's largest manufacturer of video poker and slot machines. Its 10/7 Double Bonus games pay 250 for a 5-coin straight flush and yield the 100.17% return referenced above. In the 10/7 Double Bonus games found in the GameMaker machines manufactured by Bally Gaming Systems, a 5-coin straight flush pays 400 coins, which raises the return to 100.53%. Correct strategy is very similar for the two games, but not identical. When knowledgeable players want to distinguish between the games, they usually talk about 10/7/50 for the IGT version and 10/7/80 for the Bally version, as 50 and 80 are the 1-coin values that correspond to the 5-coin payouts for 250 and 400, respectively.

Several versions of Joker Poker are found throughout the country. The game found in Nevada returns even money for a pair of kings or aces, so it's usually called Kings or Better Joker Poker, or Kings or Better Joker Wild. The best version pays 20 for 4-of-a-kind and 7 for a full house. When it pays 4,000 coins for a royal flush, the game is worth 100.65% and when it pays 4,700 coins for a royal flush, the game is worth an even 101%. This is a very different game from any version of Joker Poker in which the lowest payout is for two pair—either game can be better than the other, depending on how much is returned for a flush, full house, and other hands. The Joker Wild game found in Atlantic City is a Two Pair or Better version. But in this game, 5-of-a-kind has a 4,000-coin payout, while a royal flush is considered to be merely a type of straight flush and is paid accordingly. This game has a different strategy from either of the previously mentioned Joker games.

Once you've determined which game you want to play, the next thing to consider is the slot club. Slot clubs are set up by the casinos to encourage player loyalty. They often reward players with cash and/or comps ("complimentaries")—such as rooms, meals, and shows—according to various formulas. These formulas often award points faster to slot players than video poker players, because slot players tend to lose considerably more money to the casinos. Frequently, employees who work in a slot club booth, and even casino hosts, neither know nor care about the fine points of their club. A successful video poker player learns the ins and outs of slot clubs so he knows them even better than the casino employees do.

"Cashback" is important for successful video poker players. When I talk about, say, .67% cashback, I mean that for every $3 a player puts through a machine, he gets 2¢ back—the cashback—from the casino (3 x .0067 = .02). But casinos rarely define it so simply. One casino might tell you that every $15 you play gives you a point and that 100 points can be redeemed for $10 cashback. Another might say that every $75 of play gives you a point and that 100 points can be redeemed for $50 in cashback. These are equivalent systems. The best introduction to slot clubs—including how they differ and how to choose the best one for you—can be found in the book *The Las Vegas Advisor Guide to Slot Clubs* by Jeffrey Compton. An updated edition of the book, with the new title *Slot Club Nation,* is due out in 2003.

Intelligent players add slot club cashback to the return on the game to determine how much it's worth. So a "1% slot club" added on to a 99.54% game results in a 100.54% return. To know what that figure means in terms of profit potential, you need to know how much money you can run through the machines in an hour. I use 600 hands per hour as an approximation. So quarter players, betting five coins for $1.25 per hand times 600 hands per hour, put $750 per hour in action. With a .54% advantage (the amount exceeding the 100% breakeven point), this is worth a whopping $4.05 per hour. Under this scenario, dollar players put $3,000 per hour into action, so the same game is worth $16.20 hourly. And five-dollar players can run $15,000 of action through a machine. For them, a .54% advantage is worth $81 per hour.

Now we're talking! Playing faster increases the return. Making mistakes decreases the return.

Casino promotions also add value to a game. Double or triple slot club points is a common type of promotion. Double pay for a particular 4-of-a-kind (perhaps 7777) is another. Paying double for the second royal hit within 24 hours is another. Sometimes you get drawing tickets for various hands. Sometimes the drawing tickets are almost worthless (as when 100,000 tickets are in the drum for one $1,000 prize) and sometimes they're worth a lot (as when 100 tickets are in the drum for $100,000). Evaluating the value of the tickets is part of the game.

For the most part, that's all you need to know to understand what I'll be talking about in the many real-life situations you'll read about in this book. Certainly, players who've been-there and done-that will get more out of the stories than those who haven't. But I've written so that anyone, no matter how much or how little he or she knows about video poker and casino life, will learn quite a bit more—and get a vicarious million-dollar thrill at no extra charge!—from the stories included in *Million Dollar Video Poker*.

Part Two

From Backgammon
to Big Vegas

Lessons from the Cavendish West

Between 1973 and 1991, I spent probably 25,000 hours gambling at the Cavendish West, located in the Los Angeles area where West Hollywood touches Beverly Hills. The Cavendish was not a casino; officially it was a bridge club. In fact, bridge, gin rummy, and backgammon were played there, for stakes ranging from small to considerable, between noon and 2 a.m. daily. The club closed sometime between 1991 and 1992. I'm not sure why. Perhaps it has been reestablished again under another name. I moved to Las Vegas in 1993 and know nothing about the current gambling scene in the Los Angeles area.

In 1973 I was 26 years old. I knew something about backgammon, but nothing about gambling. For the next 18 years I spent way too much time learning about gambling. Although my game of choice has changed more than once, many of the lessons that prepared me for being a successful professional gambler today were learned the hard way at the Cavendish. Let me share some of those lessons with you.

• It's possible to make a living gambling. It's not easy, but it's possible. For every 100 "wannabes" there's probably one "will be" and 99 "won't bes." Not a very good chance of success. But good enough if you have some talent, can learn from your mistakes, and have a tremendous amount of drive.

• Learning to win doesn't come quickly. My game was backgammon and I'd mastered the literature, such as it was. (This was before the publication of Paul Magriel's masterpiece *Backgammon*. Today there's a large amount of information about the game written by very knowledgeable players.) But mastering the problem hands in a book is a lot different than playing live opponents. In a book, you just try to win. In gambling, if you win, someone else (or the house) loses. Not all losers are gracious about it. And losers take steps to prevent losing again in the future.

• When you reach a position about which you're unsure, your chances are better when you're grounded in the basics. No one knows everything about every game—although perfection is attainable in some of the easier video poker games, such as Jacks or Better. Even in that game, progressives and promotions will come along that will change the correct strategy slightly. The longer you've been involved in the learning process, the more likely you are to have encountered such a situation before.

• As players learn more about the games, the games get tougher to beat. Players study and talk to each other. Players write about their experiences. I've heard many players complain that the games were better in the "good old days." Players like the fantasy that they'll be able to improve while all their opponents (including casinos) remain sitting ducks. This, of course, would be the path to Easy Street. But such is not the way of the world.

The best backgammon players today have considerably more knowledge about the game than the players who played twenty years ago. The same is true in blackjack, poker, sports betting, and video poker. You can piss and moan that things just aren't the same or you can buckle down and keep up.

• The best players continue to study. I knew three backgammon world champions well and three others casually. I also knew several of the top money players. These players would frequently make note of positions to study later. Most would play "propositions," which entails taking a real-life position about which players disagree on the best way to play, and playing it out for money, over and over again, until there's a lot more certainty about the intricacies of that position. Some of the players were computer programmers who would devise ways to analyze the game. When I was playing backgammon, personal computers were not common. Today a variety of programs are available that make computerized learning and analysis affordable and within the grasp of everyone.

There were some players who stopped studying and just kept playing. These players generally found their skills deteriorating while their opponents got better.

• Referees are important. Picture three-on-three playground basketball where you call your own fouls. Self-rule enforcement works pretty well on the playground, although sometimes the arguments get heated. However, introduce a $500 wager on the game and see how calling your own fouls stands up. Now the arguments get more frequent and more heated. For this reason, I'm glad for the Nevada Gaming Control Board and similar agencies in other states. I like the idea that I can appeal a casino's actions to a reasonably fair referee.

There are still states where there's virtually no regulation and every Native American tribe sets its own rules. If you think a machine is unfair, you're welcome to complain to the tribal council. And good luck. The lack of regulation is the reason I've been hesitant to engage in Internet gambling. Who's watching whoever is offering these "fair" games? I don't like it. But as regulation comes to that industry, perhaps someday I will determine that the Internet is a safe (and legal) place to gamble.

• Knowing a lot about a game and being a winning player are different things. There were excellent players who could figure out any problem you placed in front of them. But they weren't winners. They would play opponents against whom they had no edge and the house rake would eat them up. They would play when tired or intoxicated. They would play erratically when losing. They would "play to the crowd" rather than concentrate on the game. They would play so fast that when a problem-hand situation arose, they would miss it.

The winning players, on the other hand, limited their gambling to the times that they were at their best. They selected their opponents carefully. They slowed down and considered their play. They might not do as well as the "better players" when it came to taking a test on problem hands, but they wound up taking the money home.

• Everyone wins some of the time. Everyone loses some of the time. You have to learn to deal with winning and you have to learn to deal with losing.

Losing streaks bring out the worst in people. Any tendency to lie, steal, or be otherwise imperfect is magnified when you're losing. My personal belief is that you don't really know someone, gambler or not, until you observe him when things are not going pleasantly. You must learn to cope with terrible losses that will make you feel like you've been run over by a big bus with license plates that read HAHAHA.

Learning to live with winning is easier and more fun than learning to live with losing. Still, many people don't handle it well. Gambling winnings spend just as well as money earned from working a job, but psychologically, they're different. New-found "undeserved" wealth is often spent on upscale toys, drugs, vacations, and other types of for-the-moment enjoyment. This is perfectly all right as long as the winning continues unabated. But it never does. This leads to the next lesson.

• Players can and do run out of money. Most players who try to survive by gambling alone eventually need to bite the bullet and go out and get a job. I was one of those who had to do this. From 1973 through 1979, I was able to scrape by as a backgammon player—partly by depleting previously saved financial reserves. But the handwriting was on the wall. From 1980 to 1989 I worked 40-50 hours a week and played relatively little backgammon. But I also continued to study. It didn't take a genius to figure out that I had to play better if I wanted to make it as a backgammon player. Simultaneously, I was learning to count cards at blackjack and would take weekend trips several times a year to Las Vegas. I didn't know what my future held, but I believed that life as a gambler was preferable to life as a database administrator.

• Gambling is easier if you don't also have to work 40 hours a week. Being at your best requires mental energy. My job was one with responsibility and stress. I liked to arrive at the Cavendish around 7 in the evening and I found that doing so after a hard day at work was an entirely different kettle of fish than doing so after waking up at 3 in the afternoon. I would have preferred the latter, but I wasn't successful enough to manage it.

In 1989 I returned to the Cavendish (still working) and began to do well. I won enough that I could have supported myself 10 years earlier, but I'd gotten used to the $50,000-plus a year my job paid and didn't want to give that up. Eventually, the decision was made for me. The company I worked for merged with another and my position was eliminated. I don't kid myself: Devoting all my off-hours to gambling (and studying about gambling) affected my performance at work. Doing a first-class job at work required a lot of on-your-own-time study, which I wasn't doing. So when they had to choose which of two workers to keep, the other guy was their choice. Embarrassingly, the choice was obvious.

• Gambling is tough on relationships. Gamblers experience larger than average mood swings and financial fluctuations. Finding a girlfriend when I was winning was easy. (I know how to dance. Being able and willing to dance means a guy never has to be alone!) Finding someone who wanted to hang around when the going got tough was more difficult. I had faith in my ability to eventually make it in the gambling world. My lady friends were less convinced. I would have liked to provide them with strong evidence that I could do it, but there wasn't any.

Me: "Trust me. I can do it. It will just take time."

Them: "Whatever you say. See you around."

• Many gamblers are physically unhealthy. Gamblers tend to be obsessive. Destructive habits such as alcohol, tobacco, drugs, under- or overeating, overspending, and carousing are frequently found among gamblers. Spend enough time around people and you'll become friends with some of them. Adopting the habits of your friends is common. But these particular habits are contrary to the habits needed for success. It's easy to believe that you're special and can succeed despite destructive habits. Perhaps you can. But I can't. And it took me a long time to learn that.

Today, I'm conscientiously at the gym twice a week. But back at the Cavendish (even when I had all the time in the world), forget it. I gave up smoking and drugs in 1979 and alcohol a few years later. I'll never know for sure, but I attribute much of my gambling success from 1989 onward to being much healthier and better able to concentrate on what needed to be concentrated on. I did stop going to the gym for a few years in the mid-1990s while living in Las Vegas and promptly developed a prominent "RFB belly"—a feature shared by many of my gambler friends. Fortunately, most of that is gone now, but I have no doubts that it will reappear if I ever stop doing what it took to get rid of it.

• In general terms, succeeding at gambling is not significantly different from succeeding at anything else. This was the toughest lesson to learn. Since gambling was so exciting and glamorous and inviting, I figured there just had to be special secrets for success. I've learned that this simply isn't true. To be sure, there are specific things you must learn, such as always splitting aces and eights in blackjack. But that's just one little detail. Overall, the secret is to study harder than everyone else, concentrate on what you're doing, save your money, and keep your mind and body fit. "Plan your work and work your plan." "Win the war before you fight the battle." Most self-help books about anything give you basically the same advice. Getting the advice is easy. Applying it wholeheartedly is the tough part.

What I Learned from Playing Blackjack

In the mid-1970s, my gambling interest was backgammon. I bought every backgammon book I could find—and most of them were very bad. (Not so today. Some very bright and competent players are writing about that game.) Winning at gambling was the goal. So I wanted to learn everything about the game that I could. The same stores that sold books on backgammon also sold books on blackjack. And many of my backgammon buddies also played blackjack and talked of their successful forays to Vegas, so I got the book *Playing Blackjack as a Business* by Lawrence Revere.

Revere's book promised that I could be a winner if I did things his way. I heard stories of guys with little success with women at home (i.e., me) who would learn to play blackjack and have these romantic all-expenses-paid-by-the-casino trips to Vegas with a different gorgeous lady each time. Sign me up!

After I learned basic strategy reasonably well, I came across a magazine ad for a place called Vegas World. It promised free room and board if I would bring in $2,500 and play $25 a hand for so many hours. This casino, run by Bob Stupak and located on a small part of the site of the current Stratosphere, didn't have very good blackjack rules. But I really didn't know how to get good deals at any casinos that did.

So I took on Stupak Thanksgiving weekend 1978. It was my first trip ever to Las Vegas. I played the whole weekend and won $2,000. (Actually I won $1,500 and received the extra money from a casino mistake. More on that later.) I was hooked. On that particular trip, most of the time when I drew a card to a 15 or 16, I ended up pulling a 4 or 5. Not bad! Other players would stand on these "stiff" hands and I'd win while they'd lose. I felt quite superior. I knew how to play and was on my way!

Since that Vegas trip had ended up positive and the books all said that I could win, everything seemed natural. I figured that most of my trips would turn out that way. They didn't. Years later, I came to realize that the game at Vegas World had almost a 1% house edge and that for 400 hands or so on a weekend, luck is more predominant than rules or even skill. My return trips to Vegas World were negative. Each weekend at a time, I chalked it up to bad luck. But I now know that with Bob Stupak's rules and Bob Dancer's skills, I had no chance.

Before I chronicle the rest of what I learned from blackjack, let me tell you a fascinating story from my first trip. I ended up being mentioned in the *Las Vegas Review-Journal* that weekend as a "high-roller gambler." I saved the article for years, but lost it somewhere along the way.

Unbeknownst to me, a sting was about to go down at Vegas World. A group of cheating players had approached a dealer and told him he would earn a great deal of money if he'd let them substitute a fake shoe (called a "cooler") with the cards stacked in a particular way. Once the shoe was in place, the team would play out the stacked shoe and take the casino for big bucks. After the shoe had been played, the cards would be shuffled and the evidence destroyed—everyone would be home free. The dealer told the gang it sounded like a good idea, then went straight to his bosses with the story. The plan was to send the dealer to the table with the best cameras located near it (including one feeding to Stupak's second-floor suite), and cram the place with undercover Metros (the Vegas police), who would be playing at nearby blackjack tables.

At the appointed time, everything was in place and would have gone down as planned, except for one thing. At just that moment, I walked up to the blackjack table that was being staked out, asked for a $500 marker, and started to play. And play. And since I was winning, I kept playing! The place was filled with very nervous team players waiting for me to leave, and Metro officers playing blackjack and losing far more than they had budgeted because they thought they would be playing for only a few minutes for cover purposes.

The dealer mentioned several times how nice the gourmet room was and that if I wanted to go, the service was best before 7 p.m. Different pit people, all in a friendly manner, told me that the key to winning in the long run was to quit while I was ahead. "It would be a shame to give that all back."

Stupak must have been fuming! When a sting is about to go down, everyone's adrenaline is flowing because there's no telling what's about to happen. If the bad guys made the cops and decided that the dealer had double-crossed them, things could get ugly fast. The police all had guns. Did the players? Who knew? If they did, would they be arrested quietly or would this be the "Shootout at Vegas World"? I played blithely on. I was totally unaware that anything was going on other than the fact that this was my first trip to Vegas and I was winning. Just like I was supposed to.

Finally, I decided to go. I announced that I wanted to buy back my marker (like the book said to do) and the pit crew was obviously more than happy to get rid of me. I couldn't figure that out. I'd won maybe $1,500, but that was nowhere near enough for a casino to worry about. Meanwhile, the people in the pit were trying not to appear nervous about what was going to happen next. I suspect they were frightened at the thought of so many guns being in their vicinity, but they were so flustered that they returned the marker and let me keep the $500 in chips too!

From talking to a dealer the next day, I found out that five minutes after I left, the table emptied. The team came, the shoes were switched, everyone on the team bet $500 or more off the top of the shoe, and the Metro officers moved in. It was over in a minute, and the cheaters went off to jail quietly. Most of the patrons there that night probably had no idea what had just happened.

Two days later I saw Stupak in the coffee shop and I asked him about it. He said he'd wanted me to leave the game, "anyhow and any way." He said he'd kept hoping that I would win more or vary my bets big or something so he could justify kicking me out of the place without raising the suspicions of the bad guys. But I kept flat-betting green chips (consistently betting $25 per hand) and winning modestly. What could he do?

I ended up with an extra $500 due to the pit mistake. Other players might have responded differently, but I kept my mouth shut and hung onto the extra money. Back then, I didn't have a fixed philosophy about what to do if the casino gave me excess money, as I do now. If a casino error in my favor is traceable to a particular person who will have to make up the money, I give it back. I reason that anyone working for wages in a casino probably needs money more than I do. But if it's going to go to casino overhead, I keep it. I figure I need the money more than the casino stockholders do. It may not be your philosophy, but it's mine.

For years I continued to fly in to Las Vegas on three-day weekends to play blackjack. Overall, I am a loser at this game. The profits I made in the year or so I played after I moved to Las Vegas in 1993 came nowhere close to offsetting the losses sustained during my learning-curve period.

People who know of my successes at video poker may be a bit surprised to learn that I'm a net loser at blackjack. After all, anyone smart enough to win consistently at video poker is probably smart enough to learn to count cards at blackjack. (And vice versa. Successful blackjack players often become successful video poker players.) And if I was a net loser lifetime-to-date, why would I move to Vegas? Did I have a bankruptcy wish?

What changed me from being marginally successful to being very successful was the use of a personal computer. I programmed mainframe computers for many years in the early '70s and all through the '80s. But I never got into PCs. The early models had so many problems, I just avoided them. Also, I heard that technology was moving so fast that by the time you got a new computer hooked up, it was almost obsolete. Since I was always trying to save money (so I could get a gambling bankroll, among other things), I didn't own a computer until 1994.

I learned to count cards manually. I got pretty good at it, but never great. How did I know if I had the right count at a particular time? I didn't, really. Unless there was an outside source counting the deck right along with me, who's to say whether I was right or wrong?

Blackjack computer programs today, of course, correct the player every step of the way. The player can input the strategy he wants to use, along with the rules and number of decks, then let the computer deal cards until diamonds grow on trees. Every time the player makes a mistake, the computer speaks up. These programs were becoming available before I quit the game, but I didn't have a computer and wasn't convinced of their value. I now believe that if I'd realized the value of practicing on a PC, my blackjack days would have been much more profitable. I can still go back, learn to count on a computer, and play blackjack, of course. But with the counter-catching tools available to casinos today and the fact that my face is already well known to people in the business, I believe that my days playing profitable high-stakes blackjack would be limited. So I don't even try.

So, then, why did I move to Vegas even though my lifetime results playing blackjack were negative? Two reasons. First, the three years prior to my moving to Vegas yielded positive results. And this made sense. My counting skills were improving and I was learning about the better places to play, so of course my results improved. By the time I made the move, I was definitely a small favorite at the game. Plus I knew of several blackjack promotions that made me a rather large favorite.

The second reason I moved to Vegas even though I was just a small favorite at my game of choice was to take advantage of coupons and casino promotions. I discuss some of these promotions in depth in subsequent chapters. For now, suffice it to say they were a big part of my early Vegas profits, but I never did capitalize enough to make up for the losses in my earlier years.

In the year and a half that my partner, Ginnie, and I played blackjack in Vegas, we made something like $12,000 from blackjack (including promotions directly related to blackjack) and $21,000 from coupons and other promotions. This $33,000 was for two people for a year and a half. It was subsistence success. But when most of the blackjack promotions disappeared, we had to make a switch to quarter video poker. Ginnie's commitment to Vegas (and me) switched as well, and she decided to move back to Southern California where she could get a guaranteed $25,000-a-year job. Things would have had to get a lot worse for me to give up and get a regular job again. And they haven't yet.

Fact is, the lessons I learned at blackjack served me well later when I played video poker. These lessons include the following:

• Play only when you have the advantage. If the house has the edge, it will beat you in the long run.

• If you don't continue to practice your skills, they deteriorate. The matrix numbers in a blackjack counting system are pretty complicated. If you don't review them regularly, they get fuzzy. Today, six years after I last played serious blackjack, I still remember about 90% of the strategy matrix. But that last 10% is gone, which probably reduces my skill by .05% or so. That's a serious amount, given the minuscule edge blackjack players must exploit.

• You'll have good days and bad days and they'll often have little to do with how well you're playing. Some days you draw to 16s and get 5s more often than you're supposed to. Those days you'll win, whether it was correct to be drawing to that 16 or not. Other days every 12 you draw to will bust. That day you'll lose—whether hitting the 12 was correct or not.

This was a tough lesson. Accepting randomness in scores is not an easy concept. It's easy to buy into the idea that if you play well, you'll win and if you play poorly, you'll lose. That concept is correct if you look at the game as being a year, or 10 years, long. I played long enough that I believe it's fair to say that the main reason I wasn't more successful at blackjack was that my skills weren't sufficient. But for individual days or weeks, I had good sessions and bad and luck was a major factor in the short run.

• It's easier to understand what casinos are doing if you consider them as business enterprises attempting to make money. I've heard fellow pros rail about casinos, "Those lousy bastards. They used to stand on all seventeens and now they're hitting the soft ones. What are they trying to do? Ruin the game for everyone?" Or later in video poker, I would read Internet e-mails berating a casino because "it used to have twelve full-pay Deuces Wild machines and now it has only four. And those machines are so busy that I can't find two side by side to play!" There will always be changes. But good players will find ways to prosper. In the professional gambling world, if you're doing things the same way you did two years ago, you're probably not doing very well!

• Playing a 100% game is no bargain. It costs money to live—cars, insurance, food, housing, clothes, etc. No matter where you live, these expenses are very real. If gambling is your source of income, you need a game that returns significantly higher than 100% to end up ahead. To those who argue that the rooms and meals provided by casinos have real value for out-of-towners, I agree, but they're not worth nearly as much as their face value or even what the casino would like you to believe. If I didn't have a free room at a casino, I'd stay home where my rent is paid by the month whether I'm there full time or not. Yes, you can eat wonderful meals in a casino "for free." But the tip alone is more than I usually pay for meals at home.

• The advice you get from other gamblers is often faulty. In blackjack, people will tell you that "you should always insure a blackjack," or that "the actions of the guy at third base are more important than anybody else's," or that "a bad player at the table can ruin the deck for everyone." I'd wager that no winning player believes any of that, but that many wannabe winning players do. You even find some of these theories in print.

In video poker it's much the same, except now the advice is, "In 10/7 Double Bonus, if you're dealt two pair with aces and eights, hold just the aces." This is also wrong, although not by much. Or how about, "If the machine has just hit a royal flush, you had better not play it because it's rare that a machine hits for two royals in the same day." That's total nonsense, but you hear it all the time. "Quit while you're ahead," and "If you're losing, quit," are both examples of nonsensical advice. The two statements offer opposite advice, so it's impossible for both to be true. But it is possible that both are false. I'll have a lot to say on this later in the book.

Here's another: "Having fun is more important than whether you win or lose." This, likewise, is a bunch of crap. If you want to tell yourself this so you don't feel so bad when you lose, go ahead. But winning players didn't get to be winners by going out to have fun, then being content to take the wins if they came along. Winning players got to be winners by working hard.

• The learning process is easier if you have study partners. I swapped notes regularly with several budding blackjack counters. This was important. If blackjack was still an important game to me, I would regularly check out bulletin boards run by Stanford Wong and Arnold Snyder. You can learn a lot from them. Unfortunately, many casino table-game executives lurk on these bulletin boards, just to see what the players are thinking.

• Finally, if learning to gamble well helps you get laid, I never learned nearly well enough! Ginnie was lovely, and so is Shirley (whom I'll marry in a few chapters!). But both of them met me on the dance floor and the fact that I could dance was more important to them than whether I knew how negative the count had to be before I hit a hard 14 against a dealer 5. There was more than a year between these two ladies and during that time, no supermodels were standing in line to meet me. So if you're looking for a profession that teems with romantic encounters, try becoming a dance teacher!

Blackjack Partner Ginnie Woo

I met Ginnie in 1991, and for the next three years or so we were an item. I probably would have moved to Vegas a year earlier than I did if I could have talked Ginnie into it. She and I made several trips to Vegas, but she couldn't quite bring herself to give up her job and friends, and trust that I knew enough about gambling to make a good life for us both. Eventually, in August 1993, we moved to Las Vegas together.

You may be wondering why I'm including a chapter about a woman who left me before I knew much about video poker. The reason is that much of my early gambling experience benefited greatly from having a female partner and I needed to go through that experience in order to get to where I am today.

Ginnie was 10 years younger than I (still is, I suppose) and was born in Taiwan. She had a permanent work visa and was planning to get her U.S. citizenship as soon as she was eligible. Shortly after we got together, she heard through some of her Chinese friends that a travel agent in San Francisco was repping a special blackjack program with the Las Vegas Hilton, and (off and on) the Flamingo Hilton, for Chinese customers. The deal was something like an offer to buy $985 worth of non-negotiable chips for $900, plus you got a free hotel room for a night and $20 worth of food credits. I think the travel agent charged $15 to create the voucher that allowed you to do this, so the deal was worth $70 cash (plus room and food) per person.

Ginnie had two names. Her U.S. driver's license said "Virginia Woo" and her Taiwanese passport said her name in Chinese, which was Shen. Whenever we did this promotion, she would sign up with both names at both casinos. She'd pick up the chips for Woo in the evening and pick up the chips for Shen the next morning. Then we'd play the chips together. Even though I was counting cards, we'd flat-bet the quarter ($25) chips until they were gone so the casino would have no idea that we were actually strong players. The double-deck game at these casinos had decent rules, so even flat betting, we had a $280 expected profit every weekend we played for about two hours work. Not to mention $80 in food coupons that never expired, plus the rooms if we needed them. Not bad.

Even after we moved to Las Vegas, we kept our California IDs and would plan trips to the Hiltons for "both" women every two weeks for as long as we could. Eventually, they said we couldn't play anymore, but Ginnie would still get promotional mail from the Hilton addressed to "Virginia Woo (barred)." We found that quite amusing. Not that our amusement helped us get back into the casino.

Our main blackjack play before and after we moved to town was at the Riviera. They had a "Gambler's Spree," whereby an out-of-state player who put in four hours at certain minimum amounts received a room, half-price airfare, all the buffets he could keep down, and a cash rebate. The rebate varied periodically, but often it was worth between $60 and $90 for play at either $5 or $10 per hand.

Our strategy was for me to count cards and tell Ginnie how to play each hand. This started out as a necessity, because she knew nothing about the game. But after awhile she knew basic strategy cold. Also, she strongly objected to me telling her how to play in front of the dealers, because it was important to her that she not appear to be stupid. After all, these dealers saw her every two weeks for two years. And if she still didn't know how to play, it might be reasonable for them to question her intelligence. I begged her to let me continue to "instruct" her when we played. I believed that a man teaching his wife or girlfriend at the table was not a threatening situation to the casino and that our longevity would likely be enhanced if we did this. If we both looked like we knew what we were doing, we might not be able to play as long. She ultimately allowed it, but she wasn't happy.

Ginny was partially appeased when we decided that she would keep the insurance count. An insurance count merely subtracts 2 for every 10-valued card (the 10s, jacks, queens, and kings) and adds 1 for every other card in the deck. If you're playing a double-deck game, and the count is +8 or higher when the dealer asks if you want insurance, you take it. If it isn't, you don't. The card-counting system I used valued 4s, 5s, and 6s differently from 8s and 9s. This made it very useful for betting and playing decisions, but only approximate for insurance purposes. The count Ginny used was 100% accurate for this one decision only, and her being involved in the decision making every one-out-of-thirteen hands (whenever the dealer's up-card was an ace) helped keep her happy.

At the Riv we used a small bet spread. Since we were playing either $5 or $10 a hand and didn't spread our bets, we were under their "looking-for-card-counters" radar. We also used a lot of coupons. At that time, the Riv gave away yellow coupon books with a $7-for-$5 and a $3-for-$2 coupon, plus many other coupons. It was easy to get these coupon books by the dozen. Although each coupon was stamped "one per day," we found that we could use them "one *per dealer* per day." The Riv had a rotation system that kept new dealers coming every 40 minutes and never the same one twice. So during four hours of play, we would each use 6 sets of coupons per day. This had an expected value of maybe $10 per person per day (we only used the coupons when the count was positive), so it added up. With a daily subsidy of $60 apiece, having an extra $10 was a significant raise.

Some of the dealers made wisecracks about our frequent use of the coupons. It didn't bother me at all, but it humiliated Ginnie. She cared a lot more about what people thought about her. I cared about getting the money.

The Stardust had a lucrative coupon book, with 6 or 8 different $7-for-$5 coupons in it—one for blackjack, one for craps, one for roulette, etc. You had to have a voucher from somewhere to get these books, but they were easy to find. For example, America West's in-flight magazine had one each issue. Several times we would go to the airport on the first day of the month and tell them that we had a friend who was mentioned in the magazine in the previous month and if they had any extra copies, we'd like them. Three times we got boxes of 100 magazines. We'd tear out the voucher and toss the magazine.

At the Stardust, we got to be friends with the ladies who gave away the coupon books by giving them some free buffet tickets for the Riviera. This wasn't a gourmet meal by any means, but for minimum-wage employees who rarely got any tokes, it was enough to let us cash all of our coupons and then some.

We would then create special Stardust coupon books, with just the good coupons in them. We could cash four or five blackjack coupons, because the tables were spread out, often two or three roulette coupons, but usually only one crap or pai gow poker coupon apiece. We would hit the Stardust three times a day (on graveyard, day, and swing shifts), so no employee would see us more than once a day, but we did this so many times that those dealers got to know us too. Their comments bothered Ginnie.

Circus Circus gave out $2-for-$1 and $3-for-$2 coupons in a funbook you got while riding their monorail between the casino and the various towers with hotel rooms. Each coupon had a value of slightly less than 50¢, but you could often get a dozen or so of them at once since customers would often drop them on the floor as being worthless. Since the Stardust and Circus Circus are both very close to the Riviera, we would make the circuit and collect the bounty. Even after we moved to Vegas, we set up imaginary "three-day trips" to Vegas every other week, so every other Thursday, Friday and Saturday, we played at the Riviera. I was "making it in Vegas." Ginnie was shamed. This was not how she wanted to spend her life.

Other casinos had similar programs to the Riviera's: the Stardust, Maxim, Hacienda, Four Queens, San Remo, and Bourbon Street. We became friends with "George," an excellent card counter who happened to sell vouchers as a sideline. He knew it when we moved to Vegas, but had no problem still selling us the out-of-state vouchers.

Eventually, each of the casinos either ended the blackjack program or decided that we were abusing them and told us we were no longer eligible to participate. We could still play blackjack without the subsidy if we wanted, but that was it. They didn't all end at the exact same time, of course, so when we started to learn video poker we were still playing a few blackjack promotions. But eventually they all went away.

Ginnie and I played a lot of coupons and promotions in 1993 and 1994. Jean Scott's *The Frugal Gambler* discusses them well and if you're a newcomer to Vegas and promotions and comps, and in the "low-roller" financial boat, it's a must-read. Jean and I became successful in Vegas at about the same time doing many of the same things at the start, but we each had our own slant on it. I've long since moved on to more lucrative ways to make money in Las Vegas and today I wouldn't cross the street to cash a $10-for-$5 coupon. But there was a time when my survival in Las Vegas depended upon just that.

Ginnie and I learned video poker together. We started by reading Stanford Wong's book, *Professional Video Poker,* and learning that strategy well. It was limited to 8/5 Jacks or Better progressives, but since we couldn't find many of those machines with a high enough meter, we used the strategy for 9/6 Jacks, too. We figured it was close enough. It was a simple case of, "When your only tool is a hammer, everything looks like a nail!"

We heard about a 4-coin quarter 9/6 Jacks or Better and a 4-coin 8/5 Bonus Poker game at the Sahara, and played them on Sundays (when four aces paid double) and Thursdays (when royal flushes hit at certain times paid double). She liked playing without me telling her what to do all of the time and I gave her a $100 bonus for every royal flush. But Vegas was my dream, not hers.

We played a lot during graveyard hours. She would tell me that her mother had always taught her that you should be awake when the sun is up and asleep during the dark hours. Ginnie's mother believed that there's a yin and a yang and it's unwise to confuse them. I suggested to Ginnie that although I'm sure her mother was very wise, she clearly knew nothing about being a successful professional gambler in Las Vegas. Ginnie couldn't refute that, but still felt that playing during the daytime hours was in more proper harmony with the universe.

After Ginnie moved back to Southern California, we kept in touch for awhile. In spring 1995 she came back for a few visits (and was an instrumental part of the "My Ship Has Come In" adventure), but I haven't seen her since then.

I learned several things from Ginnie. One was that I needed to find a partner who could sign up for the same dream I had. However pretty she was. However good she made me feel to be around. If we weren't pulling in the same direction, I wasn't going to make it. I'm someone who needs support. When it later came from Shirley (and Jeffrey and Liam and Anthony and Dean and others), I was in a position to blossom. If you're able to succeed without good people to support you, you have life figured out a lot better than I do.

I also realized that I needed to get my act together if I wanted to attract the right kind of lady for me. Running around collecting coupons worth 50¢ each is a lot of fun when you're 21, but when Ginnie left I was 47! The ladies I was used to seeing in California were bright, educated, and successful. A 47-year-old guy with a net worth of less than $10,000 and just learning a trade that cleared $10 an hour wouldn't be considered a catch by the women I wanted to be with. I used Ginnie's leaving as a wake-up call and for the next year and a half I spent 80-hour weeks studying video poker, analyzing it on a computer, and playing. When I met Shirley in mid-1996, I can tell you that she wasn't what I thought I wanted, but five years later I can also tell you that she was just what I needed!

Another thing I learned was that my blackjack playing skills improved when I had to teach them to someone else. I figured that if I could continue teaching, I would continue to get better and keep my skills sharp. So I vowed to continually write down what I knew as if it were going to be published in a book. Whether it was eventually published or not was not the point (at that time). My thinking was, unless I could write down what I knew in a way that others could understand it, I didn't understand it well enough myself. Without this one insight (which at first I didn't really believe deep down in my gut), I never would have been in position later to earn the million dollars.

And one last important thing I learned while playing with Ginnie is that if you show the casinos over and over again that you can beat them, they will take measures to prevent you from continuing to be able to do that. This came back at me big time in 2001. I'll delve into that in Part Four.

An Efficient Time to Get Barred?

One of the casinos with a blackjack non-negotiable chip-rebate program was the Dunes. Ginnie and I played it a lot, with a conservative bet spread so the casino wouldn't get wise to the fact that we were advantage players.

When the Dunes was bought by the Mirage Corporation for the express purpose of imploding it, the casino's last day was announced months in advance. About two weeks before the Dunes closed shop, Ginnie and I began playing the blackjack program more aggressively. After all, if we were barred, why would we care? The casino was about to evaporate in a cloud of dust.

Sure enough, three days before the closing we got run off. I went around boasting to some of my friends about how efficient this was and how I was able to squeeze the last drop out of the place and play almost until the end.

A week after the Dunes closed, the pit boss who ran us off got a job at the Aladdin, which was another casino with a rebate program. He recognized us and came up. "The Aladdin has different rules than the Dunes had, so I won't kick you out just yet. But I know you're good players. And I'll be watching and putting a notation on your rating card."

I no longer felt so smart. I'd forgotten that even though the casino would be imploded, the employees wouldn't. Blackjack pit personnel are rewarded for their ability to recognize and remember players and most of the Dunes employees ended up working for other casinos. Turns out there's no good time to get barred.

Scouting for Stanford

For more than 20 years, Stanford Wong has been one of the most respected of gambling writers. Although he has books on a number of games, he's known best for his work on blackjack. His *Current Blackjack News* (*CBJN*) has for many years provided monthly updates on blackjack playing conditions at several hundred casinos across the nation. When I played blackjack, I subscribed.

In late 1993, Wong wrote in *CBJN* that he was looking for scouts to evaluate Las Vegas casinos. Each month, the scouts would go to every casino on their route and report on the number of blackjack games offered, along with the conditions of play, such as number of decks dealt and level of penetration, which means determining how closely to the end of the deck the dealer deals before shuffling. In addition, the rules of play had to be checked. I applied for the $150-per-month job and was hired.

My route, at first, extended along Las Vegas Boulevard from the brand-new Treasure Island to Boomtown (now Silverton), including a few nearby off-Strip casinos. Later, Wong realigned the routes so mine shrunk somewhat.

The job sounds fairly simple, but I didn't find it to be. Counting the number of games was easy enough (separate counts for single deck, double deck, four decks, etc.), although these counts change several times during a day and more games are open on weekends than on weekdays. And some of the rules, such as whether or not the casino takes another card when dealt A6, are printed right on the table, so you can check them immediately. But some rules are obscure. For example, all casinos allow you to split aces once, but only a few allow you to re-split them. A scout can't know for sure how a casino plays this rule until he sees aces being split—and it can take awhile for this to come up. Likewise, determining whether a casino offers doubling after splitting also takes time.

You can ask about the rules, of course. But questioning a dealer about 10 or so different situations makes you stand out like a sore thumb. Part of the "act" of successful blackjack players is to blend in with the crowd. So I'd sit down to play and say something like, "It's been a month since I was in town. Anything different rules-wise?" Sometimes I'd get accurate information and sometimes I wouldn't, but it was a starting place. I'd play for low stakes for 15 minutes or so and watch to see if there were any changes from the month before.

While I was in these casinos, I also kept a lookout for anything else that had changed. And almost every month I found an interesting promotion or two somewhere that made sense for me to play. At the start, these were all table-game promotions, because that's all I cared about. But as I learned about video poker, I looked for those advertisements, as well. The most lucrative situation I found while scouting for Stanford was at Vacation Village, which I'll describe later in this section. It ended up being an opportunity worth thousands of dollars that I wouldn't have found if I hadn't been walking through the casino with my eyes peeled.

After a few years, Wong and I parted ways. As a result, I also cut way back on my own scouting. Since I was no longer being paid $150 a month to walk through casinos, I didn't do it. This, it turns out, was penny wise and dollar foolish. Scouting requires a big investment of time and it doesn't always result in finding value. But sometimes it does. And when it does, it can pay very well, making up for all of the fruitless searches.

When Shirley and I were playing years later at the MGM, she asked one of the best out-of-town players how often he walked the Strip. "Every time I come, if it's been at least two weeks since my last trip. Things change all the time. I've been the first to find more than a dozen different juicy opportunities." Walking the Strip proved to be time well-spent for this pro—and for me, too.

Vegas World Revisited

Vegas World was a product of the marketing genius of its owner and founder, Bob Stupak. Vegas World advertised extensively for "free" Las Vegas weekends. This promotion was marketed to a totally different audience than the deal that required $2,500 front money and four hours a day of $25 betting that I'd tried before. That deal was probably still available, but I was no longer interested.

The typical offer in this new promotion had a purchase price of $398 and returned something like $400 in "casino action chips" and $600 in special slot tokens, plus a two-night stay in the hotel. And you always got two free pulls on the million-dollar slot machine. And some free keno tickets.

A lot of people signed up for this "VIP Vacation," including me. It turns out that the casino action chips were worth slightly less than 50¢ on the dollar and the special slot tokens were worth about 10¢ on the dollar. The free pulls were worth less than a penny apiece. And the keno tickets were worth about a nickel. So this "$1,000 vacation costing you $398" was worth only $250 or so in gaming value, plus a not-very-special hotel room for two nights.

Vegas World was located on Las Vegas Boulevard at the site of the current Stratosphere—north of the end of the Strip and south of downtown. With its eclectic mix of topless bars and wedding chapels, the area might charitably be called "seedy." Once out-of-towners arrived on one of these packages, they generally didn't want to leave the casino. The games at Vegas World were, for the most part, considerably tighter than anywhere else in town, so players on this package typically lost everything they brought with them (plus the original $398).

The Nevada Gaming Control Board cited the casino periodically for deceptive advertising and Stupak was the regular *winner* of the "least popular celebrity" category in the annual "Best of Vegas" survey conducted by the *Las Vegas Review-Journal*.

Doesn't sound like an opportunity for profit. But it was.

After a customer got taken on one of these packages, he generally wouldn't return, of course. So Vegas World kept mailing him better and better come-ons. The best ones were offers of $1,000 in casino action chips (worth $480 or so), plus $1,000 in slot tokens (worth $100 or so), plus a hotel room, plus the almost-worthless extras, all for the same $398 price. *This* was a good deal, as long as you had the discipline to *leave* the casino as soon as you cashed in the package.

Toward the end, Vegas World also offered a "charter membership" in the Stratosphere project, where in addition to getting plenty of good things, you were given a line pass, which allowed you to go the head of the registration line and other lines on all subsequent visits. This was very valuable.

What's more, you could sign up your "friends." And as long as you had a note saying you were authorized to play for them, you could cash their packages, too.

I would sign up for four packages at a time (the most they allowed), then call back a few hours later and do it again. I invented family members, so the mail would still come to my house. I signed up for Abe, Ben, Charlie, David, Elaine, Frank, Grace, etc., all with the same last name. I probably cashed more than 100 of these packages over the years. I rotated eight different styles of stationery, four different colored pens, and six different writing styles so when I wrote variations of "Please allow Bob Dancer to cash my package," they didn't all look the same.

I had a credit card that rebated 5% of all my purchases when I bought my next General Motors car and each package included $20 worth of "car credit." When I purchased an Oldsmobile in 1996, about $3,000 was pre-paid thanks to the credit card. At least two-thirds of that was earned at Vegas World buying these packages, which gave me an advantage and essentially no risk.

When Ginnie and I moved to Las Vegas, I still had 20 or so uncashed packages, and for awhile, more could be purchased from resellers. We used the California address of one of Ginnie's girlfriends and every weekend we'd each cash a package or two.

We did this until they were no longer obtainable.

To ensure our win, we placed half our promotional chips on the don't pass and half on the pass line in craps, with the appropriate amount on the 12 for insurance. A smarter bet would have been to just play the money on the don't pass, as the house bite would be lessened. However, the results would fluctuate more.

Was this fun? Not at all. And this also bothered Ginnie. You had to go into a crowded casino filled with people annoyed at being suckered into the (original) $398 deal. By then, the crap dealers all knew us. They also knew we were earning a hundred or so "free dollars" every time and resented us for it. No matter; we continued to do it as long as we could. It was, after all, bankroll, and as far as I was concerned, it beat working a regular job.

There's an old joke about a kid shoveling manure as fast as he can, knowing a pony must be in there somewhere. In gambling, I've sometimes had to deal with a lot of manure. I've found a few ponies. They *are* there, in some of the most unlikely places. Even today, while Shirley and I enjoy a much higher standard of living than I knew at the time, I'd still cash these packages if the option were available. Spending two hours and getting a guaranteed $200 every time? You bet!

Playing at the Sahara in 1994

I studied Stanford Wong's *Professional Video Poker* and memorized the strategy. However, Wong's strategy was for 8/5 Jacks or Better with a 12,000-coin royal flush (from a progressive meter) and I was using it on 9/6 Jacks or Better games with lower royals. Furthermore, Wong's belief at the time was that speed at this game was more important than complete accuracy, so his strategy was simplified. For example, all suited high card-ten combinations were grouped together, so I had no idea that JT was superior to QT, which was superior to KT. Similarly, Wong put all combinations of two unsuited high cards together—and ranked below high card-ten (that is, from Q♥J♠T♠, hold JT)—so I had no idea that AK, AQ, and AJ were actually lower in value than KQ and KJ, which were both lower in value than QJ.

The game I began with was 9/6 Jacks or Better at the Sahara. It required four quarters to play and the royal paid $1,000. A 4-coin game paying a $1,000 royal is equivalent to a 5-coin game paying $1,250 (a "5,000-coin" royal flush)—without the tax forms. (There were also a couple of 4-coin 8/5 Bonus Poker games, but they paid less, so I didn't attack them first.) The 9/6 game returned slightly over 100%, but the Sahara held promotions that made it worthwhile. Before I could modify the strategies to handle the promotions, however, I needed to learn the basics of this game.

Coins in the Tray

During my first few years in Las Vegas, I constantly looked for coins abandoned in trays and on the floor. I probably found $200 or so in all—certainly not a lot considering the hours I spent looking, but when you feel your survival is at stake, every extra buck or two is manna from heaven.

There's an art to picking up spare coins. Because if a casino identifies you as a "silver miner," you can expect a security guard or two to show up pronto. Casinos want people who bring money into the casino and are willing to pay for their gambling excitement. "Scavengers" are not good for business.

So, if I spotted a dollar or more in a tray, I'd sit down at the machine for a few seconds and act like I was playing. I'd put my slot club card into the machine and sometimes even load $10 into the bill acceptor. Then I'd press the cashout button so all of the coins would mix together and there would be no way to tell which were there originally.

If the coin was a quarter or less, I'd generally just pick it up. If a security guard told me I couldn't keep it because it wasn't mine (which has happened two or three times), so be it—this small amount of money wasn't that important. But for a dollar or more, I'd spend a minute to increase my chances of getting the dough.

My stance on strategy simplification was (and is) different from Wong's. I had more time than money. I had the ability to figure things out. I had a new computer (my first personal computer ever) and both of Wong's video poker programs. I figured that, for me, accuracy was more important than speed. The goal was to prosper in these games and build a bankroll. I figured I couldn't do that unless I stressed accuracy over all.

I'd also picked up Dan Paymar's 8th edition of *Video Poker Precision Play*. His Jacks or Better strategy was an eye-opener. It was considerably more complex than Wong's, but, as I learned as I went along, full of mistakes. Still, it gave me added insight.

In a footnote in one of Paymar's appendices, he'd written that you should hold a suited high card-10 over two unsuited high cards unless there was another card suited with the high card-ten. By now I knew that you had to look at all five cards to make the proper playing decision, rather than merely compare two combinations. I had been grouping cards into categories (high pairs, three-card straight flushes with no high cards and one gap, etc.) without realizing that the value of those groupings wasn't fixed. Paymar taught me that the play of A♥Q♠T♠9♥4♣ was different from A♥Q♠T♠9♥4♠, though he hadn't taught me why. (I later figured out the easy-to-overlook fact that the value of Q♠T♠ was higher if there were still 11 spades in the deck than if there were only 10.) As it turns out, Paymar's rule was wrong more often than it was right, but this was my first glimpse into the effect of "penalty cards."

Even with this insight, my strategy never got to be completely accurate. But it was close. And I was working on four games at once. On Thursdays, the Sahara paid double for royal flushes hit in the first 10 minutes of any hour. On Sundays, it was double pay for four aces. With four aces doubled, Ginnie (she hadn't left yet) and I switched to the 4-coin 8/5 Bonus Poker machines where aces paid an extra $80 compared to an extra $25 on the 9/6 Jacks game.

So I was working on the 9/6-5,000 Jacks or Better, 9/6-10,000 Jacks or Better (because of the double royal), 8/5-10,000 Bonus Poker, and 8/5-5,000 Bonus Poker with double pay for four aces. It was a mess. There were a lot of similarities between the games, but also many differences.

The first time Ginnie hit a royal flush was on an 8/5 Bonus Poker machine at about 9 p.m. on a Sunday when we were trying for the aces at the Sahara. A thousand dollars was a lot for us at the time so I was happy, and Ginnie knew she'd receive her $100 bonus, so she was happy. She wanted to go to a movie to celebrate. Since the promotion ended in three hours and we didn't have another video poker or blackjack promotion until that Wednesday, I asked if we could please continue to play and celebrate on Monday or Tuesday. After one of her "you love money more than you love me" pouts, she gave in to the logic and we each managed to hit four aces before we left that night. (The next night we did go to the movies. We would watch a movie once, then stay in the theater after everyone else left. I would take a half-hour to explain some of the scenes to her, because she never caught all of the words. By then the movie was running again and she would catch enough to enjoy it. I was always surprised by how much more I also saw the second time through.)

The double pay for four aces worked like this. The machine paid once. Then you turned on the change light and the floorperson paid a second time. That was $80 for aces—twice. (If you're a Bonus Poker player used to aces paying $100, remember that this was a 4-coin, not a 5-coin, machine.) One night Ginnie hit the aces and a new floorperson came over. He did the math and figured that the total amount due us was $160. He paid us the $160 in cash and walked away. We still had the $80 in credits. What to do?

We decided to keep the money, but leave for the evening. If we hit aces again and the same floorperson happened to be paired with someone else who knew that we should get $80 instead of $160, we might have been required to return the money. But if we came back a week later, it's likely that no one would remember. The extra $80 came out of casino overhead and was unlikely to be traced to the floorperson, so we had no qualms about keeping it.

For the Thursday royal flush promotion, our strategy was to play the one 4-coin 9/6 Jacks machine non-stop, but to use the 10,000-coin-royal strategy during the 10-minute intervals at the top of every hour when the royal flush paid double. This machine was slightly positive even without the promotion, so we had no problem playing it through. (We should have had a problem, though. The edge was pennies an hour with considerable risk.) Since there were two of us, Ginnie played one of two 4-coin 8/5 Bonus machines slowly (slightly negative without the promotion). If she was dealt four cards to the royal, she stopped playing that machine and saved the good hand until the top of the hour. She'd switch to the second 8/5 Bonus machine if it was available. If I happened to get four cards to the royal during the off period, I switched over to the 8/5 Bonus machine if I could.

Waiting with the 4-card royal preserved a 1-in-47 chance to collect an extra $1,000, which is worth $21.27 on average. That's not a lot, but since the entire promotion was worth less than that per hour, it was *always* a good idea to wait. We both brought books and if we got the hands, we waited. We waited 20 times or so over the months that this promotion was alive, but never benefited from the waiting. Not a big surprise, but a disappointment nonetheless. When you make a smart play to squeeze out a little extra, it's better when it pays off once in awhile.

On one Thursday, Ginnie and I were playing and someone else had one of the 8/5 Bonus machines. We watched him play and because he was using the appropriate strategy for the higher royal, we figured he knew what he was doing. It happened that he hit a royal flush at about five minutes before the hour. The guy knew that if he called it to the floorperson's attention right then, he would receive only $1,000. But if he got away with waiting for another six minutes, he might be paid $2,000. So he decided to chance it.

When you hit any jackpot, the colored "candles" on top of the machine start blinking. So the guy put a couple of plastic change cups over the candles and hung his jacket over the change cups. Ginnie and I were curious about what would happen. It's one thing, we thought, to silently let a casino pay you more than you're entitled to, but it might be another to doctor the evidence to get the extra pay. It's a gray area, perhaps, but we didn't want to be involved.

He looked at us and said, "You know what I'm doing, don't you?" I said that we did, but we had no intention of either lying for him or turning him in. Soon a change girl showed up and said that it was too bad he'd hit the royal a few minutes early. He turned to her and said, "If you tell them that I hit it after the hour, and they buy it, I'll pay you one hundred dollars." The change girl agreed.

At five minutes after the hour, the player took his jacket off the machine, removed the cups from the top of the candle, and started to whoop and holler with excitement. The floorperson came over and asked the change girl if it had happened before or after the hour. "After" was her response.

The floorman shook his head and said, "It's pretty close. I'd better go check the cameras." The player knew that when they looked at the cameras, he was a dead duck. Who knows, he might be arrested for fraud. He was sweating. The change girl was sweating. Ginnie and I were uncomfortable, as well. We didn't want to be witnesses one way or the other, but the floorperson knew us and knew we'd been there when it happened.

The floorman came back and he had the shift boss with him. The shift boss said, "We have a problem with the cameras in this section of the casino and we can't tell if it was before or after the hour, so we're going to pay you."

The player came to life and glibly lied, "No matter. You would have come to the same conclusion if you had seen the tape." So he was paid and after the bosses left, he slipped $100 to the change girl. He offered to pay me $100 as a reward for keeping my mouth shut. We sure could have used the money, but I wasn't sure what to do. Ginnie tapped my leg and when I looked at her, she shook her head very slightly. So I refused. Soon midnight came and we all left.

Would I have done the same thing in that player's place? I honestly don't know. I've passed such an "integrity test" many times in my life, but I've also failed on occasion. I certainly know the right thing was to tell the truth, but I also know that I was under considerable financial pressure and may well have succumbed. I *also* know there was a risk of serious consequences. When you're caught failing an integrity test, you might find yourself spending time in jail, and definitely *not* writing about how you won a million bucks. I'm not a saint, and throughout this book I fess up to occasionally having my own feet of clay. But I suspect that many people struggle with such dilemmas in gambling situations. I can't say mine is always the best way to do things, but if you've been there, I can tell you you're not alone in your struggles.

A week later, I was playing a quarter 8/5 Jacks or Better progressive at the Sahara on a Thursday morning. The meter was at about $3,500. The shift boss was talking to me as I played, and I hit the royal. We both looked at our watches: 8:58. Sigh! Two minutes too early. He went away to supervise the paying of my jackpot.

When he came back, he told me that the 10-minutes-an-hour rule was causing more trouble than it was worth and that the Sahara was now paying the extra $1,000 all day Thursday. They hadn't announced it yet, but it was definitely a policy and I was the first recipient. Congratulations!

This was welcome news, and not only because of that instant $1,000 bonus. The promotion had just become more lucrative. In round numbers, an extra $1,000 for a 25¢ royal adds about 2% in return, which is $15 dollars more per hour. The bonus is worth only $2.50 per hour if it's restricted to the first ten minutes. The change in rules meant my expected income had just shot up an extra $12.50 per hour.

Still, when I did the math I realized that playing these promotions wasn't going to cut it for me. My "nut" (my recurring monthly living expenses) was more than my intake. Ginnie put in her full hours playing, but hitting the normal number of paydays on these deals wasn't enough.

It was then that I discovered Deuces Wild. I'd never even looked at this game; until then I'd examined only variations of Jacks or Better. Deuces Wild is totally different. But I knew from Paymar's book, as well as from a book by Lenny Frome (an early video poker guru who actually coined the often-used term "full-pay") what the full-pay schedule was. There were four of these machines at the Sahara and I figured that, with the promotion, the games were worth $25 an hour on Thursdays. If Ginnie and I could each play 16 hours every Thursday, this game would bring in $400 a week apiece. With the couponing and the occasional blackjack promotion, that would be enough for us to survive.

But first I had to learn Deuces Wild, both with a 4,000-coin and an 8,000-coin royal. I knew from experience that Frome's and Paymar's strategies would not be acceptable for me as a final product, but they were a good place to start. I had a week before the next Double Royal Thursday came around.

I spent upwards of 50 hours in the next six days learning the game and teaching it to Ginnie. We got to the Sahara at 11:50 p.m. the next Wednesday night, ready to play for eight hours straight, only to find every seat full. Damn! We hadn't counted on that. It was the first time we'd run into this particular fact of life—if a casino is offering a juicier-than-average promotion, *a lot* of people will show up to try to take advantage of it. If you don't like crowds, make sure you play only when a promotion isn't going on.

The Deuces machines were all taken, so we played the 4-coin machines. They weren't as good as the Deuces, but still a good deal. It was here that we ran into another fact of life: When you switch between games as radically different as Jacks or Better and Deuces Wild, making mistakes is very common.

We played until 9 or so the next morning, then took a room to sleep for a few hours. (The Sahara didn't have a well-structured slot club at that time, but as known regulars, Ginnie and I could get rooms whenever we wanted them.) We slept, ate, and were back at the machines by 4 in the afternoon. There was one Deuces Wild machine open, so I played it and Ginnie played the 9/6.

One of the harsh realities of Deuces Wild is that the swings are bigger than they are playing Jacks or Better. If you don't hit

How Are the ...

Assume you're looking at the following five cards: 5♥5♠A♠4♠9♠ and you decide to hold the spades (the correct play for most games). You draw and get the 5♦ in the first position. Players often wonder if they would have gotten this same card had they held 55.

The answer is yes. In all video poker machines manufactured by companies licensed in Nevada, the sixth through tenth cards come out in the identical order, no matter which cards were originally held. So if you'd held 55, you would make 555 at least (and have a chance for four 5s).

The main reason players ask is because they want to know if it's legitimate for them to feel bad that they could have made a paying hand, rather than end up with the actual worthless hand. I'd say that you have the right to feel bad whenever you want. But just because a 5 came out first doesn't affect the fact that holding the spades was the correct play to begin with. The right versus the wrong hold decision must always be made *before* you know the results of the draw.

The method of dealing cards just described is called "serial." Many players mistakenly believe that five cards are stacked directly behind the original five cards after the deal—a method called "parallel." For most purposes, it really doesn't matter other than facilitating the fruitless shoulda-woulda-couldas when another draw would have worked out better.

However, there is a situation where knowing the way the cards are dealt is important. Say you were dealt K♠Q♥K♦K♣5♥.

a royal or four deuces, you get stuck pretty quickly. I ended up losing $500 that night and Ginnie lost $300. On the earlier shift we'd lost $400 between us. Instead of being up $800 for the day, as we'd budgeted, we were down $1,200. When your entire bankroll is $7,000 and you need part of that to pay rent and buy gas, a loss of this magnitude represents a big hit. It was also the straw that broke the camel's back for Ginnie; she moved back to Southern California two days later.

... Cards Dealt?

You hold the three kings and draw. After the draw you see K♠7♦K♦K♥3♦. This looks like a normal unsuccessful draw until you examine the card in fourth position carefully. It was the K♣ before the draw and now it's the K♥. What happened? The K♣ became "un-held"—perhaps because of a sticky button or maybe it just wasn't hit squarely. If you believe the cards are dealt in a parallel fashion, then one 3-of-a-kind is as good as another and you'll go on to the next hand. But if you know that the cards are dealt in a serial fashion, you'll figure out that the final hand should have been K♠7♦K♦K♣K♥. This is a big difference in payoff and most casinos will pay you for the quad if you mention it right away (modern video poker machines can view the before and after images of some number of recently played hands).

Sometimes the cards being dealt in a serial rather than parallel fashion ends up costing you. Assume you are dealt Q♠7♣Q♥6♦5♥ and hold the Q♠. As before, assume the Q♥ becomes un-held and you end up with Q♠A♣4♥3♥Q♣. Should you be paid for a pair of Qs or for 3-of-a-kind? I argue that the pair is fair because if the Q♥ hadn't slipped away the hand would have ended up Q♠A♣Q♥4♥3♥ and the Q♣ would have never appeared.

Should you try to get paid for a 3-of-a-kind anyway? I would have during the early years of my career. Today I wouldn't, because a knowledgeable manager would know I was "taking a shot" and wouldn't appreciate it. Why risk threatening my welcome over a few coins?

Interestingly, though, her leaving led to a turnaround in my fortunes. Within two weeks I hit three Thursday-royals and broke even for the rest of the time, so my bankroll doubled. It was tempting to say that all I needed to win was for Ginnie to leave, but I knew better. *When* the royals come is largely luck. It was just a fluke that they bunched up that way. I missed Ginnie, but I had to make the best of whatever the rest of my life would bring.

I Meet a Knowledgeable Man

Note: In this chapter, two separate men have been combined into the character I call "Pete." Neither would want their real names or strong identifying characteristics bandied about in print.

For the first six months of 1995, I was at the Sahara every Wednesday night by about 10 p.m., playing Deuces Wild using the $1,000-royal strategy until midnight. When the promotion began at 12:01 a.m., I'd switch to the $2,000-royal strategy and play for as long as I could (stopping when I could no longer operate proficiently). At nine or ten in the morning, I'd either check into a hotel room for a few hours or drive home. I usually managed to put in a second shift Thursday afternoon or evening. Ten o'clock Wednesday night was always early enough to get a seat. If I'd failed a time or two, I would have gone in at 9 or earlier.

On two occasions I was dealt four to the royal before midnight, so I pulled out a paperback and started to read. The second time, the shift boss came around at about 11:55 and told me that I might as well play, because if I hit the royal, it wouldn't count for a double pay. I asked why and he told me it was because I was abusing the "spirit of the rules." I looked at him funny and he said, "The rules say 'Management Reserves All Rights.' You're not going to win this argument." I shrugged, played on, and the royal wasn't there.

There's a time to fight and a time to walk away—this was the latter. Even if I'd waited until after midnight, hit the royal, and gotten Gaming Control to agree I deserved the extra thousand (a long shot to be sure), the victory would likely be Pyrrhic. It did me no good to anger Sahara management sufficiently for them to ask me to take my business elsewhere. Casinos always hold that card and I didn't want to put them in a position that would force its use on me.

It was at this point that I realized that casino promotions aren't always black and white, and are often cat-and-mouse propositions. Apparently, the Sahara had been burned a time or two by people sitting on 4-to-a-royal until the promotion was in effect. So now management was walking around prior to midnight and telling players that royals made on hands originally dealt prior to midnight wouldn't count. From the casino's point of view, it was the old adage, "Burn me once, shame on you. Burn me twice, shame on me."

Another player came by every week about the same time I did. It was Pete. I'd seen Pete around for a few years. He'd provided information for a few of Stanford Wong's books, was in the process of programming the "best video poker computer trainer ever," and was constantly on the lookout for casino games to beat. Since we'd played backgammon against some of the same opponents in the past, we struck up a friendship. Our unwritten arrangement was that he would expound on things he knew (moreso after he'd had a few drinks) and I would help him with some hands, because I'd studied $2,000 Deuces Wild more than he had.

One of the first things Pete taught me was unintentional on his part, but it was valuable nonetheless. Each new promotion required study to determine how to take advantage of it. Pete's attitude was that if a promotion paid enough, it was okay if he didn't play every hand perfectly, because he was still a favorite. This approach, however, turned a potential $25-per-hour promotion into a $15-per-hour promotion. Still a good deal. Still the best thing going for him on Thursdays. But nowhere near what it could be. Pete constantly had his eye on the future and the killings that he could make, but he gave up a sizable amount in the present. My philosophy was that in order to have the bankroll in the future to take advantage of whatever comes along, you need to take care of the present.

I told Pete that I'd created the $2,000 Deuces Wild strategy using *Stanford Wong Video Poker,* a software trainer. He told me that *SWVP* was good, but another program was better. What was this? I gradually got out of him that a company called Panamint produced a program called *Video Poker Tutor,* and that it was the best out there. Of course. Pete's own program would be better still. I wound up getting Panamint's fine program and will write more about that in other chapters. Whether or not Pete's program actually was ever finished, I don't know.

Pete taught me about "scares." Say you're dealt A♥K♥J♥5♠4♦, and draw, in order, T♥5♣. That would be a scare, because the last card could have made you a royal flush (had it been the Q♥). Compare this to a draw in which the last two cards, in order, are 5♣T♥. This is as much a 4-to-the-royal hand as the previous one, but that wouldn't qualify as a scare, because the 5♣ "ruined" your chances for the royal. (Some players call such hands "80-percenters." When the next-to-the-last-card ruined the royal and the last card was a royal card, Pete called it a "Polish scare.")

"It takes forty-seven scares on average for every royal you make," Pete told me. "So if each royal returns two thousand dollars, each scare is worth a little over forty bucks. Since I've had two scares today, I figure I'm eighty bucks ahead of what my actual score shows."

"But if on your next hand your scare turns into a real royal, then you'll still count it as forty dollars, right?" I responded. "If you get a royal next hand, you'll count it as being up a hundred twenty rather than two thousand?"

Pete smiled. "Yes. That's one downside to giving yourself credit for scares. People want to assign an average value for every scare, but then count full value for the royal. They only end up fooling themselves."

"So why do it? I've seen several players making a mark in their notebook for every scare they get."

Pete thought about this. "Lots of reasons, I think. Some players have a strong belief that there are unfair machines out there. Presumably, if they kept track of scares, they could sometimes identify those gaffed machines, although I'm not sure how they would do it and I believe that machines in Nevada are fair anyway.

"Second, people like to whine. And they believe that adding precision to their whining makes it better. I think they believe that saying something like, 'I've had one hundred thirty-seven scares since my last royal and that makes me unluckier than you!' makes people feel sorry for them. Not likely!

"Third, people need some kind of salve to help them through the losing streaks. If they know that they have a lot of scares, it might be likelier that the machines will 'catch up with their royals' someday. So in some way, the losing streak doesn't seem as bad as it otherwise might.

"Fourth, if each scare is given a type of time stamp and saved in a permanent notebook, then they believe the IRS will accept their logbooks more than if they didn't have these intermediate verifications. Probably true."

We didn't talk only about video poker, of course. We'd each recently lost a girlfriend, and there were the NBA playoffs (it was the year that Michael Jordan came back just before the playoffs, but the Bulls lost early anyway), and a whole lot of other subjects. But the video poker information I picked up was very valuable.

For example, I learned how to calculate progressives. "Remember," he said, "if there are three cards to be drawn, as with a suited KQ, there are sixteen thousand two hundred fifteen possible combinations. Every dollar added to the progressive has to be divided by that number to determine its effect on the KQ. If there are two cards to be drawn, such as an AKQ, the number is one thousand eighty-one. And if there's only one card to be drawn, such as AKJT, the number is forty-seven. Keep that in mind and you'll be able to figure out the rest for yourself." He was right.

Just as I was playing at the Sahara on Thursdays, I was also playing at Vacation Village on Sundays and Mondays. I told Pete that I was working on a 10/7 Double Bonus strategy and would probably publish it someday. He wasn't happy about that.

"The more people who know how to play, the tougher the games will get and the harder it will be for pros to make money," he said. "You can likely earn more money by using what you've figured out and keeping it to yourself than you can by enlightening the world." (This view was echoed to me by dozens of pros over the next several years. Many of them encouraged me to stop publishing information for the masses. Even some who learned from me in 1999 and 2000 came to me later to say that they were glad they had the information, but now please stop teaching others. I think this is a shortsighted view and will explain why later.)

Pete also explained the rationale behind team play. At the time I was considering whether I wanted to be connected with a team. After all, the idea of getting paid to play, without worrying about the risks, had a certain appeal. But as he went through the math, I decided that as long as I had the bankroll, it would be much more profitable for me to play on my own. I experimented a few years later with running my own team and found I wasn't cut out for it (I tell about this in "Trying to Go to the Bahamas.")

Pete helped me a lot, as have several other pros since. Most of them don't want their names published and many have requested that what they tell me not be printed until whatever it's about is dead and gone. I've respected these wishes. But the absorption of knowledge is an important part of the process of becoming good at anything, which is why I couldn't have been as successful as I've been without going through it.

Other potentially successful gamblers who will start by standing on my shoulders (and Wong's and Paymar's and Scott's and TomSki's and Zamzow's and Compton's, etc.) will still need to find others to learn from. Why? Because casino managers stand on our shoulders too. It would be nice, perhaps, to learn what we need to know without others becoming aware of it too, but I know of no way for that to happen.

Vacation Village in My Early Days

The year 1995 was still early in my video poker career. At this time, the only games I knew reasonably well were 9/6 Jacks and Deuces Wild, and my gambling bankroll was about

$12,000. Ginnie had moved back to California and I had yet to meet Shirley.

Vacation Village (VV) was a barn of a casino, located on Las Vegas Boulevard about two miles south of the last casino on the Las Vegas Strip (the Hacienda at the time, now Mandalay Bay). VV closed in early 2002 and as I write has not re-opened.

I came across my first "card-of-the-day" promotion there. The way it worked at VV was that every 4-of-a-kind in the card of the day paid double: four 3s on Sunday, 4s on Monday, etc., until 9s on Saturday, then they started over again. I knew that doubling the pay for a low quad at 9/6 Jacks added only .44% (which brings the total return to 99.98%—not nearly enough if you had to support yourself, which I did), so I walked the casino and looked at every machine to see if there was a better game to play. I didn't look at just some of the machines. I looked at every single one.

The best quarter machine was 10/7 Double Bonus (returning 100.17% to start with), and the best dollar machine was 9/7 Double Bonus (returning 99.11%). Doubling four 4s added 1.37% to either game. It might seem obvious that adding 1.37% to 100.17% would be much better than adding 1.37% to 99.11%, but it's not that simple.

Assuming 600 hands per hour, on a 25¢ game you put $750 per hour through the machine. And a 101.54% return (which is 100.17% + 1.37%) on $750 implies an hourly win rate of $11.55. The same 600-hand-per-hour rate means putting $3,000 an hour through a $1 machine. That amount times a 100.48% return (99.11% + 1.37%) implies an hourly rate of $14.40, which is considerably higher. So quarters had a higher return rate, but dollars paid more per hour. Since my total gambling bankroll at the time was about $12,000, I decided to play for quarters. I didn't have a firm grasp on bankroll considerations at the time, but I knew that being down more than two royals (i.e., $8,000 when playing for dollars) was not that uncommon.

A big hurdle for me at this point was that I didn't know how to play Double Bonus and I couldn't find any good books with the strategy. Paymar didn't discuss the game. Lenny Frome's books had a simplified strategy, but his errors on Deuces Wild and Jacks or Better caused me to distrust it. I *was*, however, willing to start from his strategy and build. Frome certainly had the basics correct, but he didn't differentiate between close hands like K♥Q♥5♥8♠4♦ (where it's correct to hold KQ) and K♥Q♥5♥9♠3♦ (where it's correct to hold KQ5). At the time, players more advanced than I told me that this difference was worth only about a half-cent per mistake when playing for quarters, so I shouldn't sweat it. I believed then, as I do now, that since I was fighting hard to build a bankroll, I had to do what I could to capture every last half-cent. Over time, I'm sure going for the last little bit has increased my bankroll by several thousand dollars.

Today, good strategies are easy to obtain, given that over the years a number of authors have published quality work. In addition, a good strategy for almost any pay schedule can be obtained almost instantly from *Video Poker for Winners!*. These resources weren't available when I began, so I had to work things out myself. And even then, before I would invest significant money playing a strategy, I spent hours practicing, attempting to memorize, and looking for errors and exceptions in it. To me it's like driving a car. I can't feel comfortable driving fast until I've tested the brakes thoroughly. And at that time for me, betting $750 per hour, hour after hour, was definitely speeding.

Even though I could play for a few hours straight on the computer without making a mistake, every so often a new hand would appear that I wasn't quite sure about. If I was in a casino, I wrote it down, went home, and checked it out. Another player at the time was also developing a strategy and we compared notes. Sometimes he stumped me and sometimes I stumped him, but we both became much better players that way.

One of the things to check during a promotion is which plays change with the promotion. For example, with T♥9♥3♥2♥3♠, the four-card flush is the best play when four 3s returns 400 coins. But how about when it returns 800 coins? I had to check. (It turns out that a four-flush is still the better play.) I found variations from standard play when 3 or 4 was the card of the day, different variations when the card of the day was 5 or 7, and still different variations when the card of the day was 8 or 9.

The Altered Numbers,
for Those Who are Interested

When quad 3s or 4s pays double, break a full house (as in 33399) to hold the card-of-the-day trips. A card-of-the-day pair is better than an open-ended 4-card straight (as in 33456). With 5s through 9s, a card-of-the-day pair is better than a 4-card straight with no high cards (as in 55789) and a card-of-the-day pair is better than a suited QJ9 or JT9. With 8s and 9s, there's the additional possibility of a low card-of-the-day pair matched against a 4-card open-ended straight with one or more high cards (such as 889TJ). On these hands, go for the straight.

In addition to the card of the day, whenever you got a 4-of-a-kind of any sort, you received a coupon worth $1.25 and a ticket for VV's every-other-hour drawing. If your name was called, you could take a guaranteed $50 or spin a Big 6 wheel for cash. Most of the spaces on the wheel were for $10 or $20, but there were a few for $50 and $100, one for $400, and one for $1,000. To determine whether it was better to spin or take the guaranteed $50, I added up all the numbers and divided by the number of spaces. The average was $57. Not a close decision at all for me; I would always spin whenever they called my name.

There were actually two barrels for drawing tickets. One was very large, and two names were picked from it every other hour between 9 a.m. and 11 p.m. The other drum was very small. They called two names from this drum at 1 a.m., 3 a.m., 5 a.m., and 7 a.m. Since you had to be present to win, and sometimes during graveyard there were more employees in the building than players, I quickly decided my odds were *much* better if I played on the graveyard shift.

For almost a year, I averaged three or four calls on Sunday and Monday graveyard shifts. Eventually, VV decided that paying so much to the same people over and over again wasn't the kind of promotion they wanted, so they discontinued the graveyard drawings.

This one play alone added $10,000 to my bankroll in less than a year, but it was a grind-it-out $10,000. I put in many hours to win tickets and made sure I was there for the drawings. My overall strategy at that time was to spend as little money as possible and bank what I could. I was very clear with myself that I didn't want to be playing for quarters forever and when good dollar and higher situations presented themselves, I wanted to be ready.

There was a curious sideline attached to this period concerning the *Las Vegas Advisor*, a monthly newsletter that tells people how to get a better bang for their buck in Las Vegas. Since I was out and about all the time, I would send the publisher, Anthony Curtis (who happens to be the publisher of this book), all kinds of information about situations I found. Vacation Village would change certain details of the promotion described above every few months and I would tell Anthony how one deal added up to $3.18 an hour and some other deal added up to $2.97 and still a third was worth $6.18 and you could do them all at the same time. To my surprise, Anthony always seemed less than impressed. What he *did* like, though, was that you could get a hot dog and beer at the bar for a $10 buy-in on nickel games. *That* was a good deal, as far as he was concerned!

My First Play for Dollars

Note: An honest accounting of "how I got from there to here" must include a few shenanigans in which I indulged early on. This story happened pretty much as presented at a real casino in Las Vegas, but the name "Firestone" is obviously made up.

I'd been playing at the Sahara on Thursdays and Vacation Village on Sundays and Mondays for almost a year when I discovered a good dollar play at the Firestone. I don't remember how I came to find it in the first place, but it wound up being a turning point in my career.

The game at the Firestone was dollar 10/7 Double Bonus with

Do You Know What it Takes to Win?

I've posed the following riddle to hundreds of people—both one-on-one and in the "Secrets of a Video Poker Winner" classes that I teach. Of the 20 or so winning gamblers I've queried, *every one* got the answer correct and thought the riddle was trivial and easy. Of the non-winners I've queried, more than half have missed it. Why? Simply because what it takes to win and what people *think* it takes to win are two different things. Here's the riddle.

Stan and Pearl are imaginary friends of mine. Every night they go to a casino and play dollar 9/6 Jacks or Better, a game that returns slightly over 99.5% when played perfectly—which they are able to do. (There is no slot club in this part of my imagination.)

Stan and Pearl are more disciplined than any players you've ever seen. Stan plays exactly 10 hands every night, then stops whether he's ahead or behind. Pearl also plays 10 hands, but if she's ahead by at least the value of a flush, she plays five more hands. If she hits a flush or higher during those five hands, she parlays those winnings by playing five more hands. And she keeps playing her sets of five hands until she finally hits a five-hand dry spell, at which time she too will stop for the night.

Stan stops and Pearl parlays. Here's the question for you: If Stan and Pearl gamble in this manner every night for a year, whose net result is more likely to be better at the end of the year? Go ahead and figure it out before you turn the page. I'll wait. ...

a .39% cash slot club. This was a 100.56% return, and since dollars allowed me to put about $2,500-$3,000 through the machines an hour, I figured that this was worth about $15 per hour. That was about the same hourly return as the quarter games at the other casinos, so there was no incentive for me to move up in denomination, especially because now I would have W-2Gs to worry about. The casino is required to issue an IRS reporting document called a W-2G on all jackpots of $1,200 or higher—which on this game was triggered by the $4,000 payoff for the royal flush.

However, there was a promotion at the Firestone that caught my eye. Every time you got a 4-of-a-kind or a straight flush, the change girls would stamp a card that had 25 squares. It looked

---

... The people who like Pearl's chances often tell me that she's playing with the house's money and that's good. Or they'll tell me that the secret to winning is to catch a machine on a hot streak, then ride it to wealth. Players who know how to win, however, know that Pearl's approach is the wrong one.

Winning players know that the key to this puzzle is that 9/6 Jacks or Better returns only 99.5% without a slot club, which means this game is a loser for the player. So the one who plays the least loses the least. Since Stan plays less than Pearl, Stan figures to lose less than Pearl during the year.

If we alter the riddle slightly so that the casino has a slot club that pays 1% cashback, everything changes. The game is now worth 100.5%. So since Pearl is the one playing more hands, Pearl is the one who will usually have the better results.

You've probably heard that you should bet more when you're ahead. You've also heard that you should quit when you're ahead. This is another example of two widely quoted rules that recommend opposite actions. It's not possible for them both to be correct, but it is possible for both to be wrong. And they are.

The secret to winning at any gambling game is to bet only when you have the advantage. If you're the favorite and you can afford the swings, go for it. If you're not, don't. Period! That's the secret to winning.

like a bingo card. There were six free squares and a completed card was worth almost $200. That meant each quad or straight flush earned an extra bonus worth a little more than $10 ($200/19 = $10.53), and since I would get about 1.5 of these an hour, the promotion was worth an additional $16 an hour.

Adding Up the Advantage

Here's the step-by-step process for calculating an edge in situations such as that encountered at the Firestone.

Step 1: Determine the advantage

Base game	100.17%
Less: factor for mistakes (I knew this game well.)	.00%
Real return	100.17%
Plus slot club cashback	.39%
Total return	100.56%

Step 2: Determine amount of action
550 hands x $5 per hand = $2,750
The low 550 hands per hour was due to the slower-than-normal play due to frequent "coin spills" (see page 63).

Step 3: Multiply the advantage times the action
.56% x $2,750 = $15.40—which I round downward to $15. The 550 hands per hour is just an approximation anyway.

Step 4: Add the value of the promotion
This is an approximation. Each bingo square was worth $200/19 = $10.52. I figured I'd get about 1.5 of these per hour, so I gave the promotion a value of $16 per hour.

Adding everything up yields the play's value of $31 per hour. There's always some amount of guesswork and approximation involved. But the objective is not to peg precisely what you will make per hour. It's to determine whether playing is worth the time to begin with and whether it's better than playing someplace else.

Now it all added up to $31 per hour. Plus, I could play any hour of any day of the week for the three months the promotion was scheduled to run. I knew Double Bonus cold (from my play at Vacation Village) and by then I'd built my bankroll up to about $20,000. I still didn't know a lot about how much bankroll I needed to survive the swings on this game—I hoped my $20K would be enough.

All of my play up until that time had been for quarters and I'd been largely ignored in casinos. Change people never hung around; quarter players require hand-pay jackpots only on royal flushes, which don't show up very often. But as a dollar player, jackpots get magnified. Every time I called an attendant over to mark my bingo card, the jackpot was at least $250. Several times a day it was $400, $800, or occasionally $4,000. To a change person, these are big jackpots. They were big to me, too, and I began toking a dollar every time I got a $250 or $400 jackpot, $2 for an $800 hand of four aces, and $10 for a royal flush. Not major amounts to be sure, but more than I had ever tipped before.

This also made me a bigger-than-average tipper for the Firestone, and the change people began paying a lot of attention to me. How was I doing? Could they call for cocktails? Did I need anything? Everything I said was treated as though I was a wit and raconteur. I responded to the attention and enjoyed being considered a sport, at least as long as it was only costing me a buck a quad!

One time I was going through a dry spell. One of the change girls came over and asked me why I hadn't turned my light on recently for her to stamp my card. I told her I was down $1,200 in the past two hours. To my surprise she said I deserved to have a couple of squares marked to make up for my bad luck. So she proceeded give me credit for two "virtual" quads. I thanked her and gave her two $1 tokens.

Whenever I got a quad, a change girl raced up to mark my card. They wanted the dollar tip. After one attendant marked it,

Coin Spills and Ticket-Out

I've played a lot of dollar Double Bonus machines that "spill" coins, instead of registering them on the credit meter, when the count is above 400. On these machines, all quads that pay 400 coins (2s, 3s, or 4s) spill into the tray, unless you have exactly zero credits when you hit them. Other quads and straight flushes that pay 250 coins create spillage if there are more than 150 credits registered when they hit. And when you get right up close to 400 credits, any 3-of-a-kind or higher drops coins into the tray.

When coins spill, you have to either feed them back into the machine one by one or transport them to the change booth. Since I'll often load a machine with hundreds and play through a spill, I've had to transport $800 or more to the change booth on dozens of occasions. Sometimes I'm ahead of the game when I do this and sometimes I'm down a thousand or two. Regardless, people see me hauling the coins and come out with comments like, "Boy! I wish I was as lucky as you," or "Where were you playing? You found a good machine!"

Since most players bring a lot less than $800 to a casino, they figure that if someone has $800 all at once it must mean they're ahead. I don't usually want to explain to strangers that I actually started with $2,000 in my pocket and am down a bundle. Or worse, that the $800 they see is nothing (and they should see the $4,000 in my pocket). So I usually smile and say something like, "I guess it was my turn." This seems to satisfy most people.

Today, many casinos are switching to a ticket-in ticket-out procedure. With these systems, credits accumulate until you're ready to leave. When you press the cashout button, you get a receipt, which is redeemable at the cashier or a change booth. Cashing a receipt for $2,000 doesn't require much more effort than cashing one for $20. And it's a lot faster than cashing coin. Best of all, it circumvents the annoyance of being congratulated when you've lost a bundle. I *love* this new system.

another would come over a few minutes later and ask if I had received credit for the quad yet. I would honestly respond, "Yes, but only once so far." Then that second attendant would take the card and mark it once or twice more. I'd thank her and toke her appropriately. It became common practice to be credited at least twice, often more, for each quad.

This was unbelievable. Every square marked on the card was worth more than $10, and the change girls were willing to sell the marks for a dollar apiece. It wasn't just a few of employees. At least ten change girls, two hosts, and four floorpeople partici-pated in this scam. Employee morale at the Firestone was, to say the least, quite low at the time. The employees felt betrayed by the casino (which was up for sale) and were willing to stick it to management every chance they got.

By the end of the bingo promotion, I was showing up to play with plenty of $5 bills on me. When I hit a quad, I'd present the card to one of my "friends," with one of the fivers folded inside. The card was returned with a lot of spaces stamped. In a typical eight-hour playing session, I should have received 12 marks (worth $125). However, I would end up with an average of two cards filled (worth $400). It probably cost me $25 a night in expenses to harvest this bonanza.

The promotion ended and I went on to different things. I figured I'd never see the likes of that promotion again. Wrong! The next year it returned, except that this time the completed bingo cards received only $100 instead of $200. Still, the squares were worth more than $5 apiece and the same change people were willing to sell them for $1 again. In addition, now we all knew how to work this game. And since no one had been caught the year before, they were willing to stamp three or four times for every quad hit.

This went on for awhile. Eventually, other knowledgeable players discovered the promotion and began playing it, too. They saw my tipping, figured out what it was buying me, and began doing the same thing. It's hard to keep a good thing quiet.

As it happened, the 10/7 machines lost money for two months in a row and the slot director figured he needed to do something about it. He decided to kick out everyone who had hit royal flushes during those two months. I was never accused of buying bingo squares.

If I were to discover such a situation today, I would walk away. Quickly. At this point in my career, I'm unwilling to risk being caught in a scandal. Remember, a lot of people knew about this and just one person having an attack of conscience could have brought the whole thing down. In this case everyone had an incentive to keep quiet about it, and it turns out everyone did, but you can never know for sure what will happen in such a situation.

At the time I was struggling. Survival itself wasn't at issue, but I'd experienced days where I'd lost as much as $3,000. Having several of these days in a row didn't seem out of the question. My bankroll kept increasing (albeit with large swings), but I wanted as big of a cushion as I could get. By then I'd developed an obsessive loathing of ever working an 8-to-5 office job again.

Today I'm not struggling in the same sense as I was then and the actions described in this adventure now seem money-grubbing and unworthy. I hope I'm never so desperate that I have to do such things again.

Most serious gamblers who have been around long enough have faced similar temptations. A few have run away quickly, though probably more have succumbed somewhere along the way. If gambling is a life you contemplate for yourself, you might want to stop and think about how you would have reacted in this situation. And then, when it actually does happen somewhere down the road, see how your actual response jibes with what you think you would have done.

Letting *Them* Do the Math

I was playing at Sam's Town during a promotion called the House Party Giveaway in 1995. Sam's Town ran this promotion for several years and every year it was different. But the year I played they had twice-a-day, three-times-a-week, must-be-there-to-win, cash drawings totaling maybe $100,000 over a month's time. Then, on the last night, they gave away a $125,000 house.

As I recall, you earned tickets as follows: Every $25-or-higher jackpot earned that dollar value in points. Every two points were exchanged for one drawing ticket. Since I was playing dollar 10/7 Double Bonus where every straight or higher earned points, I qualified for a lot of drawing tickets.

I played in the high-limit slot area and kept track of the hands I got. Since every 4-of-a-kind was worth between 250 and 800 points, if I played a few hours, it was quite common for me to end up with 1,000 points or more. And if I took a 1,000-point voucher to the Town Hall slot club booth, they would exchange it for the 500 tickets I'd earned. But I could also take the voucher to the cage, where one cashier didn't understand the instructions clearly. She would pay two tickets per one point rather than one ticket for two points. So the same 1,000-point voucher was worth 2,000 drawing tickets if I took it to her. And take it to her I did. Not every time, but often enough so that I ended up with maybe twice as many tickets in the barrel as I was entitled to according to the rules. I did have one of my tickets drawn for $3,000, but that was all I got after being there the majority of the month and playing a huge number of hours.

My philosophy then was the same as it is now: If a casino employee makes an error in my favor that cannot be attributed to that employee and thereby get her into trouble, I keep the benefit. But if the casino employee makes an error in the house's favor, I correct her every time.

Some slot clubs have difficult formulas for determining how many dollars of cashback you get. Before I cash in points, I calculate how much I'm entitled to. Then I let the employees come up with a number. I've found several "mathematically challenged" employees who regularly overpay players. When I discover such a person, I go back to him every time.

Cashback or Bounce-Back Cash? Which is Better?

There are two primary ways casinos rebate cash to players: same-day "cashback" and "bounce-back" cash. Cashback is a rebate that is a fixed percentage of coin-in (or sometimes coin-out). Bounce-back is usually less precise. You play at a casino and you begin getting coupons in the mail.

If you're a tourist or an infrequent visitor to a casino, same-day cashback is much better than bounce-back cash. After all, if you're not returning, you'll never be able to collect your bounce-back money. For such a player, a bounce-back cash system is tantamount to no cash rebate at all.

On the other hand, if you visit a casino regularly, bounce-back cash is better. Why? Because much of the bounce-back cash that is issued will never be collected, which means the casino can afford to offer more. For example, if a casino can afford to offer .25% in same-day cashback, it might be able to offer .5% or so in bounce-back cash. For the casino, it adds up to the same amount because of the "breakage" (i.e., the non-cashed checks), but for the regular player who'd be there anyway, .5% is definitely better than .25%.

Does it bother you that you'll get twice as much bounce-back simply because some other players will get nothing at all? It doesn't bother me. My decisions are usually made according to what works best for Shirley and me. If it doesn't work so well for someone else, that's not my problem.

It's been my experience that slot club booth personnel are more likely to make a mistake in the casino's favor than in mine. I don't know if this is typical or not. But if it is, players who take the casino's word for such things are, on the whole, losers because of it. It's smart to do the math yourself as a safeguard.

If a slot club attendant miscalculates my cashback in favor of the house, I see this as an opportunity. First, I let him know that I think he's made a mistake. Sometimes he calls a supervisor over and sometimes he doesn't, but usually he gets it correct the second time. Not always, though. Sometimes the error is in my favor the second time.

Some players tell me that they're not good at math either. Fair enough, but if you go to casinos a lot, it's worth your while to learn how to do this arithmetic. Get a supervisor at each slot club to explain how the system works. Then bring a small calculator with you. I can tell you that doing the math myself beforehand, then letting the casino employees do it, has been lucrative, netting me an extra $30,000 to $40,000 in seven years. I would say that this kind of return adequately compensates me for the nuisance of having to figure it out myself. Wouldn't you?

How Are Your Flushes Running Today?

One weekend I was playing at the Firestone and a face from my past walked by. A lady I had dated eight years before (when I still lived in California) and her husband of two years were in town for a visit. I was genuinely happy to see them, as we had remained friendly. A few months earlier I had mailed them a copy of my 10/7 Double Bonus report (which was still in draft form), because I knew they played that game.

Janice and Tom came over, said hi, and asked if they could watch me play. I suggested that Janice sit down and play with my money and I'd give her pointers along the way. Since they were normally quarter players, playing for dollars was an exciting prospect for her.

Janice sat down and began playing; I had about 300 credits. The first hand that came up was actually quite easy to play, but it sure gave us something to talk about. She was dealt 4♥4♣8♥J♥A♥. The choice, obviously, is between the low pair and the 4-card flush. This is an easy play in Double Bonus. The 4-flush is worth $3.21 more than the low pair. But Janice looked at me and said: "How have your flushes been running today?"

"Huh?" I didn't have a clue what she was talking about. She was never the type to talk about bathroom matters.

"Well," she explained, "if flushes haven't been running for you today, it's a big waste of money to play for them."

"I've been getting my fair share," I stammered, and she held the hearts.

Of course, I subscribe to the opinion that what has happened earlier has absolutely nothing to do with how you should play a hand. You will never see on a strategy chart, for example, "play this way if you are winning and that way if you aren't." But not so for Janice. She sees this game as one of streaks and is forever attempting to catch a machine in a giving mood.

It took us about ten minutes to lose 100 credits. For me this was no big deal, but Janice was feeling mighty uncomfortable. Soon we had another easy hand that gave her problems. We were dealt J♦J♠4♥4♣7♦. Holding JJ44 is better than JJ by about $1.54. This upset Janice a lot. She mumbled that I could never get 4-of-a-kind making such a chicken play. "No wonder we're losing!"

She was correct that holding two pair precludes getting 4-of-a-kind, but that's a minor factor. The increased chance of getting a full house more than makes up for this. This tradeoff is not unusual in video poker. Every time you make a choice on how to play a hand, you give up the chance for certain other hands. Knowing when to give up something in order to go for something else is part of playing winning video poker.

We kept losing. Soon we were down to 100 credits. This is not particularly unusual at Double Bonus, which is a very streaky game. But Janice was now playing v-e-r-y s-l-o-w-l-y in an attempt to change the rhythm of the machine. "Hurry up," I urged her. "Each hand is worth almost four cents. Your slow play is costing us money."

She looked at me like I was crazy. Play faster? As far as she was concerned, losing on a machine was a good reason to quit altogether. As far as I was concerned, the score over the last few hours or days had absolutely nothing to do with whether or not you should continue playing. I knew I had the advantage. Let's go. Time's a wasting!

Soon we were down to 20 credits. Janice continued playing very slowly, until she was dealt A♣A♥A♠5♦5♣. Quick as a wink, she held all five cards. "Not so fast," I said. "Hold just the aces; it's the best play by fifty-seven cents."

"I can't do it. You'll have to do it yourself. Fifty bucks is just too much to mess around with when you're losing!"

I reached over, un-held the fives, and drew. I got a six and a four, ending up with three of a kind, worth $15.

"See!" she said triumphantly. "Your idiotic play just cost you thirty-five dollars. I hope you're happy!"

I smiled and said that I was comfortable that I'd made the right play. I knew that once in $23^{1}/_{2}$ draws I would connect for an $800 payoff for four aces, which would make up for all the $35 losses, and then some.

About this time Janice was dealt A♣K♦Q♠9♥6♣. She held KQ, which is certainly a reasonable play. But AKQ is better and I told her so.

"What! Tom would kill me if he saw me keep the ace. He says always toss the ace from AKQ."

"In that case," I kidded, "perhaps you'd better not tell him." I explained that Tom was right in most games, but in Double Bonus it depends on whether one of the other two cards is a 9.

In a few more hands, we were down to zero credits. As far as Janice was concerned, my crazy playing was responsible for the loss. As far as I was concerned, this was just a normal swing and nothing to worry about. I pulled out a $100 bill and promptly put it in. She was dumbfounded.

"You used to be such a cheapskate! Now you're throwing money around! How can you continue to waste money on a machine that has clearly shown you who's boss?"

I told her I was still thrifty, but that this game was the best one I knew about on this day and I was going to continue to play.

She played some more, and it got testy again when we had these hands back to back: K♥Q♥8♠5♥3♣ and K♠Q♠9♥7♠3♦. Getting her to play KQ in the first hand was easy. Getting her to play KQ7 in the second was impossible. "Do you want to know why you should hold all three spades?" I asked her.

"Nope! You'll just give me some smarty-pants answer that's too confusing. Why can't you play like a normal human being?"

I didn't have a good answer for that one. I never thought of my plays as being super-human—or even sub-human for that matter. My goal was to play as perfectly as a computer. If other people didn't understand my plays, that was their problem, not mine. I guess I still feel that way, although I do spend a lot of energy teaching others to play.

Janice and I remain friends today, but we'll never agree about video poker. I believe that there is only one mathematically correct way to play every hand. I believe that today's score doesn't matter. I believe that you should make every decision based on an assumption that you are in the long run. And I put my money where my mouth is.

Janice, on the other hand, has a totally different set of beliefs. And she puts her money on the line backing those beliefs. (Fortunately, she married a man with money!) Video poker is a game that you're welcome to play using your own theories. As long as your supply of quarters doesn't run out, you can make any playing decision you like.

I Learn How Comps Add Value

Note: The character "Arnie" is based mostly on one player. It's a bit of a caricature, though, in order to preserve some of Arnie's anonymity.

I knew Arnie from dance classes we took together in Bellflower, California. Every Sunday morning in the early 1990s, we both attended an intermediate West Coast swing class that drew 20 or 30 people, fortunately about an equal number of men and women. Several times after class, Arnie and I had lunch and swapped Vegas stories. We were both blackjack players trying to play with an edge. He knew more about some valuable coupons than I did and I knew about the great deal at Vegas World. We shared information.

In early 1996, I was debating whether my bankroll was big enough to play in some promotional video poker events at Treasure Island and Arnie asked me if the return would be good enough if the slot club paid double—in other words, 1.33% cash-back rather than the .67% it actually paid. I told him that that would make it interesting, but how could I get the extra pay?

I'm making up the numbers here, because I don't remember the real ones. But it was something like this. Arnie told me that for every 600 points I earned (requiring $9,000 coin-in), Treasure Island would give me a *Mystère* ticket if I asked for it and I could still keep my points. *Mystère* tickets could be sold for $60, which is exactly what the slot club paid for earning 600 points. Hence, this had the effect of doubling the slot club rate.

"But how do I sell the *Mystère* tickets?" I asked.

"Easy. Every night there's a line of people who want tickets to the sold-out performance. You just sell them to people in the line. There's a sign saying that selling the tickets for more than sixty dollars is scalping, so you don't. You can pick up the tickets and sell them very quickly."

"But doesn't the casino mind? How many *Mystère* tickets can I convince them I'll actually use myself?"

"I expect they would mind if you asked them. But so far I've received more than sixty tickets and no one has said a word."

I was amazed. I set out to try it once, but I was so afraid I'd be busted that I decided it wasn't worth it. Arnie, on the other hand, probably got more than 100 of them before the casino felt forced to make special "Arnie rules" to prevent this kind of abuse.

As I progressed in my play, Shirley and I began generating a huge number of comps issued on a use-'em-or-lose-'em basis. During weekends at the Mirage, for example, we might have earned $2,000 worth of comps above and beyond the cost of our suites. That's a lot of gourmet dinners, complete with $500 bottles of wine. But we don't drink, so $100 for dinner feeds us superbly. On occasion we've ordered a nice bottle of cognac from room service and taken it home to give away. But when you've accumulated 40 bottles, why do you need more?

Casinos frown on the selling of comps. If I want to drink a $1,000 bottle of wine, that's fine with them—especially if I go play immediately after drinking it. But if I take that bottle and sell it to someone for $200, the casino feels it's being cheated. If they catch someone doing this, it isn't unusual to see their privileges restricted.

Sometimes we get rooms for relatives, which is perfectly fine with the casinos. More than once, we secured rooms for friends for non-cash consideration (perhaps a trade of a favor or service). We've done this a little. But not a lot.

We became more and more careful about this as we played for higher stakes. Most of the comps we transferred were for extended family—and Shirley and I have big families. Plus, we feel that as long as we don't receive money for comps, we're technically all right. So we make good use of the barter system. Our chiropractor has seen several Las Vegas shows and treats us for free. Our dry cleaner worked for awhile on the same basis. If our host asks if we're selling comps, we can honestly say "no."

Is this comp abuse? It all depends on whom you ask. Casinos tend to see the issue as far more black and white than players do. Casinos are always trying to cut costs, and players feel that if their play warrants such benefits, they should be able to decide for themselves how to disperse them. Either side can get self-righteous about it.

Just remember that if you do this, you must be discreet about it. Sometimes a casino will warn you before it restricts you and sometimes it won't. And be aware that even if you can justify (to yourself) the practice of giving away, bartering, or even selling comps, you'll never be able to convince casino management that what you're doing is right.

Dieting at the Buffet

It's tough being on a diet in Las Vegas. The casinos compete with each other for the claim of having the best restaurants. And casino comps are frequently open-ended, so you can order up as much as you like and even take some back to your room in a doggie bag.

My early meals in Vegas were predominantly at buffets. "All you can eat" is a good way to go when you're eating only one meal a day because of finances. I overate at these buffets for many years.

Today, cost considerations aren't a big issue for me, but I still eat at buffets. Why? Because now I find that buffets are often the healthiest places for me to eat. I can load up on salads and vegetables and skip the rest. I can usually find some healthy food prepared simply—turkey breast, for example. At the casinos I frequent, the buffets tend to serve the same food every day. And since I've eaten at each of them numerous times and seen everything, nothing looks so good that I can't pass it up. If I want to eat healthy, it's easy to do, and no one I'm with has to suffer, because they can have whatever they want.

This technique isn't for everyone. Some people are too tempted by the lavish desserts and other goodies. But for those with will power, the buffet diet produces good results.

My Ship Has Come In

After Ginnie moved back to California, she came back to visit me a few times. We were in a neither-fish-nor-fowl relationship for about a year—not together, but not totally apart, either. One spring we traveled together to the wedding of Ginnie's best friend. About four in the afternoon the day before the wedding, we were passing through a resort area with casinos. We hadn't been at the "My Ship Has Come In" casino for awhile, so we stopped in to check things out.

The video poker inventory wasn't very impressive and the $5 and higher inventory was pathetic. The best we could find was 9/6 Jacks or Better for dollars. Since the casino slot club returned a half-percent in cash, this was a breakeven game. Not interested. Still, we decided to stop by the slot club booth to see if a promotion (that would make playing worthwhile) might be going on.

There were two: double points, which added another half-percent, and double pay on four 6s, which added another .44% for Jacks or Better.

I was used to playing with a 1% advantage, and this situation was getting close to 1%, so I did some calculations: 99.54% (base return for Jacks or Better) + .50% normal slot club return + .50% for double points + .44% for quad sixes. "This adds up to only 100.98%," I told Ginnie. "That's thirty bucks an hour; a waste of time." But Ginnie pointed out that it was close to dinnertime and we needed a place to stay the night. She figured we could probably get full comps if we played a few hours, so we sat down.

A half-hour into our play, a slot host came up and offered us dinner in the coffee shop and the casino rate on a room. He also mentioned that if we played a bit more, the casino rate would go down to zero. This was a casino with very few dollar players and most of the dollar machines had bad schedules. The casino knew it made money on dollar players, so any who fell in the door were treated like royalty to keep them from falling out again.

We were a little behind, not crazy about the promotions, and hungry, so we cashed out and went off to find the coffee shop. On the way, we noticed two $1 GameMaker machines we hadn't seen before. We didn't expect to find a good schedule, but we checked anyway. Surprise, 10/7 Double Bonus. "I'm not hungry anymore. Let's play!"

A 10/7 Double Bonus game normally returns 100.17%. But this was a Bally GameMaker machine where 5-coin straight flushes pay $400 instead of the normal $250, for a return of 100.52%. Additionally, 6666 on these machines paid a bonus of $250 rather than the $125 on Jacks or Better. Nice.

I whispered, "I think we're up to 102.4%. That's $72 per

hour apiece. Sit down and play fast!" (I figure my dollars per hour by assuming perfect play and 600 hands per hour. On a dollar machine, that means $3,000 per hour; $3,000 times 2.4% = $72.) Ginnie whispered back that she didn't know all of the strategy adjustments for this game.

"Doesn't matter much," I said. "Just play!"

After another hour, the host came back and changed our coffee shop comp to the gourmet room. "I'll have to limit your wine to only fifty dollars, but other than that, you can have whatever you want."

After another hour or so, we asked to have the machines "locked up" (held for our return). "These are our lucky machines," I explained. "We're down now, but we want to get our money back after dinner. Okay?" Like heck we were down, but I find that it often pays to tell the casino staff what they want to hear.

On our way to dinner, I stopped by the slot booth to get our cashback. They gave me quite a bit more than I was expecting. I took it (*of course*), but went away scratching my head, trying to figure out why.

Over dinner it hit me. This casino paid twice as much cashback for slots as it did for video poker. The GameMaker has both slots and video poker on it and the whole machine must have been set to pay at the slot level! Doubling the cashback added another full percent. Now our expectation was up around $100 per hour—it was the highest-paying game I'd played up to that point.

"Ginnie, let's skip the wedding."

"Bob, you promised."

"Yeah, I know, but this promotion is too good to last."

"She's my best friend."

"If she's such a good friend, she'll forgive you."

"I'm the maid of honor. I have a brand new dress."

"Yeah, but ..."

"Bob, we're going!"

"Yes, Ginnie."

We drove to the wedding the next day and had a good time. Knowing that we'd have two more days of the promotion on the way back, I pulled out my laptop and got to work while Ginnie drove. We knew 10/7 strategy cold, but we hadn't played much on the GameMaker version, and definitely hadn't played when 6666 paid double. I wanted to see what strategy variations we needed to make to take advantage of these promotions.

For example, with 6♥6♠7♥8♠9♦, usually you hold 6789, but now 66 was the correct play. And with J♦T♦9♦6♦6♠, usually you hold JT9, but now 66 took precedence. It wasn't that quad sixes were going to pop out more often during the promotion—drawing to a pair, it's a 360-to-1 shot to convert regardless. But when you do connect, the promotion boosts the payoff to $500 instead of $250. So it makes sense to go for it more often.

The higher straight flush called for a few play changes, too. For example, from K♥Q♥J♥6♥5♠, KQJ becomes correct instead of KQJ6. And with Q♦J♦T♦9♦8♣, it now makes sense to give up the made straight and try for the straight flush.

There were several other plays on my chart by the time I got through, but I knew that they didn't make much difference. Using standard 10/7 strategy and missing these plays would put us within $1 per hour or so of the return for a perfect strategy. On a $100-per-hour promotion, this wasn't much to give up.

After I finished my strategy calculations, I sat back and thought about the situation. I was uneasy. Someone else might discover the value of this machine. The casino might wake up and realize that it was giving away the store. I knew that worrying about it wouldn't help matters, but thinking about it made me more alert to the possibilities.

I also spent time deciding what act to use. I knew that this casino didn't see much dollar play, so if two players were camping out, they'd certainly be noticed. It wouldn't be too long before the casino figured out it was paying too much and the promotion would be history. I decided that a distraction was necessary. Since it was impossible to be invisible, we'd be the most visible gamblers in the entire place! Ginnie and I would be happy-go-lucky "crazy" people. Whenever we were dealt three 2s, 3s, 4s, or 6s, we'd go into a loud chant: "Hoiya! Hoiya! Hoiya! Hoiya!" People would gather. If the quad hit (for either $400 or $500), I would stand up, go kiss a grandmother-type I didn't know, and give her $5 for bringing us luck. I did this with three aces, too. If the aces came (a 2-in-47 chance), I'd pay $10 to my new assistant and give this *lucky* grandmother two kisses (they all took the money, but some strongly resisted the kisses) … and $10 to the change person and $10 to the floorperson.

If we didn't hit anything in a half-hour or so, we'd each walk around our chairs three times (bumping into each other in the process). I'd explain to the crowd that this was important to confuse the machine and get it to pay again.

We came, we played, we acted crazy, and we prospered. And everyone, including the casino staff, enjoyed the show. In the 20 hours Ginnie and I played this promotion on our way back from the wedding, I probably dished out $250 in these extra tokes. But I knew our expected win was $4,000 (we actually did a bit better than that, because Ginnie hit a royal) and we didn't want the casino to pull the game. On the contrary, the casino *loved* this action.

Nearing midnight, I knew the double points would end soon. This would reduce our take by $30 an hour. But we were told that a new "Easter egg promotion," whatever that was, would start the next day. Even if it added nothing, the game was still worth more than $70 per hour and certainly worth sticking around for. Besides, Ginnie didn't have to be back at work for three more days.

I came down at six in the morning and the machine with the good schedule was still there. I'd learned that the Easter egg promotion allowed players to open up an Easter egg when they hit jackpots of $250 or higher, and inside the egg was a certificate worth money. Probably $5 or so, I figured, but that was still better than nothing.

At 6:20, I hit four 8s. Great, that was $250. On went my change light. But when I asked for my Easter egg, the only thing I got was: "Huh? I don't know what you're talking about."

I asked for the supervisor, who came over and explained that the promotion didn't start until 8 a.m. "Really," I responded. "I have the announcement right here and it doesn't say anything about 8 a.m. It says, 'Starts Tuesday' and this is Tuesday."

"I'll be right back," the supervisor said, looking a bit confused.

Five minutes later, he returned and said, "It's only for hand pays. Your machine paid you the two-fifty, so it doesn't count."

"Really," I said again. "I have the announcement right here and it says two hundred and fifty dollar jackpots. It doesn't say two hundred and fifty dollar *hand-paid* jackpots. I think I should qualify."

"I'll be right back."

While the supervisor was gone, I considered my strategy. I didn't want to press my luck too hard, because the promotion was worth so much even without the stupid Easter eggs. I was willing to lose this battle, but I'm not the type to just roll over and play dead. If I could get them to do it my way without alienating them, so much the better.

The supervisor returned. "We just forgot to say hand-pay. Surely we're allowed to make a mistake."

"Well," I countered, "if you want to post a big sign, I suspect that would cover you for future jackpots, but I think you owe me one egg anyway, because I hit it before any sign was up."

"I'll be right back."

Finally, the supervisor came back with a compromise. I would get to open an egg for this jackpot and any I hit after 8 a.m., but if I hit another before 8 a.m., I wouldn't be given an egg, as I now knew the rules. Also, I'd have to wait, because the Easter Bunny didn't start work until 8. "Okay. Fair enough. I'll be right here."

I hit another quad at 7:55 and decided I'd wait until 8:05, turn on my light, and claim another egg. Unfortunately, the supervisor and the Easter Bunny walked up at 7:58 and saw me waiting. "Waiting for eight?" the supervisor kidded. I suspect I looked like a kid caught with his hand in the cookie jar. "Don't worry about it. You've been such a good sport, I'll let you have it anyway."

Surprised, I thanked him and picked two eggs. I opened them up. One was for $25 and the other was for $50. Oh my! I promptly toked the supervisor and the Easter Bunny $5 each. Since Ginnie and I were likely to get these more than once an hour each, this could run into some nice change and I wanted the Easter Bunny to *want* to come over to my machine. My Ship Has Come In. Indeed!

By the time Ginnie came down a little after nine, I'd collected two more eggs—for $5 and for $10. I told her it was a great promotion and she started to play. We hit a few more quads, opened a few more eggs, locked up our machines, and went to eat. We wanted to discuss how to make the most of this opportunity.

Ginnie had noticed something that I'd missed. The eggs were just cheap plastic. We knew that the $5 prizes were printed on blue paper, the $10 on purple, and the $25 on red. Maybe we could see the color of the prizes through the eggs. If so, it would be a simple matter of avoiding the blues and purples. Anything else had to be valuable. We wolfed down the rest of breakfast and hurried back to test our theory.

The next time I hit a quad, I chatted away and kept the Easter Bunny distracted while Ginnie examined the eggs. When it was time for me to pick, Ginnie said, "Why don't you try the yellow one in the corner? I get lucky vibes from that one."

"I certainly believe in my wife's lucky vibes," I laughed as I opened up the yellow one with flair. "Wow, two hundred and fifty big ones!" (No, Ginnie and I weren't married, but we presented ourselves to casinos as a married couple. The casino didn't really care whether we were married or not, but that was part of the act we'd decided on.)

We worked out a system. When one of us hit a 4-of-a-kind (about every 20 to 30 minutes), that person would chant "Hoiya! Hoiya! Hoiya!" and do a war dance around the chair. The other person would check out the eggs and suggest which one to pick. The first day we drew $500 twice, $250 three times, and $100 about ten times, mixed in with some lower pays. We earned $3,500 on the first day from the Easter Bunny alone, plus we were up on the game. My Ship was Still Coming In!

The next day disaster struck. When I came down in the morning, someone else was playing one of the machines. I didn't recognize the lady, but after a few minutes I realized she knew how to play. In the first five minutes I saw that from K♥Q♠8♥3♥4♣, she held KQ, but from K♥Q♠9♥3♥4♣, she held K93. Both correct, and plays I suspected would not be made by more than 1% of the players in this town. It was likely she would know enough to figure out how lucrative the machine was—although I wasn't going to help her.

Maybe she didn't know the machine was paying out 1% cashback instead of the .50% it was supposed to pay. Maybe she didn't know that 6666 paid double. Maybe she didn't have the eggs figured out.

It turned out that she and her husband were knowledgeable players. They were passing through, saw Ginnie and me playing, and correctly analyzed the game. They didn't know about the higher slot club points, but the regular points on top of the 6666 was attractive enough for them. But they couldn't figure out why they kept drawing $5 from the eggs, while Ginnie and I were averaging more than $50. "Beats me," I shrugged.

Ginnie and I switched to a tag-team format. For example, when I hit a quad, I chanted, picked out one of the eggs, and cheered wildly while Ginnie took over playing. Then Ginnie played until she hit and the roles were reversed. The other couple took turns on their machines. They were very studious and couldn't understand why Ginnie and I were making such a commotion and tipping so lavishly.

Easy to "Join" the ...

One afternoon while Ginnie and I were at the My Ship Has Come In casino, I was visiting with someone I'd made friends with while he was playing dollar 9/6 Jacks at the bar. He didn't belong to the slot club. I explained that this was a mistake, but he didn't want to be bothered.

As has been explained, the casino was offering double pay for four 6s. Sure enough, my friend hit them. Now he understood why he needed to join the slot club—he had to be a member to collect the additional $125. What to do? Simple. My friend quietly pulled out a $20 and asked the bartender if there was an extra slot club card lying around. Sure enough, a card was found. The bartender pocketed the $20 before the floorperson was called and my friend was paid.

All casinos have rules against using a slot club card belonging to someone else. Usually, this is impossible to enforce, except when the player has a hand-pay and the ID presented doesn't match with name the player-tracking system recorded

---

Later that night, the casino shift boss came over and asked the other couple to leave the casino.

"Why?" they asked, not believing their ears.

"We think you're professional players and we'd rather you didn't play here."

"What about them?" they inquired, pointing to Ginnie and me.

"Obviously, they're not pros. They're winning because they've been lucky. We'll get it back."

Ginnie and I were amazed. Though we were glad our act was paying off, we were shocked when the other players were backed off. This is a rare event in video poker. Much more common methods of dealing with the situation would have been to exclude the machine from the promotion or simply change the pay schedule.

Ginnie was incensed and wanted to boycott the casino. "Right," I scoffed. "We're making a hundred and fifty an hour

---

... Slot Club

on the jackpot ticket. (A "jackpot ticket" is the document printed by the player-tracking system and used by the casino for accounting purposes. It varies by casino, but typically includes the machine number, the size of the jackpot, and the name of the person whose slot club card is in the slot when the jackpot hits.)

I've used Shirley's card in a number of casinos and have never had a problem. Once they know that Shirley and I are married, they don't care which of our cards I use. This is great, because I play considerably more than Shirley does, and considerably more than the amount required to get A+ benefits at most casinos. So it makes sense for me to play enough on Shirley's card so she can receive those benefits, too.

I've heard of one instance where a player, during a promotion, had his wife's card inserted when he hit a bonus quad of 8s and was denied a $100 award. The casino was within its rights, but this surprised a lot of experienced players.

---

and you want to boycott. Boy, that'll sure teach 'em!"

"Maybe we'll wait until the promotion is over and then we'll boycott," Ginnie offered.

"Yes. That's a much better plan."

The last day of the promotion, Ginnie and I left for home. Although the game was still good, the promotion wasn't. Seems that only $5 eggs were left. Imagine that! Also, it would be good for future opportunities if the casino were to get some bad players on these machines. We were up $6,000 on the game (plus $3,000 from the slot club and $7,000 from the Easter Bunny). Unless some losing players sat down soon, the casino couldn't help but notice the loss.

It had been a nice week. We turned a good profit. We'd been out of town (with new restaurants and things to do), attended a fun wedding, and had a nice "date." But Ginnie had to be back at work in California, so we left.

I was glad to get home. And when I checked my mail, there were two letters from hosts at My Ship Has Come In.

"Come back. We miss you. It seems so quiet since you left."

Players React to the Rio

In both 1995 and 1996, the Rio ran the "Cash is King" scratcher promotion between Thanksgiving and Christmas. Casinos often run specials during this time of year, which traditionally is a slow period in Las Vegas. People all over the country are shopping and going to parties at home rather than traveling to Las Vegas.

During this promotion, when you connected on a jackpot paying $25 or higher, you turned on your change light and a change girl (or sometimes a floorperson or supervisor) came by and gave you a scratch card. The cards were good for either a cash amount or entry into a drawing.

The returns on these cards were something like this:

• 70% of the cards: drawing only
• 25% of the cards: $5
• 4.99% of the cards: $10 or $20
• Some very small percentage: $50, $100, or $1,000

The drawing, held on the last night of the promotion, was worth $50,000. The first year, as I recall, there was one winner for $25,000 and the balance was made up of 25 $1,000 winners. The second year, there were 50 $1,000 winners.

After awhile, we estimated a card's average value at about $2. This was a guess, because we didn't know the exact percentages of the availability of each award. Nor did we know how many cards would be in the must-be-present-to-win drawing. The guess was pretty close, I suspect, but who knew for sure? There was also a football contest going on, which I'll talk about later.

I didn't hear about the promotion at the start, which was a good thing. Players who saw the announcements in advance carefully evaluated every machine in the house to identify those that were worth the most, taking into consideration the value of the cards. One of the best machines was a 98.9% version of Deuces Wild, which returned 5 for 4-of-a-kind but only 12 for 5-of-a-kind. (Liam W. Daily and I refer to this game as "pseudo-full-pay Deuces Wild" in our *Winner's Guides*. Some choose to call it "Fooler Deuces," but we'll stick with our name and see if it catches on.) What made it good was that 4-of-a-kinds paid exactly $25 and they came around an average of every 15.3 hands. So in 100 hands (or $500 coin-in), you expected to lose $5.20 playing the machine (minus about a third of that from slot club cashback), but win seven scratchers worth $14. If you could play 500 hands per hour (which depended on how fast the change girls could bring the scratchers), you could make $40+ per hour. Not bad.

The Rio slot department suddenly noticed that a lot of strangers had descended on a bank of machines that previously almost no one played and change girls had to stand right there to hand out one scratcher per minute. Since each ticket had to be signed, once a change girl got to the area, she could never leave! Also, since more players wanted to play these "gold mines" than there were machines, impromptu teams were formed with players taking six-hour shifts. That is, John would play from noon to 6, Carlos would take over from 6 to midnight, then Mary would take over … and so on.

This wasn't what the casino bosses had in mind at all, so they took countermeasures. They changed pay schedules on the machine so that 4-of-a-kinds paid only $20 instead of $25, which eliminated their attractiveness immediately. Also, I was told, players who hit these machines heavily the first two days had their slot club privileges severely restricted. Some said they were kicked out of the casino totally, while others were simply not allowed to participate in the promotion. Either way, I was lucky not to be caught up in it.

The other machines of choice were dollar 10/7 Double Bonus. Since straights pay $25 on these machines, you got a scratcher for every straight, flush, full house, and higher. This happened every 25 hands or so—not as often as on the Deuces game, but often enough. Plus, the game was worth over 100% to start.

The Rio left these machines in play, but made countermoves here as well. First, they disabled the machines' credit meters. If you hit a full house, 50 coins fell into the tray. And before you could play the next hand, you had to hand-feed five more coins. If you made a straight, 25 coins would tumble. It was tedious.

In addition, they slowed the speed of the machines big time. On IGT machines of that era, speed controls from 1 through 9 determined how fast the cards were displayed, both on the deal and the draw. Level 3 was normal in most casinos, which displayed the cards in about a second. At Level 1, the cards displayed in about a quarter of a second. This pace is unnerving for a beginner, but professional players often prefer it. The Rio set the machines at level 9, which took 5 seconds for the cards to display. Five seconds is a *long* time: Thousand one. Thousand two. Thousand three. Thousand four. Thousand five. It was awful.

On top of that, you had to wait for the scratchers. The staff was pretty good about bringing them promptly, but each change girl had a big area to cover and sometimes it took awhile. All non-professionals gave up on this very quickly. Recreational players play for fun, and a machine that's this slow is not fun.

I played from about 10 at night until 8 in the morning. I could usually get at least two machines, and sometimes three or four. Playing two machines at once when they're that slow isn't difficult after you practice a bit. I could play three or more at once when there was a straight or better on one or more machines and a change person hadn't come by yet. Occasionally I'd have all four change lights lit up waiting for scratchers.

Those of us who played did so for dollar-per-hour reasons, but we hated the Rio while we did. The employees also thought the casino's reaction was lame. After awhile we started tipping and the employees began handing out extra scratchers. The going rate settled on 50¢ per extra scratcher.

"You Have to Learn to Trust People"

One year during the "Cash is King" promotion, the Rio ran short of change cups. Normally, cups would be stacked up near all the machines, but someone forgot to order enough and this year they were scarce. So I made a point of gathering 10 or so cups before I began playing, just in case. If I waited until I actually needed the cups, I'd have to tip a change person to either guard my coins while I searched, or to fetch the cups for me.

Obviously, if I needed to search for cups, other players did too, and if I had cups stacked next to my machine, others would come by wanting to help themselves to a few of them. Usually this was quite innocent. After all, a stack of 10 cups looks like a supply provided by the casino rather than an individual player's horde. But I also had several cups full of coins in the same place, so no way did I want unknown people coming near my cash cache. Whenever someone reached, I firmly and loudly ordered them to get away. They all professed innocence, insisting that they were reaching only for the empty cups. "These are mine," I'd say. "I'm not sharing. Look elsewhere."

One guy took serious issue with my selfishness and decided it was his job to teach me manners. My problem in life, he lectured me, was that I was too suspicious, and if I wanted to succeed, I needed to learn to trust people. "Most people," he assured me, "are quite honest."

Maybe so. There are places you can live where no one locks their doors. But Las Vegas is not one of them. In every casino town, there are people who are always trying to get money by any means possible—fair or foul. And you can't always tell the good guys from the bad guys at a glance. So I keep *everyone* away. I've heard lots of stories about people being ripped off in casinos and I believe that many of these stories are true.

Do I come off as rude sometimes? Of course. Will some people be offended by my actions? Yes. But the person with primary responsibility to protect my bankroll is me. And I take that responsibility seriously.

Another trick we came up with was to get paid twice for the same jackpot. We'd hit two jackpots and turn on both lights. A change girl would hurriedly hand out the scratchers, then rush off to handle someone else. At that point, we'd turn off both lights but resume play on only one of the machines. Thirty seconds later, we'd turn on the light for the machine we'd already collected on. It still showed a full house or whatever and the next change person didn't know that it was a jackpot that had already been seen. Since six or more staff members all gave out tickets in the same area at any one time, it was easy to get paid multiple times.

Did we feel guilty about this? Not a bit! The Rio was Mickey Mousing its promotion, so we felt justified in using tactics of our own. Of course, this was a self-serving rationalization. We were stealing from the casino and we knew it.

It took me awhile to recognize that there was one strategy change I should be making during this promotion. Aces full (e.g., A♥A♠A♦5♣5♥) pays $50 if you keep it, but holding only the three aces is worth $50.57 on average. So drawing two cards to the aces is normally the correct play. But in this promotion, AAA55 was worth $50, plus a scratcher worth two bucks, plus a football ticket. Although you could expect to earn a certain number of scratchers starting from AAA by either drawing the last ace or ending up with another full house (which happens a little more than 10% of the time combined), the better play was still to keep the made full house.

As I mentioned, a football contest was also in progress, and a flush or better earned one entry into the contest. You had to pick the winners of the following Sunday's professional football games straight up, which means just picking winners—the point spread isn't taken into consideration. The winner got $10,000 each week.

With 13 games, there were 8,192 possible outcomes. You get this number by multiplying 2 x 2 x 2 ... x 2 a total of 13 times, which takes into account that either team could win game 1, either team could win game 2, on so on. Three of us combined

---

I'm So Glad I Didn't Hit It

One early morning during the scratcher promotion at the Rio, a woman sat down a few seats over and began playing one of the dollar machines. She'd play one coin, two coins, three coins, four coins, and, very rarely, five coins. Needless to say, this is not how winning players play.

After a half-hour or so, she was dealt A♥K♥Q♥J♥5♠ with four coins bet. She held the hearts and drew the 7♣. "I'm so glad I didn't hit it," she proclaimed. "It would be so awful to hit a royal with only four coins in."

Awful? Really? Hitting the royal would have given her $1,000. As it was, she got nothing. I don't understand someone preferring to win zero to winning a grand.

I assume she felt that she would hit a certain number of royals in her life, and "wasting" them on less-than-max-coin situations would cost her money. This is nonsense. Whether she hit a royal on that hand or not had absolutely nothing to do with how many she would hit in the future. It was a bad decision to bet four coins, but once the hand was dealt it was too late to do anything about. Hitting the royal would have been the best result possible at that point.

---

our tickets, so we'd have about 1,000 entries per week. That wasn't enough to cover all of the possibilities, but it handled many of them, especially if we were smart about it. On games where one team was favored by 10 points or more over another, 90% of our tickets were on the favorite and 10% on the underdog. On games where the spread was 3 points or less, we'd split our tickets 50-50. And a 6-point spread might be split 70-30. You get the idea.

Our little syndicate won once and just missed a couple of other times. But it took 10 or more hours each week to fill out the tickets and we were each playing as many hours on the machines as we could. The last few weeks, another group bought our tickets from us, both to eliminate us as competition and to get more tickets for themselves. I don't remember what we were paid, but the combination of the guaranteed money and the relief of not having to fill out all those tickets every week made it an easy choice.

The big drawing was held on the last night of the promotion. The first year, it was a disaster. First, the room they held it in was far too small to hold the thousands of players with tickets in the barrel. There was a loudspeaker out by the swimming pool, but it was 35 degrees outside and most people hadn't come dressed to hang around outdoors. One player I know had more than 10,000 tickets, but was shut out because he couldn't get into the room. When he found out later that his name had been called for $1,000, he was furious, but there was nothing he could do. A security guard initially prevented me from entering as well, but I was just outside the door so I could hear Rio Rita calling the names. After a few names were called, I told the guard that one of them was mine and he let me in. It wasn't my name, but I got through the door.

The Rio learned from its mistake. The next year, the announcements were aired over a loudspeaker heard throughout the casino. There were about 10 supervisors wearing yellow T-shirts. If your name was called (and they called them 10 at a time) you had two minutes to get to one of the yellow T-shirts, each of whom was in contact with someone in the drawing area. This system worked well.

Both years, I was part of a group that pooled tickets and won $1,000 in the drawing. We had a lot of tickets and were optimistic for a better result, but it didn't happen. Over the two months the promotion ran (one month in each of two years), I netted more than $30,000 from the Rio.

Finding a Backer

The Desert Inn used to run its video poker a little bit differently than other casinos. In late 1995, I learned that it had $5 9/6 Jacks with a 1% slot club (which means 1% cashback). This was a very good deal. Unfortunately, I didn't have the bankroll to play it.

Using the 3-to-5-royals formula (see page 92), I figured I needed *at least* $60,000 to play this game. There was also a three-coin machine, and for that I needed *only* $36,000-$60,000. I might have had $36,000 by this point, but I certainly didn't want to invest it all on one play. When you build up your bankroll at quarters (and recently, dollars), you realize that it can go quickly at the $5 level. So I talked to Arnie about it and he volunteered to be a backer.

Arnie would put up the money and I'd do the playing. As the backer, he proposed taking half of the return and being responsible for all of any losses. As the player, I would also get half of the return, but be responsible for none of the losses. I wasn't real happy with this rate. "With a one-percent club, we're almost guaranteed to profit," I pointed out. "Why should you get half of it when there's so little chance of a loss?"

His response was, "If you feel that way, maybe you should put up all of the money yourself. That way, if it goes as well as you think it will, you'll get one hundred percent of the profit."

I was even less happy with this suggestion. Arnie was the only potential backer on the horizon, so I agreed to his terms.

As it turned out, I put up some of the money, too. We each invested $10,000 with the understanding that we'd be 50-50 money partners until all of that money was gone. Since I was doing all of the playing, I'd get 75% of the win and take 50% of the loss.

Next we had to tackle the sticky question of when to settle. Arnie wanted it to be "lifetime to date," which meant that if we *ever* ended up on a positive note, he would make money. The only way he could lose was if we quit losers forever—which was certainly possible, of course.

I thought we should take things six months at a time. It was an arrangement that would result in substantially more risk for Arnie, because he would have to incur half the loss during any six-month losing period, whereas he would collect only a fourth during a winning period of the same duration.

He didn't like this at all. "Not for me," he said. "If you insist on that one, find someone else. My original offer stands. Take it or leave it."

I took it. I wanted to play the bigger machines and this looked like the best way to do that. If I could play $15,000 per hour through the machine, the 100.54% game (the base return plus the 1% cashback) would return $81 per hour. Even three-quarters of this was $60 per hour—a good deal for me.

We agreed that until we got used to the situation, I would

A Rule of Thumb for ...

The exact bankroll you need to play any video poker schedule is a complicated mathematical computation involving the optimal return on the game, the game's volatility (i.e., how big are the normal ups and downs of the game), and how much the slot club returns. It even matters how "risk adverse" you are, which is fancy talk for how big of a disaster it would be to you psychologically if you lost everything.

There are mathematical formulas, but I never use them. That's because the underlying assumptions (e.g., "I'm willing to face a 10% risk of ruin" versus "I'm willing to face a 1% risk of ruin") are just too nebulous for me. I use the "3-to-5 royals rule," instead.

Assuming that the game (including all extras) returns over 100%, this rule says it takes a bankroll equal to the amount of from three to five royals to play safely forever and ever, amen. That is, for quarter play, a bankroll of $3,000 to $5,000 is necessary. For $5 play, you need a bankroll of $60,000 to $100,000.

The rule is greatly simplified. It understates the bankroll needed for highly volatile games (Loose Deuces or Double Double Bonus) and overstates the bankroll needed for games returning 101% or more. Nevertheless, this is the only bankroll rule I have ever used.

play one of the two three-coin machines. One paid $12,000 for the royal and the other paid $12,500. Since we figured that a royal would show every 70 hours or so, one machine paid $7 per hour more than the other. No contest. We went for the twelve-five.

Early on, the machine dealt me a royal and we decided that I should move up to the five-coin machine. I played it for three months and went up a total of $16,000.

At this point, I decided to reevaluate my position. The way the deal was structured, being in plus territory changed my 75%/50% dynamic. Now I was getting a straight trade on the play of the money we'd won: I was still getting 75% of the

---

... Bankroll Calculation

Understand that the 3-to-5 rule addresses total bankroll requirements, not what you need on hand for a given session. That's another important question for which getting the answer requires one of today's sophisticated software programs. Here's an example of the calculation. Let's say the game is NSU Deuces Wild, the denomination is quarters, playing 2,000 hands (which is the amount you'll play in 3-4 hours), and the cashback rate is .50%). Enter this information into the software and let the computer play out this scenario any number of times (say 10,000). The program will give you a distribution of results.

When I did the above run, it gave me numbers for each of the 100 percentiles, of which five are listed here.

10%	-245
30%	-150
50%	- 66
70%	+ 50
90%	+283

This tells you that 10% of the time you will lose $245 or more. Half the time you will lose $66 or more. You will win $283 or more only 10% of the time—very valuable information when you're planning a casino visit.

profit, but also bearing 75% of the risk. And since we now had a $16,000 cushion, there was a good chance that we would always be plus. Had we been $16,000 minus, the deal, as it stood, would have been much more attractive to me. But I figured that I now had the bankroll to play the three-coin machine by myself, so I terminated the arrangement.

I paid Arnie $4,000 (plus his original stake of $10,000) and kept $12,000. Not bad, considering I couldn't have done it without him. Although he preferred to keep going, he was in no position to force the point when I told him the deal was over.

Six months later, I discovered two $5 15/10 Loose Deuces machines at the Frontier (if this terminology is foreign to you, refer to "What You Need to Know About Video Poker to Understand this Book" in Part One). This was a game that returned 101%, plus slot club points. But I knew from playing this game for quarters at other casinos that it had wild swings. Four deuces paid $12,500, but when you didn't hit, you could easily lose $2,000 an hour. I was afraid of the swings, but attracted to the $150-per-hour profit potential. So I called Arnie again (the play is detailed in "Loose Deuces at the Frontier").

This time around I really learned how important the negotiation process is to playing successful video poker. Arnie and I discussed our arrangement for weeks before it was finally set in stone. I wasn't happy with the percentage he wanted. He wasn't happy about my being able to bail out whenever I got ahead enough to do it on my own. Coming to an agreement took work.

Negotiation situations don't arise only between players. In fact, they're more often necessary between players and casinos. Often during promotions, situations come up that are not effectively covered in the rules. And whether they're resolved in the player's favor or not can involve major bucks. (An example of this was the Easter egg episode detailed in "My Ship Has Come In.")

Some players use the it-never-hurts-to-ask form of negotiation. They go after everything they could possibly be entitled to … every time. This works well enough if you never have to deal with these people again—perhaps you're on a cross-country drive in a part of the country you expect never to revisit. But if you have to deal with people over and over, you don't want them to feel that they were bludgeoned in the last go-round. I've found that it's better to leave something on the table for the other guy.

Loose Deuces at the Frontier

The casino that's now the New Frontier was called the Frontier when it was owned by Margaret Elardi and run mostly by her son Tom. I played blackjack there for a long time; they had a single-deck game where the player had an advantage off the top. The good blackjack rules ended in 1994, but for a few years after, they had some of the best video poker in town—especially when the Frontier union employees were on strike.

Throughout the approximately six-year-long labor dispute, the casino tried to get customers to cross the picket lines by offering good games. Many of the players had no desire to take sides. We simply did what was best for us and figured the union and casino would eventually make their peace (they never did; the strike was settled only after the Elardis sold the casino).

Two of Las Vegas' last dollar full-pay Deuces Wild machines, a $25-per-hour game, brought in the pros and semi-pros. We worked out a form of rotation so we all got to play. My time was from about midnight to 8 a.m. If the Deuces games were full, however, I could also play dollar 10/7 Double Bonus. The Frontier mailed out gimmicky coupons every month (four 10s gets an extra 100 coins, a full house of fives over threes gets an extra 200 coins, and the like), so the 10/7 game was an acceptable alternative while waiting for the Deuces machines to open up. The coupons weren't valid on wild-card machines, so playing them on the half-percent-less 10/7 machine was comparable to playing Deuces without the coupons.

During the summer of 1996, I noticed they'd installed two $5 15/10 Loose Deuces machines (returning 101%). I was familiar with them, having hit quarter Loose Deuces hard at the Las Vegas Hilton. This game is *very* streaky. Compared to full-pay Deuces in terms of average value, increasing the return for four 2s from 200 to 500 almost exactly offsets decreasing the return for 4-of-a-kind from 5 to 4. The problem is you get a 4-of-a-kind every 15.4 hands and you get four deuces every 4,700 hands. Even regular deuces is streaky, but on Loose Deuces you lose an extra five coins every 15.4 hands and make it up every 4,700 hands—or about 8-10 hours. On the 25¢ game it was scary. On this $5 game it was petrifying! When you didn't hit a royal (for $20,000) or four deuces (for $12,500), you could expect to lose $2,000 or more per hour. What was the required bankroll? I didn't know. But I knew I didn't have it.

I called Arnie. When I approached him to back the game at the Frontier, he wanted to start from where we'd left off (at the Desert Inn). That is, he'd return the $4,000 I'd paid him, I'd put back $12,000, and that would be the bank until we lost the $16,000.

I wasn't interested. I told him that on the Frontier's Loose Deuces we had a 1% advantage, $150 per hour, and he stood to make quite a bit of money. He let me prevail in this round of negotiations, but only after I agreed to let him use my slot club card to get free haircuts and manicures in the hotel beauty shop. Since the swings were bigger on this game, we agreed to put up $15,000 apiece. If we lost the thirty grand, we'd powwow and decide what to do next. As before, if I lost we would split it 50-50 and if I won, since I was the one putting in the hours playing, we'd split 75-25.

Before I started, I went back to school. I'd learned this game when I played for quarters, but I revisited the close hands in case I'd missed something. And I had. When I was playing for quarters, I hadn't spent a lot of time studying exactly when to hold a suited KQ, KJ, or KT with various kinds of interference. Some authors claimed that it was optimal not to worry about such things, but they weren't playing for $25 a pop. I wanted to know the strategy perfectly. I probably failed in this, but I wound up a lot closer than if my goal had merely been to be good enough.

As it turned out, I got lucky right from the start. My first afternoon, I hit a royal *and* four deuces and wound up ahead $24,000. I immediately contemplated ending my deal with Arnie right then and there. My share of the $24,000 was $18,000, and I reasoned that, combined with what I already had, it was probably enough to make the solo play. I talked myself into it, though I shouldn't have. If this game went bad, I'd be in trouble. But with the confidence of the naive, I bought Arnie out for his $6,000. This wasn't the deal he wanted, but again he couldn't complain: He'd now cleared $10,000 from our relationship.

I also considered quitting this machine altogether. After all, I'd beaten the odds and gotten an early head start, but it would be easy to give it all back. So maybe I should quit. I was accustomed to these thoughts. The important fact was that the game still presented a $150-per-hour opportunity and that was the decision variable that drove my actions. I hadn't quite formulated my theory that "today's score doesn't matter," which I'd expound so many times in the future, but I'd certainly grasped the basic concept.

I continued to gradually increase the win, with very large ups and downs. Losing $8,000 a day became commonplace, but a few times I hit four deuces twice in the same day. I ended up well ahead of the game.

After several weeks of play, a professional team began monopolizing both machines and I usually couldn't get a seat. I could still play dollar Deuces, but when you're psyched up to play a $150-per-hour game and have to settle for only $25 per hour, it's a letdown.

I had an interesting side adventure with one of the Frontier floor ladies, Julie. I was toking fairly generously then and was used to casino employees being extra friendly. But her attention seemed to have additional, not-too-subtle, overtones. How nice.

This was long after Ginny and just before Shirley and I was ready for some female companionship. But Julie was wearing a wedding ring. I was ready, but not that ready! A saint I ain't, but for me, messing around with a married woman is totally out of the question. A college roommate had been shot and killed by a jealous husband and I'd known a number of people who had been emotionally devastated by infidelity issues.

Still, Julie continued her flirting and it was fun. I'd been nose to the grindstone and eye on the prize for the last year, and getting some testosterone flowing felt pretty good.

I began to consider the possibility that her ring was a dodge. It occurred to me that if an attractive single woman didn't want to be continually hit on by guys in the casino, she might wear a wedding band to discourage some of them. This was the only scenario that made sense to me. Acting on the premise that she wouldn't be flirting so brazenly if she wasn't available, I finally asked, "Are you married?"

Her face fell and she admitted that yes, she was, but she was unhappy. She'd decided that as soon as she found a new man who loved her, she'd leave her husband and get a divorce. Apparently, she was willing to try me on for size. This was flattering, to be sure, but on further reflection, it didn't sound like anything I wanted to get involved with. We flirted as long as I played there, but I never asked her out.

This may sound like little more than an insignificant titillation, but at the time it was very distracting. I was trying to concentrate on a game with huge swings, and there I was, saddled with crotch-level fantasies. Not smart. The play for 5♥6♥7♥7♠8♠ is different in this game from 5♥6♥7♥7♠9♠ and they're easy to confuse (hold 77 and 567, respectively). I needed to concentrate. But how do you turn off your hormones? If you have that one figured out, please send me your solution.

The distracting thoughts aren't always erotic, either. I could be angry at someone, physically uncomfortable for whatever reason, or even writing a magazine article with half a brain while playing with the other half. When I find this happening, I stand up, have a drink of water, stretch a little, then go back to the game.

It doesn't always work, to be sure, but my results are better than if I just try to power through it.

I know I get only one chance to play each hand. And though 98% of them are no-brainers (once I've practiced enough), I have to be ready for the other 2%. I don't know when they're coming and if I make a mistake, the machine doesn't give me my money back.

A few weeks after I split with Arnie, I learned that one pro had lost $80,000 on the Loose Deuces play at the Frontier. Wow! I had no idea that a loss of this magnitude was possible. If I had, I wouldn't have terminated my partnership with Arnie. This pro (who I believe played every bit as well as I did—maybe better) hit no royals over two cycles (about 90,000 hands at Deuces) and only about 13 sets of four deuces, rather than the 18 to which he was mathematically "entitled." This was a very unlucky parlay, but it happens. Meanwhile, I hit two royals in 50,000 hands (instead of the normal 1.1) and 12 sets of four deuces rather, than the normal 10 or 11. I wound up $30,000 ahead after I paid off Arnie.

If this pro and I were playing baseball, his result would be called a slump and mine a hitting streak. In baseball, results are always attributed to a player's abilities or attitude. I would also be considered to be the better player at the time.

Though people often use sports lingo and analogies when talking about video poker, it's wrong when they do. In video poker, you can't judge how well someone is playing merely by looking at his score over a short period of time. This pro and I were playing every hand identically. But the royals showed up on my machine and not his. That's life in this game. Over the course of a year or two, he and I will hit pretty close to the same number of royal flushes per hands played. But over any particular month, either one of us could be way ahead of the other.

This reality is no big deal … as long as you can afford it. I couldn't have lost $80,000 at the time. I didn't have that much— and I probably would have backed off this machine totally if I'd lost the $30,000 stake Arnie and I had originally put up.

Cycles for Common Games

The "cycle" for a video poker game is the number of hands it takes on average to hit a royal flush. The number 40,000 is commonly used, but it's correct only for Jacks or Better. Other games have different cycles.

When a game has a large payoff for a hand other than a royal flush, that hand also has a cycle. In Deuces Wild, we talk about deuces cycles, which is the average number of hands between hitting deuces. In Double Bonus, players are concerned with the aces cycle. And in Kings or Better Joker Poker, the 5-of-a-kind cycle is important. You can speak of a 3-of-a-kind cycle if you like, but it's low-paying enough that players generally ignore it.

This chart lists the relevant cycles for the games discussed in this book.

Deuces Wild	4 Deuces	Royal Flush
full-pay Deuces Wild	4,909	45,282
15/10 Loose Deuces	4,703	45,236

Double Bonus	4 Aces	Royal Flush
10/7/50	5,030	48,048
10/7/80	5,034	46,727

Jacks or Better		Royal Flush
9/6 Jacks or Better		40,391

Joker Wild	5-of-a-Kind	Royal Flush
20/7/5 with 4,000 royal	10,713	41,214
20/7/5 with 4,700 royal	10,725	38,614

Why does it take longer to hit a royal flush in 10/7/50 Double Bonus than it does in 9/6 Jacks or Better? Because the strategies call for different plays. For example, playing Jacks or Better with the hand K♥Q♥J♥7♣3♥, KQJ is the correct play, which produces a royal flush slightly less than once in 1,000 hands. In 10/7/50, KQJ3 is a better play, and starting from there you'll *never* hit a royal.

Courting Shirley on a Budget

During this same summer, I met Shirley at Sam's Town's Western Dance Hall (which has since, sadly, become a smoke shop). Shirley came to town every month or so on business (she worked for a dry-cleaning company and supervised the stores over much of Southern California and Las Vegas) and liked to dance. After two dances, I asked her if it would create a problem for her or anyone else if I monopolized her for the next hour or so. She smiled and said that would be fine. Things clicked, so at the end of the evening, I gave her my card and suggested she call me the next time she was in town. I'd given my card to two other ladies I'd met dancing in the previous few months, so now I had three cards out there.

What Does Your Business Card Say When You're a Professional Gambler?

When I met Shirley for the first time, mine said "Dance Instructor." I'd had this card printed up before I moved to Las Vegas three years earlier. I was a part-time instructor in California and expected to get a teaching gig at Sam's Town or one of the other nightclubs once I got to town. It never happened, but I still had the cards.

For casino-consulting clients, I have cards that say "Gaming Analyst."

Today, I no longer pass out cards socially.

Two months later Shirley called and said she'd be in town the following week. She wanted to know if I was interested in going dancing? I said yes, though I didn't want to make it a late date, because my shift at the Frontier dollar Deuces Wild machine began at midnight. So I suggested we eat first at Papamio's, the Italian restaurant at Sam's Town. She agreed.

There was one problem. I didn't exactly remember which of

the three ladies was named Shirley. At this point, it actually didn't matter to me. It's a long way between a dance date and a meaningful relationship, and from experience, I knew it was unlikely that this particular lady would turn out to be *the one*. Still, you have to take the time to find out—one lady at a time. Any of the three would have been an acceptable place to start.

To figure out which of the three she was without shooting myself in the foot, I took a stab with, "Let's meet at the restaurant at eight. By the way, you haven't gone and dyed your hair or anything like that, have you?"

She responded, "Nope. I'm still the same tall blonde I've always been."

Thank you for the information! Now I'd narrowed it down to two. And the odds were strongly against them both showing up at 8 o'clock at Papamio's on that particular Tuesday. "That's good enough for me," I said. "See you Tuesday at eight."

We met and chatted over dinner for a fairly long time. She was both fascinated and skeptical about my gambling stories. It turned out she had several family members who gambled heavily and every one of them was a loser to the casinos—some by quite a bit more than was prudent. But they all liked to tell stories about the successful gambling trips they'd had. (Although Shirley's family hadn't had much success at gambling up until the time I came along, a few of them are having considerable success six years later. I provided some impetus at the beginning by pointing them in the right direction and proving by example that a living could be made from gambling. But for the most part, they've improved from their own hard work, without my direct assistance.)

By the end of the evening, things had gone well enough for me to suggest she come back to Vegas for Thanksgiving weekend to see what gambling with a knowledgeable player was all about. I told her we'd play with my money and all she had to do was follow directions. She'd have her own hotel room, nice meals, and we'd see a couple of shows. This intrigued her, but then I fed her the real bait. "We'll even have time to go dancing one night." She was hooked!

And I delivered. She stayed for two nights in an Atrium suite at the Frontier, then one night in a standard room at Treasure Island. Both rooms were much more comfortable than what she was used to on the road. And we went to the Magical Empire at Caesars Palace (thanks to a comp from a friend) and *Mystère* at Treasure Island (based on my own play).

It was a fantastic weekend, so I told her that I was invited to Treasure Island for New Year's Eve for a formal dance and asked if she was interested. Silly question! I also told her that between Thanksgiving and New Year's, Treasure Island was having a "Santa Bucks" promotion paying a type of double cashback, split between normal cashback and gift certificates at the hotel gift shops.

So, having already checked earlier to make sure I could do this, I took her to Damsels in Dis'Dress at Treasure Island and let her pick out her own Christmas presents to put on layaway. After earning the gift certificates two weeks later, I'd redeem the merchandise.

A bit awkwardly, she asked, "How much should I pick out?" Fair question. Neither one of us knew at that point how long this romance would last. After all, we'd only had a few dates and although they'd been promising, who knew for sure? I left myself an out. "I usually play enough to earn four hundred dollars or so in these certificates. Why don't you pick out about twice that much, but make it several pieces so I can pick and choose among your selections and still surprise you. Do you mind?" Silly question!

The truth was, I usually played enough to earn about $1,000 in these gift certificates over a weekend. But I was also concerned that if the relationship lasted, Shirley might come to expect thousand-dollar gifts every year, and who knew if the casino would offer the same promotion in 1997 and beyond? For someone trying desperately to build a bankroll to play the machines on a full-time basis, $1,000 in Christmas gifts sounded horribly extravagant if I had to spend real cash.

Luckily, $400 at a hotel gift shop was a generous present as far as Shirley was concerned. Besides, if the basic relationship weren't interesting to her, $5,000 in Christmas presents wouldn't have made a difference. Conversely, from the right guy, a nice Christmas card would have been enough.

And I knew that if I promised her $400 worth of gifts and delivered twice that, she would be ecstatic, and ecstasy in a new relationship is always to be encouraged! But if I promised her $1,000 and she had to settle for only $400, I was sure I wouldn't like those results nearly as much.

As I recall, our play over Thanksgiving in the "Santa Bucks" promotion and on New Year's cost me about $10,000. This was a significant loss for me, because I was still primarily a dollar player. I wondered if falling in love was distracting me too much to concentrate on what I had to do. On the other hand, I'd also earned quite a bit more than $10,000 during that same time period at the Cash is King promotion at the Rio.

Right after my New Year's celebration with Shirley, I played at Bally's and did well, so there was plenty of money to play $5 machines as much as I wanted. Since Treasure Island held promotions almost every month, Shirley tried to arrange her Las Vegas trips to be in town during promotion weekends.

Treasure Island is an upper-middle-class hotel and for us it was heaven. We didn't get a suite during New Year's (when a whole lot of people try to squeeze into a fixed number of suites and all but the biggest players get downgraded), but after that we always did. We started out with one of the Caribbean suites. What luxury! There were actually two large bathrooms in it.

As our relationship progressed, so did my level of play—and the level of suites. Soon we were in the Buccaneer suites, which were the same size as the Caribbean, but more lavish. When we started playing at the Mirage, we got suites there, too. Of course, earning the suites at the Mirage required considerably more play than those at Treasure Island, but the Mirage was definitely a first-class hotel.

From the time we met until we married, about a year and a half elapsed. I remember this period as one of the sweetest times in my life. I got the girl, stayed in a variety of luxury casinos, and made more money gambling than I ever had previously. Shirley would come to town during promotion weekends and for that entire period, our lives were a big fun dance.

During June of that year, we took a week-long trip to Nashville to go to Fan Fair, the biggest event of the year for country-western music fans. Although we both liked the music, the real reason for the trip was to see if we could enjoy being around each other without the casino suites, gourmet meals, and video poker machines. Turned out we could.

A Second Woman Enters the Picture

In the spring of 1997, Shirley and I (still unmarried at this point, but dating exclusively) signed up to play in a giveaway weekend at Treasure Island. During these weekends, invited guests earned drawing tickets Thursday through Saturday. Shirley couldn't come in from California until Friday evening, but I started playing Thursday night. That way we'd have more time together after she got there.

At around 2 a.m. Friday morning, I hit a royal flush on a $5 machine for $20,000. Yes! You can never get enough of these. Surprisingly, at that particular moment the high-roller area was deserted, strange for a giveaway weekend.

It usually takes about 15 minutes to get a jackpot of this size paid and I was sitting quietly while I waited. Grinning like a Cheshire cat, probably, but quietly. Sometimes at moments like this people walk by and ask, "How much is it?" I wish they wouldn't ask. I don't like advertising the fact that I'll soon be walking around with a ton of cash on me. But when they do, I usually answer civilly, though not in a way that invites further conversation.

This time, however, I heard another question. "Hi there. Are you married?" What was this? I turned around and saw an attractive well-dressed woman of 45 or so smiling at me. I had recently turned 50 and was under no illusions that women thought I looked even remotely like Tom Selleck. A presentable appearance? Yes. Love-at-first-sight-material? *Not.*

All this woman knew about me was that I had just won $20,000. That, apparently, was enough to interest her. (And if that was what made me interesting to her, it was enough to make me totally uninterested in her, Shirley or no Shirley.) I've thought of a number of snappy responses after the fact, but at the time I was speechless for about 20 seconds. I finally came up with the not-so-dynamic, "No, I'm not. Why do you ask?"

"I just wanted to know if you were available," she purred.

My mind raced. She was trim, sharply dressed, and appeared to be intelligent with a sense of humor. In short, perfect. But, perfect or not, I had a girlfriend who was close enough to perfect. "Nope. Not available, but thanks for letting my mind pleasantly wander for a few moments. You're the second nicest thing to happen to me in the past ten minutes." She laughed and walked on.

That was it. Totally over in less than a minute—though an unforgettable minute.

Of course, it wasn't over. Shirley arrived late Friday afternoon and we started off the weekend with dinner at Madame Ching's, a fine Chinese restaurant at Treasure Island. I listened while she told me about her day and week, patiently awaiting my bombshell-dropping opportunity.

When the inevitable "How did your day go?" came, I calmly answered, "Nothing unusual, really, other than getting a marriage proposal from a very nice lady." Now it was Shirley's turn to be speechless for 20 seconds. Her response, when it finally came, was dripping with icicles. "I drove three hundred miles to hear this? I hope you'll both be very happy, you #%@&%$!"

It took some time to explain that it wasn't a serious proposal and that I didn't even know the woman's name or how to get in touch with her and that, in total, only a few dozen words had been spoken. Shirley gave me a look that meant "it's not a good idea to fool me like that," but then all was forgiven.

And once she'd calmed down, she became aware of the rest of the story. "Wow! Twenty thousand! What are you going to do with it?"

"Nothing really. Maybe mutual funds. It's not real money, you know."

"What do you mean it's not real money?"

I explained that I didn't know when my next royal was coming. I could conceivably lose $100,000 or more before it hit. Without getting into exact probabilities, I told her that a loss of that size would be unusual, but not impossible. If I didn't bank almost everything I made as I played, a $100,000 loss would come close to wiping me out. And I wanted to move up to $10 machines, which meant I'd need twice the bankroll required to play $5 machines. In short, any money I got I was planning to save, other than spending a modest amount for living expenses.

"How much do you figure you'll need?" she asked.

I told her that a $100,000 bankroll would provide a reasonable cushion for playing $5 machines full time. Though, I reminded her, playing $5 machines was not my ultimate goal.

"You mean that you have to save up until you have two hundred thousand before you can spend anything?" she asked incredulously.

"Actually," I replied, "the comps are so much better when you play the twenty-five dollar machines that I'm trying to accumulate half a million."

This is an unusual way to look at money, at least for most people. If she wanted to be part of my life, Shirley would need to either come to grips with my point of view or convince me that it needed altering. I didn't like her chances for the latter.

Shirley looked at me long and hard and decided I was leveling with her. Which was good, because I was completely serious. "In that case," she told me, "we better go out and get a royal flush for me too this weekend."

We didn't hit another royal that weekend, which was no

surprise. Royals are rare events and you never know when they'll pop up. In fact, we lost about $4,000 while putting points on her card, but won $2,500 and a Sony 54-inch TV in the drawing Saturday night. Not bad, especially since I was up more than eighteen grand from the play on my card.

Reducing the Outflow

So far in this book I've told proportionately more stories about hitting royal flushes than about being on losing streaks. Both events are part of video poker, but for obvious reasons the successes are more fun to write about than the failures.

When Ginnie and I moved to Vegas, I had about $6,000. At various times in my life I had more. Much more. Turns out that getting to Las Vegas was the easy part. Earning enough to stay and enjoy the good Las Vegas life was much harder.

My goal was to increase my gambling bankroll and I was serious about it. It's easy to read stories about my successes at the Desert Inn, Frontier, or Rio and conclude that my bankroll must have been increasing, but it was actually more complicated than that.

Think of a gambling bankroll as a lake of money. The goal is to make this lake bigger. The river of money coming in is from gambling jackpots and whatever other sources of income are available—i.e., employment, investment, interest, pension, inheritance, Social Security, etc. Everyone has a slightly different income stream.

But there are also many rivers of money going out. In addition to the obvious, gambling losses, money must be spent on rent, food, clothes, transportation, insurance, recreation, and whatever else is needed. Everyone has a slightly different expense stream.

Whether the income stream is $10,000, $100,000, or $1 million, you can't know if the lake is growing or shrinking until you know how large the expense stream is. If you make $10,000 and spend $5,000, the bankroll is increasing. If you make $100,000 and spend $120,000, the bankroll is decreasing.

I believe that for me, the gambling side of the income-expense formula will always end up positive if I can wait long enough. I'm betting only when I have the advantage and the long run is short enough that I'll come out ahead. I don't sweat the daily or weekly gambling scores.

But expenses are something I can find ways to reduce. I currently don't pinch the expense pennies as much as I used to, but when I was coming up, I was thrifty. My father was of Jewish heritage and my mother's ancestors were Scottish. Both groups are stereotyped as being fiscally tight. The stereotype is untrue for many members of each group, but in the case of my parents, and later me, it fits pretty well.

Being thrifty is a mindset. It can be based on necessity and fear. This was the case for my mother, who grew up struggling to make ends meet on a farm during the Depression. For the most part, her job when I was growing up was to be a good mother to five children. And she was, although at times she took part-time jobs to help pay the bills. By the time she died in her late fifties, my folks were comfortable financially—although my dad was still working long hours in his real estate business.

Being thrifty can also be based on looking to the future. This was the case for my father, who always wanted lots of kids and to be a millionaire, and believed that any extra money should be invested. As I write this, he's in his mid-eighties and has considerable assets. He also has no hobby, other than going to work to make more money. He has set up a charitable foundation and he's now consumed with the belief that if he can leave $20 million to this foundation when he dies, his life will have been better spent than if he leaves only $10 million. If the stock market proves friendly enough and he lives long enough, I'm sure he'll wind up believing that leaving $30 million to the foundation is better than $20 million. He has very little use for money in his own day-to-day life.

My philosophy on earning a gambling bankroll was similar to my father's, although he used his bankroll to buy real estate. Devising a way to spend less money (while maintaining perfect credit) was just as valuable as finding a way to earn more money. As they say, take care of the pennies and the nickels and dollars will take care of themselves.

At the same time, I was not at all interested in growing old with no hobbies. So I maintained my habit of dancing once every two weeks or so. Part of this was a true love of dancing. I'd taken several hundred hours of dancing lessons over the years and was fairly good at it. Part was the belief that this was where I was most likely to meet a suitable lady friend. And part was the fear that if I didn't maintain some sort of hobby, I would end up just like my father. Although I admire him in many ways, I believe my life will be happier if I can enjoy some of the things that money can buy.

My first gambling goal was $100,000, with a promise to myself that I would reevaluate things when I reached it. This was the amount I believed I'd need to play $5 machines forever. And until I reached this goal, I'd put as many expenses as possible on hold. I never paid for food; I could get all I needed at the casinos for free. Alcohol, tobacco, and drugs were money sewers that I was better off without. Cars work just fine for at least eight years. Owning fine clothes isn't that important. Tips for jackpots can be modest if you're friendly. A haircut once every two months is enough. I never spent money on valet parking or bellmen. And I've been using casino soap, shampoo, and other toiletries for years. Cable TV was not worth paying for—there's plenty to watch on the networks.

You get the idea. I wanted my bankroll lake to keep filling by minimizing the outflow. And I was successful at this. Meanwhile, the results from my video poker play were better than average (because most people didn't work at it as hard as I did), but not exceptional. Several other players hit just as many royals and 4-of-a-kinds as I did. The reason my bankroll increased faster than theirs was because I lived extremely frugally.

Although it was an important goal for me, I never knew exactly when I made it to that $100,000 bankroll. My money was in mutual funds and cash, and counting it every day isn't my style. My gambling results went up and down, but mostly up over time. Mutual-fund returns in the mid-to-late 1990s also went up and down, but mostly up. Besides, even when I had more than $100,000 all at once in a mutual fund, I wasn't sure how much was bankroll. I'm still not.

Bankroll is something that, if things go bad, you're willing to keep investing until it's gone. I don't know how close to zero I'd be willing to get. No one does, really, until he goes through it. Whatever decisions a person with $100,000 in the bank might make about what he'd do if the money wasn't there cannot possibly take into consideration the exact circumstances surrounding an impending bankruptcy.

After awhile, I knew my bankroll was more than $100,000. Then I had to reevaluate my miserliness. By that time, Shirley was a part of my life and she had a big vote.

When it finally came time to consider whether Shirley and I would get married, the fact that she had about $30,000 in the bank was a major consideration, although not for the obvious reason. I personally had $150,000 or so by that time, and although I was always eager to add another $30,000, Shirley's money wasn't what I was after.

What I wanted was someone who knew how to *save* money. I felt that if she could save $30,000 on a $30,000 salary, she had the basic skills to help me preserve and build my own bankroll—which was about to become our bankroll, after all. This was more important to me than how pretty she was or how well she danced.

I was extremely tight until I got to $100,000, and that tightness has paid dividends ever since. My bankroll is still in mutual funds (actually more in index funds now) and other investments where it can grow without me doing anything extra. My miserliness softened somewhat after I surpassed $100,000. The bankroll kept expanding, but not at the same rate it would have if I'd continued to pinch pennies. Today, after earning a million dollars over a six-month period, we still haven't decided what the acceptable level of spending-versus-saving should be. It's a nice problem to have, but we're still working on it.

Big Time at Bally's

In mid-to-late 1996, Bally's Las Vegas had full-pay Deuces Wild for very high denominations. By very high, I mean three-coin $25 machines and three-coin $100 machines. With the slot

---

The Benefits ...

Assume you have plenty of bankroll, video poker knowledge, and discipline to play only games where you have the advantage. You go to a new casino and can choose between two options:

Option 1: On Trip 1 you lose $500. On Trip 2 you lose $500. And on Trip 3 you win $1,000.

Option 2: On Trip 1 you lose $50,000. On Trip 2 you lose $50,000. And on Trip 3 you win $100,000.

Which is the more profitable option? At first blush, they seem equivalent. In both cases you break even.

Shirley greatly prefers Option 1. For her, the pain associated with losing $50,000 twice is much greater than the joy of winning $100,000. So even though she breaks even, the stress factor with Option 2 is too high for her "psychological bankroll."

I, however, greatly prefer Option 2. Why? Because when you lose large amounts, casinos rush in to nurture you. Casinos *like* players who can lose $50,000, pay off their debts, and come back and gamble more. So to ease the pain, they'll often rebate 10% of a large loss if you ask for it. They figure it's well worth $5,000 today to have you come back and lose $50,000 again tomorrow.

At the end of Trip 2, they'll usually give you another $5,000 or so if you ask for it. You are, after all, an extremely valuable customer. And they're still $90,000 ahead, so they like their position.

club (around .15% cashback at the time, plus another .075% that had to be cashed in December), it put this game's return just fractionally below 101%.

Arnie and I considered teaming up to tackle the $25 machine. We figured a taxable jackpot would happen only on wild royals and higher, which occurs slightly more than once every 500 hands. The machines would hold only 47 credits at a time, so they'd spill into the tray frequently—or so we hoped!

The 47-credits limit existed because 48 $25 coins adds up to

... of Losing

Though I've been using the $5,000-rebate figure like it's a fixed amount, it's not. They might offer you $2,000 first. Maybe you'll squeeze $8,000 out of them. Some casinos won't give you anything. But 10% of your losses is approximately correct at most places.

At the end of Trip 3, you get to keep all $100,000 you've won. You don't have to return the two $5,000 rebates. So with Option 2, you end up $10,000 ahead, which is far superior to breaking even.

Now let's consider a new Option 3: Trip 1, you win $100,000. Trip 2, you lose $50,000. And trip 3, you lose $50,000 again. ("I'll take that one," Shirley says, "except I'll quit after Trip 1." Not a choice.)

When you lose $50,000 on Trip 2, you're unlikely to get a rebate. The casino will look at it as if you're still playing with its money. It's worth a shot, so go ahead and ask. But don't be too surprised when you get turned down. Your odds improve on Trip 3 (now you've had two $50,000 losses in a row), but it's still iffy.

The best strategy for getting this rebate is to be in the red lifetime-to-date. If you're skilled at the strategies and are playing the right games, this won't be the case at too many casinos. But it will be at a few (personally, I'm probably behind at 20 or so casinos throughout the country). At those where you're losing, if you're behind a bunch, ask away. You're a favorite to get lucky.

$1,200, and it used to be that machines would never hold $1,200 or more in credits at a time. Apparently, when they set this up, someone confused accumulated credit totals with the $1,200-in-one-hand W-2G minimum. On this particular machine, full houses paid 9 coins ($225), 4-of-a-kinds paid 15 coins ($375), straight flushes paid 27 coins ($675), and 5-of-a-kinds paid 45 coins ($1,125). If I had 30 credits accumulated and hit a straight flush for 27 more, the total would add up to 57 coins. Since the machine held only 47, the 27 coins would spill into the tray and the meter would retain the remaining 30 coins. On the next hand, I'd bet three coins so the meter would decrease to 27 coins. If I collected on a straight or less on this hand, the credits would rack up. If I hit a straight flush or 5-of-a-kind, 27 or 45 coins would spill, respectively. These coin spills took a lot of time—partly because when you hit several of them in a row, the machine hopper would empty out and there'd have to be a fill. The better your less-than-wild-royal results were, the more time was wasted with the spillage. Other time-consuming factors included the necessity of a hand-pay for a wild royal or higher and the need to constantly feed the machine with either coins or hundred-dollar bills.

If I could get $30,000 (400 hands) or more through the machine per hour, which we figured would be manageable because three of the machines were side by side and I could switch off while waiting for a hand-pay, this was a $300-per-hour opportunity—plenty of money to share if we could work out the details of the partnership. I couldn't take this play on myself. My bankroll was somewhere between $50,000 and $70,000 at the time—a nice chunk of change, to be sure, but nowhere near enough to play this game. Or so I thought. I knew from a lot of experience at quarter Deuces that when you don't hit four deuces (paying $15,000 in this game!), you're in for a long expensive day. I wasn't nearly brave enough (perhaps foolhardy would be more accurate) to want to tackle this solo. But by the time Arnie and I had worked out the details for our joint venture, the games were gone. Another player had beaten up the casino pretty badly,

The "Royal" Couple

Bob and his host, Mary, take third place in a polka competition.

Bob and Shirley at the Treasure Island Super Bowl party in 1998.

Spinning the Wheel of Fortune for
a cash prize during a video poker
"giveaway weekend."

Some advantage techniques are more obvious
than others. In this giveaway, Bob maximized
his return by choosing envelopes (full of cash)
that were the fattest .

**Treating guests to big weekends is one of the perks of play.
Here, Bob's father joins Bob and Shirley at
an invitational tournament at the MGM.**

**Bob and Shirley at one of the monthly
invitational parties at the Mirage.**

Shirley, Bob's father, and Bob attend a Hollywood Extravaganza slot tournament at the MGM Grand in 2000.

The 1999 New Year's Eve party at the Mirage was a big event for the casino's best customers.

MGM GRAND
2001
A MUSICAL ODYSSEY

Another slot tournament party at the MGM Grand —formal attire required.

Cash drawings, elaborate dance parties, and themed snapshots are the order of the day at casino invitational tournaments.

There's no telling what props the tournament party photographers will come up with.

Dealt royals paying $100,000 always made Bob smile. This one came at the MGM Grand, about seven months before his million-dollar six months began.

The big hand at the MGM— Shirley pops the royal flush on a $100 machine!

I suspect. It wasn't me, but I knew that someday I'd have the bankroll and the nerve to try such machines.

Shortly after New Year's 1997, I heard that the games were back—sort of. Same denomination, but now the machines were 10/7 Double Bonus in the Bally GameMaker version. Double Bonus is the same game I'd played for so many hours at Vacation Village, "Firestone," and the Rio. I knew it cold. But I'd been playing the IGT version, which paid only 50 per coin on the straight flush. The Bally version paid 80 per coin. This enhancement added more than a third of a percent, so the game was worth 100.52%. With the same .225% slot club, it totaled almost 100.75%, which was about three-quarters as good as the earlier play. Still not bad—more than $200 an hour.

Overall, my life was going very well about then. My bankroll had grown since the time of the first play, Anthony Curtis was about to publish my book, and Shirley and I had spent a spectacular New Year's holiday after visiting with her family over Christmas. I decided that this was as good a time as any for me to take a shot at these machines.

I decided to put $8,000 at risk. This was not a scientifically determined amount. It was simply the amount of cash I had on hand at the time without going into my checking account or mutual funds. If I could hit enough good hands early on, this $8,000 might blossom into something big. On the other hand, if I had two bad hours in a row at the start, my $8,000 bankroll would be wiped out. And I'd decided that if the $8,000 went, I wouldn't chase it. At least I hoped wouldn't. I usually kept promises to myself, but not always. I was more than a little nervous. The biggest game I'd played previously was for $5 units, which took $25 per hand. Loading up a three-coin $25 machine takes $75, so I'd be risking three times as much as I ever had before.

I first had to learn the game. When the straight flush pays more, there are several differences in strategy. To find out what they were, I tried to check the hands systematically, investigating those with straight flush potential. I first looked at 4-card straight flushes compared to 5-card straights—hands such as 4♥5♥6♥7♥8♣. It turns out that it's still slightly better to keep the straight, as long as all cards are ten or below. However, if there are one or more high cards in the straight flush, as in 8♠9♠T♠J♠Q♥, it's better to try for the straight flush. The presence of the three jacks remaining to be drawn (and return even money) is enough to make the difference in the play.

I then checked the 3-card royal flushes compared to high pairs, as well as 3-card royal flushes compared to 4-card flushes. There were a lot of these and they weren't easy to figure out. For example, from K♣Q♣J♣5♣4♦, you hold KQJ in the 10/7/80 version of this game rather than the KQJ5 in the 10/7/50 version, but from K♣Q♣J♣5♣J♦ or K♣Q♣J♣5♣9♦, you hold KQJ5 in both games.

I knew that double inside straight flushes with no high cards were close in value to either a J or an A, depending on straight interference. So I checked those. And I checked many other hands too. I spent at least 10 hours finding and memorizing these differences. As I look back on the notes I took then, I see now that I missed quite a few of the strategy changes. I know a lot more about various kinds of interference than I did then and the available tools (for analysis) are better now. Still, I went forward at the time with the best tools I had.

At about 8 o'clock one evening, I took my eight grand and went off to Bally's to seek my fortune. Their high-limit room, called Champagne Slots, was essentially empty. A host was idly chatting with a cashier when I walked up and asked to buy $5,000 in $25 tokens. This got their attention. Before I could sit down I had the host's card in my hand with a promise that he'd be available 24/7, forever and ever, to get me anything my little heart desired. Well, maybe he didn't promise quite that much, but it sounded like it. I tried to be cool, as though I did this all the time. "I'll get back to you. Right now I'm more interested in getting four aces than I am in eating."

"Okay, fine. But don't forget, I'm right here."

It took all of 20 minutes for the machine to swallow the $5,000. *Slurp slurp* and it was all gone. Feelings of dread began to spread over me. I started feeding hundred dollar bills into the machine, each one worth only slightly more than a single bet. The cashier came over and asked me if I wanted to buy more tokens. I told her that I'd try the bills for awhile. "Maybe it'll change my luck."

Two minutes later, I was dealt four 3s for a $6,000 payoff and I was even again. Phew! I now knew that $8,000 was a *pitifully* small bankroll with which to attack this machine, but I kept going anyway. I moved over to the adjacent machine and before I'd been paid for the 3s, I hit four kings for $3,750. I started to breathe normally again. This might turn out to be an okay experience after all.

I now had a small cushion. Very small. In 15 minutes I was back to my original $8,000. Then I hit another quad. In the next

---

Cash or Coin?

When the Bally's floorman came over to handle the $6,000 payment for the four 3s on the $25 machine, he asked me if I wanted cash or coin. Since these machines were balky in terms of accepting coins, I asked for bills. When the two floorpeople brought over the $6,000 (there's always a witness for transactions of this size), they had $5,000 with a paper strap around it and ten $100 bills.

They asked if I wanted the $5,000 counted in front of me. I was amazed by the question. Even when I'd hit a $20,000 royal at the Frontier earlier, everything was counted out. I was told that at Bally's, a lot of the customers didn't want to waste time with counting. And besides, two people had counted it already. I told them the "strap" was fine with me, although as soon as they left I counted the money anyway.

A side note: I've since received several hundred $5,000 or $10,000 straps from high limit-cashiers in several different Las Vegas casinos. I believe that I've never been shortchanged.

hour, I hit for three more 4-of-a-kinds, one of which was "special" (paying $6,000 rather than the $3,750 for the "non-special"), so I was up ten grand. Life was beautiful!

Over the next few hours I gave most of that back. Shortly after midnight, I hit four aces: $12,000 all at once. Yes! Since this jackpot was more than $10,000, it had to be verified by a "suit"—i.e., a slot supervisor or a shift boss. No problem. There were two vacant machines just sitting there and I had cash and tokens.

While waiting to be paid on my aces, I was dealt aces on the adjacent machine. Another $12,000. I whooped. I'd never won this much money at one time and I was excited. A minute or so later I'd calmed down enough to move over to the third machine, where it took me five minutes to line up a straight flush for another $6,000. Amazingly, all three machines were now out of commission with jackpots requiring hand-pays. *My* jackpots. I couldn't play, so I just sat there, alone, at one in the morning, basking in the glow of $30,000 that I'd amassed in less than 15 minutes. Plus, I still had coins in my tray and a strap in my pocket. I was ecstatic.

At this point, I considered getting a room at Bally's for the night. Although I lived less than 10 miles away, at that moment I wasn't sure I could drive safely. But by the time I got paid, I was fine.

This was when I learned the rules for leaving money in the cage. I didn't want to take possession of 30 grand in public, but I was required to fill out a line-of-credit application before I could put the money on deposit. I filled out the form. They kept the money and gave me a receipt.

(Once you have one line of credit in Las Vegas and a history of paying it off on time, getting more lines is easy. You don't need to fill out all the forms. The casino at which you're applying just calls Central Credit, the credit-overseeing organization that most Las Vegas casinos use, and they set you up fast.)

I played several more hours and finished at 5 in the morning. My net for the day was +$22,000, and I had a big stack of W-2Gs.

I'd had one session this big before—at the Frontier—but this was still special. I had to call Shirley. Today, I've hit enough of these jackpots that I just let her sleep, but not back then. Besides, she was a new girlfriend—people do things differently under those circumstances. Shirley was surprised when her cell phone rang at 5 a.m. in a motel room in Fresno. Initially, she was frightened, thinking it must be something bad for anyone to wake her up like that. But when I told her the story, she forgave me for calling.

I had trouble going to sleep. When I finally did, my dreams were filled with straps of hundred dollar bills. It was exhilarating! When I woke up, however, I faced a big decision. I'd taken a potshot and gotten away with it. I was willing to lose $8,000 the night before, but this was a new day. Twenty grand was a good-sized addition to my bankroll, but I still had less than half of what I needed to play that game safely. (Based on the 3- to 5-royal rule of thumb and a $60,000 royal, I figured I needed between $180,000 and $300,000 to play the game forever.) I'd lost half a royal in one day several times while playing for lower stakes. Half a royal on this machine was $30,000. One average bad day could wipe out the results from the best day in my life so far. What to do?

I decided to continue to go for it, but at the same time, I'd also lock up some of my profit. I put away $13,000, putting me $5,000 ahead of where I'd started. That left me $17,000 for another potshot.

I'd been around gambling for 25 years. I knew that locking up profits had very little, if any, mathematical basis. Nothing was sacred about where I was when I took the first potshot, so neither was my new bankroll of $5,000 more. At the same time, I knew I was gambling for bigger stakes than I could afford. I was out on the skinny limbs of my bankroll and my nerves; thus, stopping points made a lot of sense—even if their only value was psychological.

So I went back the next night, and lo and behold, I won again—though this time it was "only" $13,000. And I won again the next night. In the first two weeks I played those $25 three-coiners, I was up more than $60,000. I had losing sessions, but not many, and they were much smaller than the winning sessions. I was in heaven. Finally, gambling for real was as good as it had been in my dreams.

After another three weeks, I'd added another $40,000. It was only mid-February and I was up more than $100,000 for the year. Quite a heady experience. By March 1, I was up $120,000. But then my gambling world turned upside down. In the next two weeks I lost $80,000. Two months previous, my entire bankroll was about $80,000, and now I watched that much go away almost instantly.

I'd expected this losing streak. It had always shown up before, and I had every reason to believe that it always would in the future. But so much. And so fast. Damn! It was devastating.

Those early-morning calls to Shirley weren't so jubilant anymore. It's a lot more fun explaining how you just won $20,000 than how you just lost $20,000. What can you say? "The machines plain died. For awhile there, even three-of-a-kind seemed like a big hand. A flush? A straight? I don't remember what they look like."

I set my stop-loss at a net profit of $30,000. How I came up with that number, I don't know. Shirley told me that if I had set my stop loss at $120,000, I'd still be up that amount. But I explained to her that ups and downs are just part of the game.

Still, Shirley was very nervous about these numbers. She was accustomed to making $20,000 after taxes for a year of hard work, and I'd win or lose that amount in a few hours. Although we hadn't discussed the M-word at this point, she'd thought about it and was trying to figure out if she could cope with these swings.

Before I reached the $30,000 stopping point and had my rainbow disappear, I found the pot of gold. I hit a royal for $60,000. Yahoo! My biggest jackpot yet. I was now up almost a hundred grand at Bally's and life was beautiful again. Shirley didn't mind that phone call one bit.

A few weeks after I started playing at Bally's, Arnie encouraged me to take a room and order booze. "You must have fifty large worth of comp credit there. Start ordering expensive wine by the case and see what happens. I'll buy it from you at forty percent of retail."

"Fifty percent."

"Okay."

So I did. I already had a room there much of the time, but now I was ordering $2,000 or $3,000 worth of alcohol a week. To be sure, the liquor prices were significantly marked up, so it was probably $500-$600 retail, but it was still substantial when I did it on a regular basis. Every day I arrived with towels from the last trip in an otherwise-empty suitcase-on-wheels and left with it full of wrapped bottles. I was ordering more alcohol than anyone in the place, but I was also betting more money than anyone. And since I don't drink, every time they saw me in the casino I was cold sober. But the total amount of comps I cashed was still less than what my play generated, so no one said a word.

Right after I hit the $60,000 royal, another losing streak began. From being up $100,000 on the play, I went down to about $60,000. To add insult to injury, my host told me that all of my comps were being cut off and he wasn't authorized to say any more. When I complained, my calls were shuttled upstairs to a vice president, who informed me, firmly but politely, that they believed I was a strong player who had an edge over them. They weren't going to 86 me from playing, but damned if they were going to let me waltz that much alcohol out of the place, too. I could continue to play if I wanted, but I had to pay retail for rooms, meals, and everything else. (As if I would pay retail for a casino room 10 miles from my home.)

Darn! Can't say I didn't have it coming, but I'd enjoyed those extras. By then I'd increased my stop-loss figure from $30,000 to $50,000. Even though I hadn't dropped quite that far yet, I decided that this was a good time to leave. The machines lasted for another month or so after I left, but eventually they were pulled.

The experience at Bally's changed my life. My bankroll got a big boost and I was never afraid to hammer away at $5 machines again. I got used to staying in nice hotel rooms and decided that if all it took to get one was to play a few more hours at a game where I had the advantage, then why not?

I used to think that all hotel rooms are alike. They're just a place to sleep; it doesn't matter what they look like. No more. I cared about the walls being soundproof. I cared about security. I learned to tell and appreciate the difference between ceramic tile and marble in a bathroom. And having two bathrooms and a Jacuzzi tub is a sweet touch. I miss these amenities when I don't have them. This isn't to say that I'd willingly pay for such things with real money, but in the casino, where you can get them with comps, they're worth a few hours extra of play to obtain.

During this adventure, I had bigger swings than ever before. I'm frequently asked how I deal with such swings. Part of dealing with them is confidence in my methods. When I played at Bally's, I'd been winning at gambling for eight years straight. My score went up and down, but I hit lifetime high-water marks again and again. This gave me confidence that I was doing the right things.

Part of it is just plain willingness to accept risk. Some people are more daredevil than others.

And part of dealing with the swings at Bally's was that I won first. There's a tendency to think of recent winnings as not quite being yours yet, so giving back recent winnings is not as big a deal as losing money you've had for a long time.

After this experience I also vowed never to abuse comps again. I did what I did at Bally's partly just to see what I could get away with. It wasn't fraud by any means or anything bad enough to go to jail over. I can make all kinds of rationalizations about why I did it at the time, but the fact remains that I'm sorry I did, and won't do it again. Lesson learned.

Living on the Dark Side

A lot of my success at video poker has come after midnight. It's not because I'm luckier in the wee hours, it's that I play far more during this time of day.

The biggest reason I like to play early in the morning is that other people don't. The casinos are considerably less busy during the graveyard shift and whatever machine I want is more likely to be available. I like people well enough, but the more people in a casino, the more smokers there are, and I try to avoid cigarette smoke if I can. A more important reason I want to play when others don't is that they tend to want the same machines I do.

Let's face it, the machines I want to play represent considerable risk for the casinos, so they're not likely to have too many of them in action. I'm not the only player smart enough to identify the good machines, so I operate during times when there's less competition.

I also find that I can usually get jackpots paid or scratchers delivered faster during the graveyard shift. Although the casino staff shrinks by two-thirds during those hours, the casino patrons shrink by three-fourths, so there are actually more workers per player. It doesn't always work this way, and frequently most change booths are closed, so you have to walk farther to turn in your coin, but often it does.

Playing two machines is easier after midnight. I usually find that there are more negatives than positives associated with playing two machines at the same time (usually only *very* proficient players do it, thus you're revealing your skill to the house), but at times I've felt it appropriate. For example, during a promotion where you have to turn on your change light and wait for a scratcher, having another machine available so you can make good use of the wait-time is more productive.

Another situation is when there are a lot of hand pays involved, and without a second machine, you have to sit idle for the five or ten minutes it takes to get paid.

Yet another is when the machines spill coins frequently. At Bally's, the $25 machines dropped coins into the tray if you had more than 47 credits. Spilling 45 coins for a full house took some time, and the machine was prone to coin jams. Having a second machine during such times was useful.

I credit discovering the benefits of playing during the dark hours to my thriftiness. The car I drove in California didn't have air conditioning. Air conditioning makes a car more expensive to buy and eats more gas, and I rarely needed it on the west side of Los Angeles where I lived. When I moved to Vegas, my car was about six years old. In Vegas, you need a/c in the summer. But installing it on a six-year-old car, especially when I was trying to conserve every penny of bankroll, didn't make much sense.

So if I wanted to drive to a casino during the summer, I drove after dark. Vegas nights are still warm in the summer, but it's 90-degree heat, rather than 110-degree heat. (For the first two summers I was here, Ginny's car was available. I got a new car just before the start of my third summer. Although my 1987 car still ran well enough and I hated the idea of spending money unnecessarily, I couldn't go through another summer without air conditioning.)

I've found that I can adjust my body to any regular schedule. If I always go to bed at 3 p.m. and get up at 10 p.m., it works just fine. During the year between Ginny and Shirley, I did just that. But when you have to deal with people on a regular schedule, you sometimes need to be up during normal hours. Teaching classes at 3 in the morning would work just fine for me, but I'd be teaching to three students max. When I'm in slot tournaments, one round is at 9 or 10 in the morning and the other is four hours later. You have to be up for both. When my consulting business requires I meet with someone, it has to be during hours that they're doing business.

So now I rely on naps. My schedule sometimes devolves into being awake for six hours, napping for three, being awake for another five hours, then napping for two. Or whatever. This works well enough. Shirley's biological clock wakes her up at 7 in the morning, and once she's up, she's up. Napping doesn't usually work for her unless she's exhausted. So we often find ourselves on different sides of the clock. It's a struggle sometimes to keep a marriage working under such conditions. So far, we've managed.

Trying to Go to the Bahamas

In the spring of 1997, I came across a good dollar pay schedule for Joker Wild at the Tropicana. It was a 100.65% game—very high for dollars. The Trop's slot club was hard to figure out (a perfect example of what Jeffrey Compton calls a "don't ask, won't tell" slot club), returning about .2% in cashback, plus comps. Since you could get $3,000 per hour through these machines, the return on the game, including cashback, was $25 per hour (.85% of $3,000 is $25.50).

The problem was that Joker Wild is an extremely difficult game to play. Bradley Davis, Lenny Frome, and Dan Paymar each had published strategies. They weren't perfect, but they were better than nothing. Paymar's was probably the best and I estimate it generated a return that was still at least .25% less than perfect. That's $7.50 an hour. Since I was considering playing hundreds of hours on this game, I needed to produce a better strategy.

At the time, the only way for me to accomplish this was by trial and error. *Video Poker Tutor* was the best computer product available. I started with a synthesis of the Davis/Frome/Paymar strategies and played on the computer until a hand came up that wasn't explained correctly. I logged all the exceptions and added rules to explain them. Eventually, I'd formulated a pretty good strategy (although not as good as the one that Liam W. Daily and I produced two years later) and was ready to play.

I played about 10 hours a week. The game was difficult and I wasn't doing well. The best thing that happened early on was that I met Liam and Katherine Daily. I'd written about this game in the *Las Vegas Advisor*. They'd seen the write-up and, by chance, were playing next to me when they mentioned either *LVA* or my name. I introduced myself and a valuable personal and professional relationship was launched.

On June 1, the Tropicana announced that it was giving away 50 all-expenses-paid trips to the Atlantis Casino in the Bahamas. These five-day mid-November trips would be given to the players who accumulated the most slot club points between June 1 and August 31. The Trop likely had a deal with the Atlantis, whereby the Atlantis would pick up some or all of the expenses for the trip in order to fill the casino with 50 proven gamblers. The Atlantis, the Tropicana, and the players were all happy with this deal. Win-win-win.

This gave me an excuse to play many hours on a game where I had an advantage. I even played two machines at once. If a slot supervisor or host asked me why I was playing so much, my answer was that I wanted to go to the Bahamas. Since they didn't believe I was actually a favorite at the game, this explanation made sense to them and they let me be.

The Trop had some $5 progressive games that accrued slot points five times as fast as a $1 game. Unfortunately, most of the time the progressive wasn't high enough to play profitably. Some players qualified this way, but not me. I didn't have to have the most points. I only had to have more than the 51st person.

For the second (and hopefully last) time in my career, I hired someone to play on my card. I paid "Joyce" $15 per hour with a promise that I would cover all W-2Gs. She put in many hours over the next three months and ended up losing quite a bit. It was certainly a possible result, although not a likely one. A few months after the promotion, she all of a sudden had enough money for a down payment on a house. Mere coincidence? I don't know. But I discovered that I'm not trusting enough to hire people to play for me.

After about a month or so, the Trop decided the dollar Joker Wild machines weren't making enough money for the casino. So they replaced them with full-pay dollar Deuces Wild machines. This was a move they thought was better for them, but I knew it was better for me. Joyce and I played 50 hours a week between us.

By late August, the Deuces Wild machines were gone, too. Also, the casino decided that three months wasn't long enough to decide who the top 50 players were. So mid-promotion, they extended it to four months. This wasn't fair to the players who'd been playing based on the old rules, but we had no recourse. We complained to the man in charge, to no avail. Fortunately for these players, the top 40 or so of the 50 places were already locked up. And since the casino removed all of the dollar-and-higher positive-equity games, anyone who wanted to earn a trip to the Bahamas had to play a game where the casino had the edge. Not many players were interested in doing that, so if you were eligible to go on August 31, you'd probably still be eligible on September 30.

Suspicious Giveaway

Midway through the Bahamas promotion, the Trop also held a giveaway drawing. I don't remember if it was for $50,000 or a new car, but it was a big prize. The more points you earned, the more drawing tickets you got, so those of us who'd been playing heavily liked our chances.

On the night of the drawing, the casino's General Manager drew the winning ticket. Then, suddenly, he just disappeared. The next thing we knew we were watching a five-minute video about the hotel. At the end of the video, the GM reappeared, pulled the winning ticket out of his pocket, and announced the winner.

The players screamed foul! When giveaway drawings are conducted, a ticket is pulled and a name is supposed to be called in full view. Here, the GM had been out of sight for five minutes. He could have easily replaced the drawn ticket with another for any player he wanted to win. Did he pull the old switcheroo? Who knows? He claims he didn't. Some players gave him the benefit of the doubt. Many didn't.

Do you have to worry about things like rigged drawings? I don't think so. Some skeptical players believe that many drawings are rigged. I don't. I'm alert, though. I watch as the drum is turned and the drawing made. And I watch to see what the person who draws does with the ticket. Sometimes watching closely helps me learn something about the person doing the drawing that will be useful next time. For example, maybe he tends to go for crumpled tickets (or maybe he *never* does). Winning drawings is part of my "job" and being successful at most jobs requires paying attention. So I do.

Of the 50 people who won trips to the Bahamas, at least 30 were video poker professionals, and most of us had come out ahead while earning the trip. These couldn't have been the players the Trop wanted to take to the Bahamas, but that's the way it turned out.

In the Bahamas, we found that the best game at the Atlantis was 9/6 Jacks or Better, with no slot club, so many of us didn't play at all. One who did hit a $20,000 royal flush, but the Atlantis

---

Don't Ask, Won't Tell

Most casinos give you a lot of information about what it takes to earn a dollar's worth of cashback. But some don't (Jeffrey Compton coined the term "don't ask, won't tell" for this type of club). During this period at the Trop, you could walk up to the booth any time they were open and find out how much cashback you'd earned. But unless you were able to physically count *exactly* 1,000 hands between trips to the booth, you couldn't figure out the rate of cashback with a high degree of accuracy (actually, you could have counted any reasonably large sample of hands, but you had to keep an exact count). And even if you could estimate the rate for one machine, there was no way of knowing whether it was the same on other machines.

Even though I couldn't get precise data about the cashback rate, I attempted to figure it out as best I could. I did it by elapsed time, using the knowledge that I played about 600 hands per hour, which adds up to $3,000 when playing $5 per hand. On one occasion, I learned I had $87 in cashback. I then played two and a half hours, after which time I had $102. Since I estimated I'd played $7,500 through the machine (2.5 x $3,000 = $7,500) and had earned $15 ($102 - $87 = $15), I put the rate of cashback at .2% ($15/$7,500 = .002 = .2%).

Calculating the cashback return is important. Don't ask, won't tell situations are rare these days, but if you encounter one, you have to devise a method to get this information. Sometimes the technique described here works, and sometimes you have to come up with a different way.

refused to pay off on the grounds that the player was in the Griffin book (of casino undesirables) as a blackjack counter. On this occasion, however, the same Trop employee who was so suspect at the drawing came to the rescue and the player was paid the next day. Still, the rest of the players stopped playing after that. Why risk anything if you're not sure you'll be paid? The casinos couldn't have been satisfied with the amount of play generated by these "proven gamblers," but they underestimated the effect of pay schedules on whether or not knowledgeable video poker players will gamble.

For Shirley and me, it was great. Neither of us had been to the Bahamas before and there were a lot of interesting things to see. Plus, the Atlantis is magnificent, especially the world-class aquarium (and it's even larger and better today). We called it a pre-honeymoon, because we weren't getting married for another month or so. We explored Nassau and enjoyed the hotel, but didn't put a single quarter into a machine. There were no games where we could get the advantage, so why bother?

Teaching Shirley to Play

When I met Shirley, she knew very little about video poker. And what she did know she didn't like. In her experience, video poker was the addictive game that kept several of her friends and relatives broke. She'd been through some tough financial times and no way in the world did she think gambling was an intelligent way to earn money. She'd heard several people expound on what good players they were (usually immediately after hitting a $1,000 royal flush), but she knew that they all ended up broke again.

I was able to get her to play by seducing her with nice hotel rooms, gourmet meals, shows, and dancing. What a stud I am!

I spent awhile going over the basics before we played together the first time. And I mean basics. Shirley didn't know a flush from a full house. She couldn't have told you how many cards were in a deck or what the four suits were. Is a king higher or lower than a queen? Shirley didn't have a clue.

After a half-hour of this, we agreed that she and I would play side by side—both using my slot club card. She'd be dealt a hand, make the play she thought best, and wait for me to say yes or no. I assured her that there was nothing to worry about. I would make all the decisions and bear all the financial risk.

The first time out, she played a $2 9/6 Jacks or Better machine while I played a $5 machine right next to her. The first evening went pretty well—meaning she got good hands on *her* machine. We started with a $100 bill and she got a few 4-of-a-kinds in the first half-hour. Every flush or higher was really exciting for her. It was my money, win or lose; still, every little success thrilled her. Of course, the fact that she had a new boyfriend (after a self-imposed eight-year hiatus from dating) and was going dancing the next night might have had a little something to do with the fun.

Soon she was dealt 5♥6♥8♥9♥A♣. She quickly held the ace. I explained that any 4-card flush was a better play than a single high card and that this particular 4-card flush was actually a 4-card straight flush. If she now drew a 7♥, she would get 250 coins. Sure enough, she connected for the straight flush and screamed. But her delight soon turned to horror. The machine began dropping coins into the tray and she was sure she'd done something to break it! I explained that this was normal when you got enough credits, but now she was disgusted that she would actually have to touch the coins and put them into the racks. After all, she'd just washed her hands!

This was Thanksgiving weekend and we made plans for her to come back for New Year's. I gave her my 9/6 Jacks or Better report to look at, along with a copy of *Video Poker Tutor*.

When Shirley came back to town a month later, she hadn't installed the program on her computer and had read only the first four pages of the report. It wasn't that she was lazy. Far from it. But she worked 80 hours or so a week and concentrating on some kind of applied math at the end of a long day just didn't float her boat (it did help her go to sleep, though).

She liked the parties and shows and dancing, so she kept coming back. We started to practice an hour or so at the beginning of every visit. I had a deck of cards and a strategy sheet and we reviewed. And reviewed and reviewed.

It turned out that she wouldn't remember much from trip to trip. I saw video poker as a source of livelihood, but Shirley saw it as something she had to put up with in order to get what she really wanted—a guy who took her to nice places (especially places to dance).

These practice sessions tied Shirley's stomach into knots. Video poker is easy if you have the mindset of a computer programmer, puzzle solver, or accountant. Jacks or Better is actually trivially easy for such a person. But for someone (such as Shirley) whose strengths lie in people skills, video poker can be quite difficult—especially if you're forced to live by the rule that "playing perfectly is barely good enough."

I made Shirley learn every last one of the rules of the game. Why you hold all four hearts with A♥K♥T♥5♥J♠ or A♥K♥T♥5♥T♠, but not with A♥K♥T♥9♥9♠, A♥K♥Q♥5♥J♠, or K♥Q♥T♥5♥T♠. When you hold a suited KT and when you throw the T away and hold the K alone. When a suited QJ is better than an AKQJ. When you hold a suited QT with an A in the hand, and when you hold the AQ instead.

Actually, there aren't many tough hands in Jacks or Better, except in Shirley's case. Where I saw a few problem hands, she saw an overwhelming number. She held a responsible position at work, but here she just couldn't remember all the nuances. You can bet I helped her as patiently as I could. I liked having a girlfriend and I had no intention of chasing her away for not learning fast enough. But it was frustrating for both of us.

Part of the problem was coming to grips with our personality differences. I'm very left-brained; word and number puzzles come easily to me. Shirley is a scrapper and makes up for the lack of raw talent with gritty determination. She believes there's nothing she can't do as long as she keeps at it long and hard enough. The result is she's reasonably accomplished at many things. And I'm extremely good at a few.

We practiced for an hour or so every visit and we always played side by side. I checked her on every hand, which she didn't enjoy. She played at least 95% of the hands perfectly, but the edge that the best players enjoy is so small, you need to play very close to 100% of the hands perfectly in order to have a chance. This wasn't the way Shirley thought. She was like the cook who made the spaghetti sauce a little differently every time and I was forcing her to make it the same way. My way. There's only one correct play for every hand. Players who accept that truth and learn to play that way are regularly called winners. Players who don't are regularly called by casino hosts.

We're getting a little ahead of ourselves in the story, but it wasn't until halfway through our million-dollar six months that Shirley first played unsupervised. And that was four years after our first Treasure Island weekend. Four years of frequent playing and me supervising every hand. As I write this, another year has passed. And periodically, I still need to review hands with Shirley. But now Jacks or Better isn't the only game she plays. We go back and forth between Jacks or Better and Double Bonus and she gets confused. Hands involving inside straights and 3-card straight flushes are handled differently between the two games. Many of these hands occur infrequently and she doesn't always remember the differences.

One thing Shirley's very good at is remembering to actively use a strategy card. I play on my own machine without paying much attention to what she's doing, but if I sense her slow down to think about a hand or see her glance at the card, I look over and supervise. She has a pretty high batting average now and knows it, but it took years of practice to get there.

A lot of things had to click for Shirley to become proficient at video poker. Most people wouldn't put up with having someone

Shirley Gets Ready for Reno

Every July, Shirley and I spend a week in Reno. It's cooler than Las Vegas and the gambling opportunities are sufficient. For three years in a row, our game of choice in Reno was Kings or Better Joker Wild. The strategy is devilishly complicated and since we played only once a year, Shirley had to get ready.

It's a regimen. First, out comes the strategy card. Even though she knows this game, to refresh her memory she scans the eight-page Information Sheet that comes with it. Then she runs through Level 1: Beginners Strategy, and Level 2: Recreational Strategy. For most players, Level 2, which is less than a quarter percent less than perfection, is satisfactory. But it's not good enough for us. Level 3: Basic Strategy is as accurate as it's possible to get without factoring in penalty cards. You can squeeze out another tenth of a percent by mastering Level 4: Advanced Strategy, but it's a tough tenth. Shirley knows that she has to master Level 4 strategy or I'll watch every hand and point out every misplay—a fate she prefers to avoid.

Next, she practices on the computer.

Then, after a few weeks, she crosses her fingers and says, "Okay, test me."

I pull out a deck of cards and start dealing hands. Shirley looks at her strategy card, then answers questions correctly. This is perfectly acceptable. Video poker is an open-book test. Strategy cards buried in your purse or pocket have limited value. Strategy cards, when they're consulted, have great value. Soon she tires of the classroom environment. "Let's go play for real."

In 2001, we headed for the Reserve (now Fiesta Henderson), which back then had a nickel four-line Joker game. We played for four or five hours over a couple of sessions, periodically checking hands against the strategy card. We lost $45 one night and won $85 another.

This is how we practice for a new game.

Our result in Reno that year was expensive, even though we'd actually spent more time practicing and then playing for nickels than we'd spent playing for dollars. Is it worth it to study this hard for a trip where you may end up losing anyway? It is for us. We're willing to work as hard as it takes to stack the deck in our favor.

monitor their every play for four years. It helped that when she met me, I was already proficient and knew I wanted to play the game professionally for as long as possible. She knew this going in, so it was no surprise down the road. If she wanted to fit into my life, she needed to come to grips with video poker. And during the inevitable losing streaks, I was always around to tell her that they would end and that we were doing everything right and that a winning streak was right around the corner.

For other people with Shirley's background, it might be impossible to do well at this game. Setting aside the fact that affordable private tutors aren't that easy to come by, for starters, convincing yourself that a game so alien to your normal way of thinking will be a good deal in the long run isn't easy. More important, developing the fundamental understanding and being able to maintain the confidence that losing streaks won't wipe you out comes only with a lot of knowledge and experience. And it's hard to get someone to bankroll you along the way toward getting this knowledge and experience.

Shirley was able to put the pieces together, but I still have to take her dancing.

Royal Coupon Adventure at the Casino Royale

I didn't want to include this story, but Shirley swore she'd tell everyone if I didn't. This story doesn't show me at my best, but I'd prefer that you hear it from me, rather than her.

Casino Royale is a small joint in the heart of the Las Vegas Strip. Tom Elardi, who used to manage the Frontier for his mother, owns it. At the time this episode took place, Casino Royale was actively courting low-stakes local players by offering a variety of short-term coupons, mailed to names in its database.

I used to play dollar Deuces Wild at Casino Royale and was a charter member of the slot club. But I hadn't played there since it changed the schedule on the Deuces machines two years prior. Many local players liked the quarter promotions, but since

I usually played $1 and $5 games, there was nothing to attract me.

Until, that is, I received the coupon to die for in the mail. This coupon, I figured, was being mailed to names on the casino's inactive player list and if it couldn't get someone's attention, that someone had already moved, died, or given up video poker.

This was the deal. For the entire month, royal flushes received a 5,000-coin bonus (certain wild card and other machines excluded). This merited looking into. Such a bonus adds almost 3% to most games, which is *huge*. For players with the bankroll to play $5 machines, this coupon was worth more than $400 per hour. The possibilities got my juices flowing, to say the least.

First, I scouted the casino and verified that it had $5 machines. They did, and they were 9/6 Jacks or Better games. This was wonderful. The 9/6 Jacks game was eligible and not only did I know 9/6 strategy perfectly, but Liam W. Daily and I had recently worked out charts on how the best play changed as the value of the royal increased.

Next, I carefully re-read the coupon. I wanted to verify that the bonus, not the entire payoff, was 5,000 coins. In other words, a total payment of 5,000 coins would represent only a 1,000-coin bonus over the normal 4,000 payoff. Sure enough, it said "5,000-coin bonus." A $20,000 royal was now worth $45,000—*if* I could hit it before Casino Royale realized its mistake.

Now I went home to study and practice. Proper play for a 9,000-coin royal is a lot different from proper play for a 4,000-coin royal. Fortunately, the computer software program I was using at the time was convenient for this analysis. In the table on the next page, the amounts in parentheses represent the amount by which one play is superior to the other when playing for a $20,000 royal versus a $45,000 royal. For example, in the first hand, playing AJ is $1.01 better than AT when a royal returns $20,000, while AT is 52¢ better than AJ when a royal returns $45,000.

	$20,000	$45,000
A♠T♠4♠J♦5♥	AJ ($1.01)	AT (52¢)
A♦A♠K♠T♠4♠	AA ($7.42)	AKT ($15.71)
Q♦J♦8♦K♣5♥	QJ8 ($1.33)	QJ (21¢)
Q♥T♥A♠K♦5♣	AKQT ($1.48)	QT (6¢)
Q♠T♠5♠J♥8♣	QJ (90¢)	QT (64¢)
K♣T♣5♣A♦9♠	AK (67¢)	KT (87¢)
A♠J♥8♣6♦4♦	AJ (11¢)	J (4¢)

This partial chart shows that several hands are affected by the change in the value of the royal.

"You can trust me," I told Shirley, "I have it all figured out. We may lose thirty grand in three or four days before we hit the forty-five-thousand-dollar payoff, but we'll probably do just fine. The odds are strongly in our favor."

"Go for it, honey," she said, swallowing hard. Shirley does trust me, but swings of this size still put her on edge. "Probably" is not a particularly comforting word. She knows the losses will come up front, but the royal is a big maybe.

There are lots of *maybes*. Maybe we'll experience one of those streaks where we lose $60,000 before we hit the royal. Maybe the casino will wake up and discover it's giving away the store after we lose a bundle, but before we hit the royal. Maybe they'll recognize me, realize I'm an expert, and kick me out. Maybe they'll exclude the $5 machines from the promotion. Maybe. Maybe. Maybe.

Nonetheless, early the next day, a Sunday, I woke up, did my exercise-shower-eat-review-strategy routine, and was at the casino by about 8 o'clock. Shirley would have played too, but she didn't have a coupon. She decided to spend the day going to church and visiting friends, then join me for dinner. In case I hit the royal early (I love her optimism!), she instructed me to call her so we could make other plans.

Hour one wasn't so bad. I was up about $1,200. Of course, hitting four 4-of-a-kinds (at $625 each) instead of the 1.5 I was mathematically entitled to didn't hurt.

This casino didn't have a high-roller section. The two $5 video poker machines were right next to the nickel machines. When the $5 tokens fall in the tray (as they do when more than 200 credits accrue), it attracts a lot of attention; to a nickel player, a $625 jackpot looks pretty big. Having several racks of $5 tokens between machines caused more attention than I was comfortable with, but for $400 per hour, I was willing to put up with worse conditions than these.

Hours two and three sucked. I lost about $3,000 during each. Since I'd only brought about $8,000 with me, I was close to running out of cash on hand. I could have gone across the street to the Mirage and cashed a marker for $5,000 or more, but this wouldn't have been wise. Asking for markers on days you don't play in a casino is risking the loss of credit there.

Surprisingly, I was the only pro around. Where were the smart players with the bankroll to play a $5 game? Perhaps they didn't get the same coupon I did. Perhaps I somehow got the coupons that were supposed to go only to the players without a clue.

I came back a bit in the afternoon. When Shirley showed up at 5, I was stuck $3,500. Not a lot of fun, but actually a better result than expected for nine hours on a $5 machine. We decided to eat upstairs, where there was a surprisingly good Italian restaurant with a great view of the Mirage volcano. Unfortunately, the comp structure at Casino Royale allowed only a $40 maximum food credit. There are no hosts and the slot club personnel aren't empowered to grant much. In any other place where I've put $125,000 through the machines in one day, the carpet has been as red as can be. Not so at Casino Royale. We begged the shift boss and finally got him all the way up to $50.

Over dinner, we decided that I didn't need to kill myself by playing long hours continuously until I hit the royal, since the coupon was good for another three weeks. But on our way down from dinner, an employee named Pete approached me: "Aren't you Bob Dancer? We took your Deuces Wild class at the Fiesta and really liked it. What game do we have here that you like?"

I told him that we'd heard nice things about the restaurant and just wanted to come by and earn enough comps to go there. I don't think he bought it. Uh oh! We had no idea how soon the information that "Bob Dancer was playing" would be passed on. It's unlikely that any high-level decision-makers were on hand on a Sunday night, but Monday might be a different story. So there would be no rest for the weary. I had to hit that machine while the hitting was good.

For the first two hours after dinner, my score—and all my cash—went straight south. I'd earned some slot club cash, so I retrieved it. And lost. Shirley had $500 in her purse. I took that too. We considered our options and decided that, if necessary, I would go cash a check at the Mirage. My line of credit would guarantee the check and it probably wouldn't count against me that I didn't play there that day. Trouble was, my checkbook was 15 minutes away. Shirley was willing (but not eager) to make the round trip. Although it didn't turn out to be necessary, we had to think about what we would do and be ready to act if we ran out of cash.

Fortunately, that was our low point. I hit a straight flush (for $1,250), which gave me some money to play with. For the next four hours, I pretty much treaded water, then managed to come back a few thousand.

About midnight, Pete stopped by to say good night and good luck. He was going home and his manner didn't indicate that he'd turned us in. We didn't know whether any changes would be made, but we figured we had at least eight hours—a minor emotional victory. Twenty-four-hour workdays weren't as easy as they'd used to be, but easy or not, we decided we had to go for it. Shirley stuck around, massaging my neck periodically and providing encouragement. She was also trying to decide which Rolex to buy when we hit the $45K.

At 3 a.m., I was dealt A♠T♣9♦8♦6♦. I wasn't sure of the right play. I knew that straight-flush draws with a gap were usually better than AT, even with a $45,000 royal. The presence of the T poisoned the value of 986 a little, but after 19 hours of concentration, I wasn't sure how much. (A couple of days later I looked it up and found AT was better by a full 1.75¢.)

I was exhausted. I wanted this ordeal to be over. I was ready to take bigger chances than this. I held AT. This time the video poker heavens opened up to me and out came KQJ of spades—the 1-in-16,215 shot I was hoping for. A royal flush! At last! It'd all been worth it.

Shirley swears that I went into my victory strut, but I deny it. It absolutely couldn't have happened; I was much too tired. Although I must admit that I produced the coupon with a bit of a flourish, I absolutely, positively, never had a "Pay That! Sucker!" smirk on my face.

At this point, I realized that I might have to wait awhile for my money. Casino Royale is fairly small and a $45,000 jackpot probably required a number of signatures. Who knows? Maybe someone would have to get out of bed to come in and verify it. But it was okay. Even though I was exhausted, I was willing to wait 'til the cows came home to get $45,000!

While I was thanking Shirley for having faith in my judgment, the shift boss came up and politely said: "I'd like to pay you the extra twenty-five grand, but you didn't qualify. The coupon says the royal must be in clubs."

I grabbed the coupon, read it, and saw that he was right. I guess I'd been so busy concentrating on whether it was a true bonus that I totally blanked on the wording "in clubs." *That's* why the other pros weren't playing.

I immediately realized I'd been making big mistakes. Three-fourths of my adjustments (those for spades, hearts, and diamonds) were just plain wrong. Fortunately, the royal came early. "Trust me," I'd said. Sure. "Check up on me" was more appropriate.

Okay, winning $20,000 is hardly a tragedy. And ending up with a significant profit on a game I wouldn't have been playing had I read the coupon carefully was a much better result than I deserved. But eating crow still isn't fun. I was supposed to be the expert. And I'm careful about reading coupons. But I'd sure screwed up on this one.

Of course, I couldn't get away without a little unwanted attention. Before I got the money, a couple of pros I knew wandered by. They had been checking out a nearby progressive. They saw that I'd held AT. They didn't know what the three cards I discarded were, but they certainly knew that this was a bad play.

"It's nice to see an advanced play rewarded," teased one of them.

"When are you going to write a report with this play in it?" teased the other. "I'd pay big money to know when to make a play like that!"

"Guys," I replied coolly. "I'm very happy to have hit the royal and can honestly tell you that it seemed like the right play at the time."

Okay, Shirley. I've written about it. Now you don't have to tell everyone. And could you please wipe that silly grin off your face and stop uttering "trust me" over and over and over.

Shirley Doesn't Always See it My Way

Shirley and I were heading to Arizona Charlie's East for "Triple-Point Tuesday" when the following riddle came over the radio: What's blue and smells like red paint? No answer came to Shirley. I got it right away: blue paint. Paint smells like paint, no matter what the color is. I thought it was clever; Shirley thought it was stupid.

We were on our way to Charlie's to play a Ten Play dollar 10/7 Double Bonus machine—a formidable game that takes $50 to fully load. We were playing it to take advantage of the triple points.

As soon as we arrived, Sherry, the assistant shift boss, came over and said hello. I asked her, "What's blue and smells like red paint?" Shirley cringed with embarrassment. Sherry shrugged. When she heard the answer, it was clear she agreed with Shirley that it was a stupid riddle.

I promptly hit a royal flush for $4,000. Royals are always nice, but they're a lot more common on Ten Play than on single-play machines, and they pay just 80 for 1 (based on the coins needed to play all 10 lines) rather than the 800 for 1 you normally receive.

When the shift boss came to pay me, I asked, "What's blue and smells like red paint?" Shirley cringed again. But this time the $4,000 soothed her embarrassment.

After humoring me, the shift boss went away and a few minutes later I hit another royal. Shirley started to develop a "theory." She argued that even though it was the dumbest riddle she'd ever heard, telling it to people seemed to bring on royals.

I replied, "That's a classic logic fallacy known as *post hoc ergo propter hoc.* The riddle preceding the royals has absolutely nothing to do with the royals being made. It's pure coincidence."

"How can you know that for sure? Maybe the video poker god has a sense of humor tonight," she insisted. Whenever someone came by, Shirley sweetly said, "Glad you're here. My husband has something he wants to ask you about paint." Now I was the one cringing, but I went along and posed the riddle.

About an hour later I hit a third royal, which, of course, supported Shirley's theory, at least in her mind. And before our session ended, I hit a fourth royal. I'd played almost 5,000 hands; on Ten Play Double Bonus, that's about one royal-flush cycle. Hitting four or more royals in one cycle happens about 2% of the time. Rare, but not exceptionally so.

Shirley didn't see it that way. "Have you ever hit four royals in eight hours before?"

"No. But I really haven't played that much Ten Play. Someday I'll be dealt a royal on one of these machines, and that will be ten of them."

Shirley still wasn't buying. "If you've never done this well before, I say it's because of the riddle. You've never told that riddle before either."

This, of course, was absolutely ridiculous. Proving something by double negative is another fallacy of logic. The fact is, superstitions come in all shapes and sizes, often when you least expect them. But riddles, clever or otherwise, are not the secret to hitting royals.

Another time, flying into Reno, we saw signs at the airport indicating that WIBC members got a 10% bonus on jackpots. What was this? We didn't know what the WIBC was, but figured it was worth our time to find out. The WIBC, we learned, is a woman's bowling organization that was hosting a tournament in Reno while we were there. A 10% bonus might not be much for a casual player, but for Shirley and me, who aren't afraid to play $25 machines, this could be enormous.

Playing Up ...

Abner, a fine player, was hammering away at a $100 9/6 Jacks machine at a major Strip resort and was stuck $80,000. Not an unusually large amount for a $100 machine, but irritating nonetheless. He asked to have the machine locked up while he took a short nap. The casino had a policy that it would lock up the machine for up to four hours at the request of anyone who'd been playing for awhile.

Abner went to his room, set the alarm, and went to bed. After three hours and 45 minutes, he returned to the machine and found it unlocked. One of the change people told him that Randy, another regular player, had tipped $100 to have the machine unlocked and promptly hit a royal flush for $400,000.

Abner knew that Randy's jackpot had nothing to do with him. Everything is random and the fact that the machine had paid out big recently was totally irrelevant to what would happen in the future. But Abner also knew that many players are superstitious, believing that a royal flush hit on a machine "poisons" it until the machine has time to catch up. He decided to play it up as though he was really mad.

Abner demanded to see the slot boss. He ranted about how the casino had agreed to lock up the machine and how the casino employee had violated that promise and, in the process,

---

"Shirley," I said, "you're about to join a bowling league."

"Oh no!" she cried. "I'm the world's worst bowler! I was forced once to join a company team and my co-workers ended up taking a collection so I could go to dinner and a movie on league nights so I wouldn't show up at the bowling alley! No way am I going through that humiliation again!"

"Don't worry. You don't have to bowl. All we need to do is get you the WIBC card so you can qualify for the 10% bonus. If we play the $25 machines, we get an extra $125 for every full house, up to $2,000 for quads, and $10,000 for a royal. And this is on top of a game that already returns over 100%. It's video poker heaven!"

... a Superstition

his trust. A lot of casinos would appreciate a player who was willing to lose 80 grand, he told them. He should probably take his business elsewhere, maybe even see a lawyer.

It was all gamesmanship, of course. Abner just wanted to see where it would get him.

He was offered $10,000 to make up for the mistake. He refused. He was then offered $25,000. He refused again. "What's twenty-five grand compared to four hundred thou?" he fumed. "That should have been my jackpot!" Abner hoped that the VPs weren't savvy enough to know that he was spouting nonsense and that they'd concentrate on the $80,000 he lost in their attempts to do whatever it took to make him happy.

He eventually settled for $42,000 and the promise that 10% of his markers would be forgiven. Not a bad payday for a half-hour of acting—an Academy Award-winning performance, in my opinion.

Abner knew that his ranting would result, at a minimum, in someone being fired. The floorperson who'd accepted the tip to open up a locked machine had to go. This didn't bother Abner in the least. The floorperson was well aware of the rules and had knowingly accepted a sizable tip to break them. Players have to be able to trust casino employees.

"But we didn't bring enough cash for a $25 game. And we don't know the rules for the 10% bonus. Surely they're not going to pay us more than $1,000 an hour in bonuses hour after hour. We should check it out first."

Shirley was right. Seeing a vague ad is one thing; reading the fine print at the slot club booth is another.

We learned from someone in the hotel elevator that Shirley could sign up for the WIBC for $11 a year. Not bad; even if we used the 10% coupon only once on a 4-of-a-kind, it was worth at least $625 to us—certainly worth the minor inconvenience of joining.

Shirley signed up and got the coupon. Turns out it applied only to the top award (i.e., the royal flush) and was limited to $1,000. Sigh. A royal comes along only 80 hours or so on a single-line machine. Possible, but not likely in our two-day trip. Of course, we still made sure Shirley played on a card with her name on it, so if she did get a royal, she could collect the bonus worth an extra $450 on the machines we were playing.

Ultimately, she didn't connect. *C'est la vie.* But Shirley was annoyed. "I now belong to an organization that wouldn't want me if they knew how badly I played and we got absolutely nothing for it. What could be more stupid?"

I disagreed completely. Collecting on lucrative video poker promotions means having to go through things like this. You have to keep your eyes open. It takes time and energy to ascertain the exact rules for a potentially promising promotion. Occasionally you cash in big time, but usually you don't.

I regularly get e-mail from readers I've never met saying something like, "I'll be in Las Vegas for four days next month. Tell me the absolute best place to play so I don't have to waste my time searching." No can do. Even if I were motivated to give out this information, I have no idea what the best situation will be two days from now, let alone next month.

The great situations are rare. And they're only great for the first few people who find them. After the first day or two, the casinos wise up and change the rules. And just who are the "lucky" people who get to take advantage? The ones who go looking and are alert to the possibilities. Many of your searches will end up futile (like this one). But always being alert means that some of the time you'll be in position to succeed. The harder you work at this, the luckier you'll be.

Invitational Giveaways

In sporting events, "invitationals" are staged for athletes of a certain level of accomplishment. They are the opposite of "open" events, where all comers are allowed to compete.

In video poker and slots, an invitational has about the same meaning. Proven players, however defined, get invited to a casino for a weekend or so where something good happens. For example, $50,000 may be given away after some sort of competition.

In the late '90s, several Las Vegas Strip casinos held monthly invitationals. The best part was that these casinos had machines with schedules that gave skilled players an advantage even before the value of the giveaway was added on. Shirley and I could be counted on to accept every invitational at Treasure Island, the Mirage, the Golden Nugget, and occasionally others. They weren't the only invitationals in town by any means, but they were the ones we enjoyed the most.

One of the nice things about these events, especially for Shirley, was that you tended to see the same people over and over again. Shirley is much more social than I am, and after she moved to Las Vegas from California, it took a few years for her to develop a circle of friends. In the beginning, her social life was these parties.

Some of the giveaways were drawings. You might earn one drawing ticket for every $3,000 or so in coin-in over the weekend. Then on Saturday night, the casino would draw tickets out of a barrel to give away the prize money. Video poker players had a huge advantage over slot players, in that they could earn tickets while playing a game where they had the advantage. A .67% slot club on top of 99.54% Jacks or Better was common at the time. That adds up to 100.21% if you played perfectly. A .21% advantage meant that for every ticket (requiring $3,000 of play) you received, you also earned $6 from play. Plus the tickets might have an average value of $8. A slot player, on the other hand, typically faced a 4% or so disadvantage. So every ticket the slot player earned cost $120—and it still had the same $8 value. Consequently, video poker players had incentive to play a lot of hours. Slot players, on the other hand, might have a budget of $3,000, or $10,000, or whatever. When they lost it, they quit. Or even if they were ahead, they played a relatively modest amount. They knew who had the advantage—and it was spelled M-I-R-A-G-E. Thus video poker players would earn dozens of tickets, while slot players earned only a few.

For giveaway drawings, I worked out the "equity" (the value of being in the drawing) as follows. If everyone got one drawing ticket, I divided the amount of money being given away by the number of players. For example, if 200 players were splitting $50,000, the equity would be $250 apiece ($50,000/200 = $250). Of course, I rarely won precisely $250. I usually won nothing. And sometimes I scored $1,000, $2,000, $5,000, or more. However, the average equity provided a good approximation of what I would make per event if I went to enough of them. If the equity was based on the number of tickets earned, our chances increased greatly, because Shirley and I earned far more tickets than most of the other players.

For a period of about three years, we averaged a profit of between $20,000 and $40,000 per year from these giveaways. And this was on top of profits from earning the entries. And eating in nice restaurants. And staying in the best suites. And dancing at the awards parties. What a wonderful life!

Although these numbers sound impressive, keep in mind that on most of those weekends, we didn't get called up on stage (to collect a prize) and we didn't hit a royal flush. Instead, we tended to lose $5,000 to $10,000 in the casino. Not every time, but losses of that size were typical. Many people gave up; they simply couldn't handle the losses financially or psychologically. And most of the players didn't play perfectly. They knew 9/6 Jacks was worth 99.54%, but they didn't master all of the fine points. On their bad weekends, these players tended to lose more than the five or ten G's we lost on our bad weekends.

For the obvious reasons, invitationals that included games where the knowledgeable players had an advantage didn't work too well for the house. After all, slot players are the profit centers of the casino, while video poker players are less so. The profitable slot players got annoyed when the same video poker players frequently won (even when those video poker players were great dancers). Eventually, the casinos had to make adjustments.

One of the major adjustments was to cut cashback in half. Now it became a .33% cash club added to a 99.54% game. We could still earn drawing tickets for the giveaways, but they now cost about $4 per. It was still a good deal, because the value of the tickets rose to $10 apiece. The value of the tickets went up because far fewer of them were being earned by video poker players after the cashback was reduced.

Some casinos stopped inviting local video poker players altogether. They reasoned that locals were likely to be much stronger players than tourists. One casino simply didn't allow video poker players period. When word of this leaked out to the player community, pros starting playing a few hours of $5 Blazing Sevens on every trip. V-e-r-y s-l-o-w-l-y. Since some casinos keep records based on time played, they wanted a high amount of time to appear on the record with as few dollars played as possible.

Today, giveaway events still exist, but they're nowhere near as lucrative as they used to be. These days, playing enough to have a yearly expectation of $20,000-$40,000 would cost about $10,000 in losses (from the negative games you have to play to qualify). Still, the strongest players have an overall advantage and the giveaways remain good deals.

Giveaways at the Giveaways

The Mirage and Treasure Island, among others, tried to find a new and unusual way to give away money every month. Frequently, the selected players would get to make blind choices of some sort and how much money they won depended on the luck of the draw.

For example, if it was a Christmas giveaway party, there might be 15 ornaments stuck with Velcro on a fake tree, with each ornament representing a different cash amount. There was no way to intelligently choose one over the other, so you just plain guessed ... usually.

I remember two events where envelopes of hundred-dollar bills were stuck up on a board and you got to pick which envelope you wanted. When it was my turn to pick, I merely opted for the fattest envelope. It didn't take a rocket scientist to figure out that $5,000 in hundred-dollar bills made a fatter envelope than $1,000, but apparently the organizers didn't consider that.

The day before most of its slot tournaments, the MGM Grand held a small cash giveaway. They'd put about $2,500 in machine tokens in a bowl and players were called to reach in and scoop them out. You couldn't look while you were scooping, nor could you use the side of the bowl for leverage. A typical amount drawn was between $150 and $300.

At one of these events, Shirley's name was drawn. Instead of grabbing the coins palm down, she did so palm up. She ended up with $615, which probably was a record. The next day, everyone wanted to see Shirley's huge "claws." Shirley doesn't have unusually large hands, she just figured out a better way to do it.

The MGM instituted a rule against this. It's not called the "Shirley Rule," but after her haul, what she did was no longer allowed. Advantage players don't use just their brains while playing the machines. They're always looking for ways to squeeze a little extra out of a situation.

Invitational Slot Tournaments

Invitational slot tournaments have a lot in common with invitational giveaways. Proven players are invited in for a few days and cash prizes are distributed among them. However, instead of earning drawing tickets via play on regular machines, players compete by playing specially programmed slot machines. The high scores win the prizes.

You can calculate your expected result in a slot tournament more easily than you can in a giveaway event, simply because it's easier to predict the number of entrants in a tournament than it is to predict the number of tickets that will be in a barrel. In addition, slot tournaments are strictly luck, so every player has an equal chance. All you need to do is hit the button and take the score you end up with. As in the giveaway events, if $50,000 is being distributed among 200 players, each wins $250 on average.

Some casinos, however, play games with the numbers. The Venetian has been the worst offender in this regard in the past few years. On one occasion, the Venetian offered $75,000 in prizes, based on 250 entries. This would have resulted in player-equity of $300. But when only 225 players showed up (90% of what the prize pool was based on), the Venetian took away 33% of the money and offered only $50,000. (They kept "$75,000" in the title of the event—so we played the "All American $75,000 Tournament" with $50,000 in prizes.) This resulted in player-equity of $222. Big difference.

Many players base much of their decision to participate on the advertised player equity. Making proportional changes to the player pool is fine (in this case, that would mean reducing it by 10% to $67,500 to compensate for the fewer entrants). But to reduce the player pool by 33% for a 10% shortage in the player base wasn't perceived as fair. This was a penny-wise pound-foolish move on the part of the Venetian. The only players who cared were their best customers. The casino was giving away money to its best customers partly as a gesture of goodwill. Why ruin it with such an overtly miserly approach?

There are no free lunches. Casinos invite only proven players, who are expected to gamble a significant amount during the tournament. A casino might expect $10,000 worth of action,

$100,000 worth of action, or even more. It depends on the place and on how much is being giving away.

How do you know how much action they expect? Ask. Ask your host what it takes to be invited to special events. If it's $10,000 per day in action, you have to decide whether it's worth it to you. This amount would be out of the question for a nickel or quarter player. However, it would require only three or four hours of play a day for a dollar player or about 45 minutes a day for a $5 player. The event may or may not come with a room and meals. But it usually has bookend parties—a reception beforehand and a full-blown awards banquet afterward.

If you determine that you can qualify, another question you should consider is how much it will cost to play during the event. Let's say it's a big tournament that requires about $100,000 of play and the equity is $1,000. If you're a slot player, a house edge of 3% might be typical. So you can expect to lose, on average, 3% of $100,000, which is $3,000. Losing $3,000 to play in an event where the expected return is $1,000 isn't smart gambling in my book. But other people have different opinions. Many players like the excitement of a Vegas weekend and a slot tournament gives them some chance to recoup their normal losses.

For expert video poker players, the question turns to what games the casino offers and what the slot club is worth. Let's say the casino offers 9/6 Jacks or Better on $5 machines and a slot club returning .33%. How would this work out?

The combination works out to a 99.87% return. So for $100,000 worth of play, you expect to get back $99,870. This means a $130 loss on the game, counterbalanced by $1,000 in equity. Is this a good deal? Maybe. It depends on how much you like the casino. It also depends on what other opportunities might be available during the same period of time.

And it's important to remember that when I talk about it costing $130 while having an expected return from the tournament of $1,000, I'm talking about averages (actually, this kind of average is known as the "mean"). Understand that some weekends you'll lose $5,000 going for this average expectation of $870. If you can survive the swings, you'll do just fine: With an average of $870 this week added to an average of, perhaps, $320 the next week, added to an average of $330 the next week, pretty soon you're talking about several thousand dollars. Sometimes you place in the tournament and hit a royal flush during play. Those are the fun ones, but usually your results aren't as much fun. It's a numbers game. Keep playing when you have the advantage and good things will happen.

Shirley enjoys slot tournaments more than I do. I find them boring—hitting the spin button for a half-hour straight requires the IQ of a turnip. I enjoy things more when I can use my mind. Shirley, though, dreams of winning and how she'll spend the prize money. She knows all the employees at the casinos where we participate in these tournaments and most of the regular players, so it's a social event for her.

Both of us, however, enjoy these events more if there's a party with a dance band at the end. Most players don't care about the band part, but for us it's a real benefit. In fact, occasionally, we accept breakeven invitations (that is, events where neither we nor the casino is the favorite), just because there's a dance.

It's often much easier to get invited to your second invitational than your first. In most cases, everyone currently invited who plays a sufficient amount gets invited again. But you need to get on the list in the first place. How do you do that?

Often, all it takes is asking. If you ask, hosts will try to find a way to say yes. They might tell you that you need a little more play first, but if you give them that play, you're usually in. I've found that being a polite squeaky wheel works well.

Triple Play—Being in the Right Place at the Right Time

When Triple Play hit the video poker scene in 1998, it was an immediate huge smash. As soon as the games appeared, players loved them and casinos couldn't get them onto their floors fast enough.

For those not familiar with Triple Play format, you bet 15 coins, which covers 5-coin wagers on three separate hands. One 5-card hand is dealt and you select the cards you want to hold just as you do on a single-line machine. The difference is, those same cards are also held in the two additional hands, which also appear on the screen. When you draw, each of the three hands receives cards drawn from separate decks. Each of the three hands stands alone and the machine pays them off according to the pay schedule of the game you're playing. That's it in a nutshell, and broken down this way it doesn't sound like such a big deal.

But it is. Triple Play is a *lot* more fun than single-line video poker and if you look at any major casino today, you'll see these machines and variations (Five Play, Ten Play, Fifty Play, Hundred Play, and Spin Poker are the most popular, with new variations coming out all of the time) making up a large percentage of all video poker machines in the casino.

When Triple Play first came out, casino-marketing types weren't quite sure how they differed from single-line machines (nor were the players, though the best players learned faster than the marketers). So the standard promotions provided a stellar opportunity for gamblers looking for an edge.

I remember Station Casinos had a promotion in which players got a drawing ticket whenever a machine paid off $25 or more. Now think about a player sitting at a dollar 10/7 Double Bonus Triple Play game. He's dealt a high pair and holds it. If he ends up with a quad or full house, the payout qualifies him for a ticket, just as intended by the casino. But if one of the lines improves to 3-of-a-kind, a not-so-rare event, the three lines combined pay $5 + $5 + $15 = $25. If the promotion is written that the "machine," rather than the "hand," has to pay $25 or more, the combination payout qualifies. So the Triple Play player receives significantly more drawing tickets than intended, in addition to being on one of the few games in the casino where he has the advantage. And, of course, more tickets translates into a higher percentage of prizes won in the drawing. This is definitely not what Station wanted to happen.

Another popular promotion paid double for the second royal flush hit within 24 hours of a first. On Triple Play machines, royals come a lot faster than they do on single-play, simply because you're playing three hands at once. This significantly changes the math on how likely a player is to get the second royal within the allotted time period. Eventually, the rules were modified to exclude these machines (or to count royals appearing on the bottom line only), but at the start, knowledgeable players did quite well on these promotions.

Most local casinos in Las Vegas installed dollar 10/7 Triple Play machines. These machines take three times as many coins to play as single-line dollar machines, but less than twice as much bankroll (see the explanation for this in "At the Orleans with the Dailys"). You can also get about twice the dollar action on a dollar Triple Play than on a dollar single-line. The reason it's not three times as much is that it takes more time for three hands to be dealt out. Also, there's the W-2G effect. Royals show up more frequently and being dealt quad 2s, 3s, 4s, or As (about a cumulative 1-in-13,500 chance) also leads to a W-2G on Double Bonus or Double Double Bonus games. When you're dealt three aces, it's possible to turn them into quad aces twice (at $800 each) for another W-2G, but that's even less common than being dealt one of these quads.

"Action" is a word that describes the amount of money put into play. "Action junkies," who get a huge thrill from gambling, want to get as much money into action as they possibly can. So do advantage players. If I have a half-percent advantage, it's worth $15 per hour on a dollar single-line machine and $30 per hour on a dollar Triple Play machine; I can get twice as many dollars through the latter. If you can afford the swings, it's natural to gravitate toward these machines, especially if it's combined with a valuable promotion.

And gravitate we did. When the Orleans or Gold Coast offered triple slot club points, you couldn't get near these machines. All seats were occupied, with players standing around waiting for one to open up. It took a year or so for the casinos to conclude that if so many players were competing to play the same game, they might not be making money on them.

Eventually, casinos began removing dollar 10/7 Double Bonus from their Triple Play machines. Station Casinos removed it a month or two after the Triple Play games were first installed. Casinos known for loose machines—such as the Orleans, Gold Coast, Arizona Charlie's, and the Reserve (now Fiesta Henderson)—took considerably longer to make the move. The last to go were those at the Santa Fe and the Fiesta; these casinos kept them until both were sold to Station Casinos. Now these same casinos offer 9/7 Double Bonus on dollar Triple Play machines and there's no problem finding a seat.

You still come across occasional quarter 10/7 Triple Plays around town and these might survive. The $30-per-hour promotions on dollar Triple Play become $8-per-hour promotions on quarter Triple Play—not as worrisome for the casinos. This hourly wage does attract some players, and some decent ones at that, but it also draws a lot of mediocre players. The video poker promotions have been juicy enough over the past 10 years to allow many players with even modest abilities to move up in denomination. But not all. Some first-rate players still, for a variety of reasons, choose to play quarters. On average, though, the players who fired up the dollar 10/7 Double Bonus Triple Plays a few years ago were considerably stronger than those who feed quarter Triple Plays today.

The second-best game found on the first-generation Triple Play machines was NSU ("Not So Ugly") Deuces, returning 99.73%. With the right slot club and promotion, this too can be a good game. Third-generation Triple Play machines had games such as Super Aces Bonus that had high returns and the good players figured them out before the casinos did. Most of the good schedules for these games no longer exist.

Today, in Las Vegas Strip casinos, the best game to play for high stakes is 9/6 Jacks or Better. The typical slot club on the Strip returns about .33% in cashback, which still renders the game a loser for the player. But with the right promotions and comps, you can scratch out a little edge. In fact, during Shirley's and my million-dollar six months, this was our game of choice. We played $5 and $10 Triple Play and Five Play at the MGM and Venetian, and we were the fortunate beneficiaries of some dealt royals (which you'll read about in Part Four).

Being dealt a royal is a 1-in-650,000 initial-hands event, whether you're on a single-line, a Hundred Play, or anything in between. This is the number for a 52-card deck. If you're playing a 53-card deck, i.e. Joker Wild, the number is slightly higher than 1-in-700,000 hands. Lifetime I've connected on four dealt royals on Triple Play or Five Play machines and Shirley has connected on one. That's probably a little better than average, but not much, considering we've played, between us, more than 2,500 hours on these machines.

At the Orleans with the Dailys

The Orleans is part of the Coast Casinos group, which includes the Barbary Coast, Gold Coast, and Suncoast. As a whole, these casinos have always had looser-than-average video poker, at least for moderate stakes.

The Orleans opened up in 1996 with a lot of dollar full-pay Deuces and a slot club that paid .2% in cash plus .1% in food comps. When Triple Play machines were introduced, the Orleans installed quite a few in all denominations up through dollars. The loosest pay schedules available on these machines could be found at the Orleans, including 10/7 Double Bonus.

Every holiday, the Orleans (and the other Coast casinos) ran triple-point promotions. (They still do, although it's now double points and the slot club has changed somewhat.) Triple points at the time meant .6% cashback on top of the 100.17% machines. Since players could run up to $6,000 per hour through the dollar Triple Play machines, triple-point days meant earning almost $50 per hour. Plus food comps. Plus coupons in the mail. No wonder these casinos were popular.

Often, another promotion ran concurrently—a drawing for a condo, double points all month, or something else. But almost always something. The Orleans was a very good place to play.

In 1998, the Orleans installed two $5 Triple Play machines with the 10/7 game. You couldn't get near them on triple-point days. Groups of pros began playing up to six hours before the start of triple points, then swapped off among themselves for the next 30 hours. No player outside the groups had a chance to get in. But when the Orleans added more machines, for a total of five, seats were obtainable. The groups weren't large enough to keep all five machines occupied all the time. (I say "groups" rather than "teams" because for the most part, these groups were put together for the purpose of playing the machine on triple-point days. Everyone used his own money and when the play was over, players went their separate ways. A team usually continues to exist after a given promotion ends and frequently pools resources.)

One time the Orleans awarded double points all month, plus a throwaway type of promotion: All dealt royals were paid double. This longshot added .12% to the game, though few would benefit due to its infrequency of occurrence. A dealt royal is about four times as likely as a sequential royal, but not something you reasonably expect to collect on. The month-long double-point deal, however, was a major incentive.

Liam and Katherine Daily are among our favorite friends from the video poker world. Liam and I were working on strategy cards at the time (since published by Huntington Press) and we corresponded regularly. They lived outside of Nevada and I suggested that they visit us so our two families could gang up on a couple of the $5 Triple Play machines at the Orleans. They were happy to oblige.

We started off with Katherine and Shirley playing, while Liam and I coached. When either woman hit a total of three full houses or one 4-of-a-kind or higher, it was time to switch. The Orleans staff was cooperative. They let Liam and me each keep a session log to record W-2Gs, and since we were open about what we were doing and that the two families were involved, the high-limit staff kept the W-2G logs more or less balanced. If Liam's had more on it, I would get the next W-2G. If mine had more, Liam would get the next one.

Session Logs

A "session log" is commonly used in high-limit rooms, where gamblers play machines that typically generate a lot of W-2Gs. Use of the log alleviates the need to sign a complete W-2G on every taxable jackpot.

Every casino works it a little differently, but the way the Orleans ran theirs was fairly typical. At the start of a playing session, you signed a blank W-2G form and they filled it out with your name and other necessary information. After each taxable jackpot, the amount was entered on the log and you initialed it, then signed again after getting paid.

At the end of your play (or at midnight—when all the logs were closed out and new ones started), they'd add up all of your jackpots and give you one W-2G with that total. It's much more convenient for both the player and the casino than filling out what could be dozens of forms.

We split the winnings and losses and figured the W-2Gs were close enough not to sweat it. Actually, splitting the W-2Gs was tougher on the Dailys than it was on Shirley and me, because we live in Nevada where there are no state income taxes. And we generated a lot of W-2Gs on $5 Triple Play (all quads pay $1,250 or more, necessitating the IRS paperwork, and a quad or higher shows up every 130 initial hands or so on these machines).

Each of us had our own slot club card, which we inserted whenever it was our turn to play. If the dealt royal came, we knew that the casino would check the cameras to make sure that the person whose card was in the machine was actually the one sitting there when it hit. We didn't want to give the casino any excuse not to pay us. Although it was a slim chance, it could be a $60,000 mistake if we didn't do it right.

The total bet on these machines was $75 per hand, which was the same as the machine I'd played at Bally's a year and a half earlier. But this play was a lot less volatile; we needed only two thirds as much bankroll to play it. The reason for the lower volatility was that we were playing three hands at once. When you bet $75 on a $5 Triple Play machine, payouts at the low end can be any multiple of $25—such as $0, $25, $50, $75, $100, $125, etc. Playing on the $25 three-coiner, the only possibilities for low-end payouts are $0, $75, $225, and $375. Also, a royal on a single-play machine is rare and worth $60,000, while royals on Triple Play machines are more frequent and worth only $20,000 each. The more-money-at-the-bottom-and-less-at-the-top apportionment of Triple Play means that there's less chance for things to go really badly. Though the two machines may return the same amount in the long run, the ride on the $25 machine is much bumpier, necessitating a greater bankroll to keep from tapping out along the way.

Looking back, this was one of the most enjoyable promotions I ever participated in, thanks, primarily, to the banter among four good friends. One time Katherine was dealt three sixes and, to wish herself good luck, began chanting, "Sixes are easy." Sure enough, she ended up with quad sixes—on two lines. Hitting two quads from this position is a rare event—actually, it only happens once out of 192 times that you start with trips. Even though we all knew her sixes-are-easy mantra had nothing to do with the fourth sixes coming, we all adopted the chant whenever 666 came up. It worked the expected number of times, but it was fun trying.

The first several days we played, we lost. Both families were down $15,000 or so. It occurred to us that if we did hit the dealt royal, one of us would need to put it on his session log and that would make everything lopsided. We decided we'd try to get the casino to put $60,000 on each log, but failing that, whoever hit it would keep $80,000 and deal with the taxes on the full amount, while the other family would get $40,000 free and clear. We further decided that each family would tip $300 if this happened, no matter who got the $80,000 and who got the $40,000.

Sure enough, one night Katherine was dealt the $60,000 royal in very lovely hearts, which, by virtue of the dealt-royal bonus, was immediately doubled to $120,000. Yes! Whooping and hollering is a lot more fun when you have friends to whoop and holler with.

We asked them about splitting the money down the middle with the W-2Gs, and after consulting among themselves, the staff determined that they couldn't do it. Okay, we'd planned for this. We then asked if we could get pictures of the four of us (one for each family) surrounding the machine with the dealt royal still visible. The casino said yes, but only if they could use it for promotional purposes.

I'd never heard of a casino insisting on this before and we thought it pretty narrow-minded in general, but I had a more practical reason to decline. I was teaching weekly video poker classes at the Fiesta at the time, and the two casinos were engaged in a battle for the claim to loosest video poker in Las Vegas. If Fiesta management saw my smiling picture on a billboard advertising the Orleans, my days of teaching there would likely be over. We decided that we could live without a picture.

This was one throwaway promotion that came back to haunt the casino. At least one other $60,000 royal was dealt that month, along with dozens of smaller ones. It was the kind of promotion that didn't attract any extra business, but the casino had to pay out an extra quarter-million dollars or so that month because of it. I don't think any casino has ever run that promotion again.

I was congratulated the next day on the Internet for connecting on the royal. "Thank you, but it wasn't me." Shirley and I have had five dealt royals on Triple Plays (including one on Five Play), but more people seem to have heard about this one than all of ours combined.

It wasn't perfect. Overall, we had poor results on this play, other than the one very big hand. We probably played 25,000 initial hands, which means 75,000 total hands, among the four of us. We should have had about 1.6 deals with one or more royals and we had one. One nice one, thank you very much, but it was still only one. In fact, among us, we were dealt only two quads. Dealt quads occur every 4,164 hands, so we should have had six or so. Plus the two we hit were both for the minimum ($3,750 rather than $6,000 or $12,000). Of course, when we talked about how bad our luck had run during the promotion, we had a hard time generating much sympathy.

The Care and Feeding of Slot Hosts—Part I

Slot hosts are wonderful inventions. A smart player can use them to get lots of goodies not otherwise available. Sometimes you get to put on your acting hat and pretend to be someone else entirely. Oooooh, what fun!

Every slot host must abide by casino guidelines. But the guidelines imposed on the slot host are quite a bit more flexible than those that must be followed by the employees in the slot club booth.

It's important to be aware of certain preferences of the casino. Casinos prefer losers over winners. They prefer slot players to video poker players (the profit margin is higher). They prefer big players ($5 and up) over small players (25¢ and down). Does this mean that you have to be a big loser at $5 slots to get anything? Of course not. But it does mean that if you appear to fit (at least part of) the favored profile, you'll do better than if you don't. For example, I never plays slots. I play a lot of video poker, but only when I have an advantage over the house. I usually play at the $5 and higher level and hosts fall all over themselves to offer me comps.

Most of my strategies for hostmanship were developed when I was a $1 player. Playing only games at which I have an edge is not the way to generate a lot of comps, but I've been known to tell slot hosts that "I was playing five-dollar Double Diamonds over at the Mirage. I hit two doublers along with a red seven— they call it 'double-oh seven.' Thirty-two hundred smackers. Wow!"

In truth, I've never played such a game in my life. But I've fed the host just enough misinformation to pay dividends. First, the casino now thinks I sometimes play $5 slots. They love that. Whether or not I won this time is irrelevant. They figure that if I keep playing, I'll lose. They also know I sometimes play at other casinos. They want to keep a sucker like me for themselves and they figure they can do that by treating me better than the other casinos do. I'm now getting comps based on sometimes being a $5 slot player—and trust me, the comps for those players are much higher than they are for $1 video poker players.

Pretending to be someone you're not is part of the fun. These days, Shirley and I are well known, so we play it rather straight. But earlier in my career, it was fun to try different personas. I can't pass myself off as Michael Jordan, Napoleon, or Demi Moore, but I can pass myself as someone with a lot of traits the casino values (because it helps its bottom line). Such characteristics are different than what is valued in normal society. If they think I'm a conservative family man who comes to town one weekend a year with a gambling budget of $250, you can be sure they'll make me pay retail for everything I get. But if they think that gambling has cost me two wives along the way and I've been known to go on binges, you can bet the red carpet will be out.

Now imagine that I tell a host, "We won yesterday and my wife wants to go home because we never end up winners. But I want to stay because you guys are treating us so well." What do you think will happen? My bet is that we'll continue to be treated very well indeed.

The Care and Feeding of Slot Hosts—Part II

Getting extra out of a slot host requires a bit of seduction. It's the type of seduction common in sexual situations, only you keep your clothes on (I do, anyway!). Flattery, small gifts, gentle talk, and other niceties all have their place. For this reason, people usually do better with slot hosts of the opposite sex. I can flirt with a female slot host and get results, but the bonding I do with a male host doesn't buy me as much.

These gifts you bring to the slot host can be tangible or intangible. I keep a file. I write down things that the hosts tell me. For example, I know that Kathy at Casino A has two kids, lives and dies by the Lakers, and is on a diet. Janice at Casino B has a sweet tooth. Sally at Casino C always wants to talk about her grandkids. Last time I was in Casino A, Kathy and I spent 10 minutes discussing Shaq's improved free throw. At Casino B, I brought a piece of strawberry cheesecake along (from a comped dinner, of course). And at Casino C, I never forget to ask how little Gina and Joey are doing. These hosts treat me as an honored friend. I make their day a little nicer, so they, in turn, help with mine.

Don't start asking for stuff in the first hour of your first trip. Coming on like a comp hustler won't buy you anything good. Remember, the art of seduction works best if you let them think they're seducing you.

It doesn't hurt to exaggerate your losses or misstate how you did last trip. Slot hosts won't always look up your action and sometimes sympathy will get you dinner in a better restaurant than what you're otherwise entitled to. Careful here. Whining gets real old real fast.

Interaction with slot hosts becomes more important as your level of play increases. For example, nickel players on traditional machines never need to be concerned with slot hosts: Their theoretical loss will never be high enough to generate much in comps. But the new nickel nine-liner slots that take 45 nickels are creating highly valued customers deserving of big-time comps. These players can easily lose well over $100 per hour.

Quarter players can usually get a meal or two off their play, with or without a host (using traditional slot club routes). And at the high end—playing $25 per coin or more—you can get whatever you want from any casino. It's the dollar and five-dollar players who have the most to gain with hostmanship.

If Casino A thinks you're also playing at Casino B and they value your business, they'll give you more. If you're setting up a competition, real or imaginary, make sure it's believable. No host at Monte Carlo will be very impressed if you tell him that you normally play at the Boardwalk. Despite being next door to each other, these casinos have few patrons in common. It also works the other way around. No host at the Riviera will believe that your choice is between them and Bellagio, two casinos in totally different markets. But Monte Carlo hosts realize that they're trying for the same customers that New York-New York gets, and the Riviera is working on the same customers who visit the Sahara. So make a claim that will help you, but be aware of what will fly and what won't.

If your slot host does a good job for you, ask if you can write to his boss to let him know that you're a satisfied customer. Then make sure to write that letter and the next time you're in, the sky's the limit when you want something.

Calling a female slot host a "slot hostess" is a good way to reduce your comps by 50%. Las Vegas is a sexist town. "Slot hostess" feeds on the stereotypes and many women are sensitive to the term.

What can you give a host for Christmas? That's a tough one. Good hosts have hundreds of customers, many of whom are also bringing gifts. Remember that the best gifts aren't bought in Las Vegas. If you live in an area of the country that's known for something, bring whatever it is and give it away. If you can make something nice with your hands, give that.

Rather than wait specifically for Christmas, Shirley and I like to do our gift-giving during the year. We get more comped show tickets than we can possibly use. Giving them away to hosts is a nice treat for them. We've even been known to offer free dance lessons to hosts—simply because we're good at it and enjoy it. I've given free hours of "one-on-one" video poker lessons to hosts as well.

It's up to you to decide what you can do that's unique. If you can't think of anything, a gift certificate at an upscale clothing store is always appreciated. Hosts usually spend a large percentage of their income on clothes and any help here is always appreciated.

Common Questions and Uncommon Answers

Q. *Why do straight flushes pay so little? They're almost as hard to get as a royal flush and they pay so much less.*

A. Tradition, I guess. The system of straight flushes paying 250 and royal flushes paying 4,000 has been accepted by the players. If a casino offers a game paying more for the straight flush, you can be sure it'll pay less for the full house, flush, or straight.

For example, 9/6 Jacks or Better normally has a straight flush paying 250 (for five coins bet). Changing the game to 8/5 Jacks or Better with a 5-coin straight flush paying 1,125 coins would yield very close to the same return. (Of course, this game would have a different strategy. For example, from 4♥5♥6♥6♠7♣, you would hold 456 in the 8/5/1,125 game and 66 in the 9/6/250 game.)

Neither pay schedule is inherently better or worse than the other. If you can learn one strategy, you can learn the other. If one strategy is too difficult for you, the other would be too. But since players and casinos are generally happy with the current pay schedule, this falls into the category of, "It ain't broke, so don't fix it."

Q. *How can I minimize income taxes on video poker jackpots?*

A. The way to reduce your taxes on jackpots to zero is to run out of the casino when you hit one. You won't collect the jackpot, but you won't owe any taxes either. Most people, though, would rather collect the jackpot, even though it comes with a tax liability.

If you itemize deductions on your tax return, you should pay taxes only on your winnings minus your losses. Accurate records are necessary for you to do this. If you don't itemize, and instead take the standard deduction on your tax return, you'll end up paying a much higher amount of tax on jackpots than you would otherwise have to. Some players have always filed a standard return, but because of W-2Gs, they now find it in their best interests to itemize.

Winning in Nevada incurs no state taxes. Winning in many other states does. And every state has its own rules. In some states winnings are offset by losses more than in other states. You'll have to consult your tax accountant.

If you play, you have to deal with taxes somehow. If this is too much for you, take up another hobby.

Q. *Why are nickel machines so much tighter than quarter machines?*

A. There are two reasons for this. The first is that it requires the same amount of casino resources to have a nickel game, a quarter game, or a dollar game. And each casino has its minimum acceptable gross profit per machine. Let's say that this requirement is $50 per day—either 200 quarters or 1,000 nickels. For a casino to have a 1,000-coin-per-day profit, it needs to have a tighter game than it does to make a 200-coin-per-day profit.

The second reason is more subtle. Nickel players are, generally speaking, less sophisticated gamblers than quarter players. And "less sophisticated" means they'll play any pay schedule that's put in front of them. So the casino puts tight machines out and the players play them.

Nickel players are frequently on limited budgets, which results in their trying to experience the thrill of gambling for as little cost as possible. Ironically, many of these players would lose less money by playing quarters, simply because the nickel machines are so much tighter.

Card-Pulling ...

Casinos use their player-tracking systems to evaluate how a player is doing. The player-tracking system is *not* the same as the slot club. The player-tracking system is computer hardware and software that delivers information to casino management. The slot club determines what the casino rebates to the players based on the information collected by the player-tracking system. A slot club may have a policy of rebating airfare only if a player has lost $5,000 or more during a particular trip. But to determine whether or not the player has lost that much, the casino uses the player-tracking system to collect the information.

For this reason, knowledgeable players have tried to find ways to confuse the systems. The most common method is "card-pulling." Here's how it works.

Assume you're playing Double Bonus for dollars and are dealt four aces. The usual player-tracking system records +$5 for the initial bet and -$800 when the aces are paid off, for a net of -$795 (these systems track the money from the casino's point of view).

How does the tracking system know which account to post the +$5 and -$795 to? It posts it to the account of the player whose slot club card is in the machine. It assumes that players use only their own cards and that players have their cards in the machines at all times.

But what if the player removes his or her card after the aces

Q. *I was dealt two royal flushes in the same weekend. What are the odds of that happening?*

A. The odds are 100% that it happened! It makes no sense to talk about odds of something happening after it already happened. A royal is dealt from a 52-card deck about once in 650,000 hands. And assuming you intend to play 10,000 hands next weekend, the odds are 1 in 65 that you'll be dealt one royal and more than 4,000 to one against being dealt two or more. But if 4,000 or so people play 10,000 hands, often one of them will get dealt two

---

... for Cover

are dealt and before the draw button is pushed? The casino still registers the $5 initial bet, but depending on the system, doesn't know which account to post the $800 against. The player still wins $795, but the casino's records show that he has lost $5. Do this a few times a day and your score will be drastically altered.

Card-pulling works on most of the older systems, but on only a few of the newer ones. To find out whether or not it works on the machines at a particular casino, you have to do a little research. First, pull your card a few times and keep track of both your real score and the score minus the hands where you pulled your card. You then go up to a host and say something like, "I usually keep my gambling money and my other money in different pockets, but I messed up and mixed them all together. So I don't know how much I lost this trip. Can you tell me?" The hosts usually have the ability to look up this information, and if your story is believable, they'll tell you. From the information you get, you'll know whether or not card-pulling works at this casino.

Slot players and others who play losing games don't need to worry about this. Likewise, players who play for dollars or less are usually exempt from this type of casino scrutiny. Very few dollar players can win more than $15,000 at any one casino in a single year, and few casinos are overly concerned about amounts like that. But for $5-and-higher players, this can make a big difference in your welcome and your comps.

royals. And you can be sure that whoever that lucky person is, he or she will go around wondering, "What are the odds?"

Q. *Which is the better choice—playing an 8/5 Jacks or Better $1 machine for $5 at a time or playing a 9/6 Jacks or Better $5 machine for $5 at a time?*

A. I don't know. Is it better to be run over by a truck or a bus? One-coin 9/6 Jacks returns 98.4%, slightly more than 1% better than 5-coin 8/5 Jacks, which returns 97.3%. Both are losers. Assuming 600 hands per hour, 1-coin $5 9/6 Jacks "invests" $3,000 per hour in action. Losing 1.6% (the resulting house edge) of that total costs you $48. Betting the same $3,000 on a dollar 8/5 Jacks or Better machine costs $81. You'd lose less playing 1-coin $1 8/5 Jacks (96.1% return, but only $600 per hour in action), which costs "only" about $23 per hour. A cheaper solution yet is to flush a $20 bill down the toilet every hour. On top of everything, these figures assume you are playing perfectly—which is a *totally unjustified* assumption. No one who has worked hard enough to play video poker perfectly would put up with a game where the house has any advantage at all.

Q. *How much should I tip when I hit a royal flush?*

A. Everyone has his or her own way of doing things, but the best theory I heard recently came from comedienne Rita Rudner. She said something like, "I don't know how much to tip. Nobody does! So when it's time to tip I just give them some money. If they look sad, I give them some more. If they look too happy, I take some of it back!" I don't recommend you actually try this. But the advice is worth a chuckle.

Part Three

Bob Dancer, Inc.

I Meet Jeffrey Compton

In 1995, I contributed every month to Stanford Wong's *Current Blackjack News* and I'd occasionally get something published in the *Las Vegas Advisor*. But in general, my livelihood came from quarter video poker and cashing coupons. One month I noticed that someone named Jeffrey Compton was also working for Wong, checking other Las Vegas casinos. That same month, the *LVA* announced that Compton had written a book on slot clubs, which was about to be published. I knew that to do well at video poker, I needed to know a lot about slot clubs. So I figured I should get to know Jeffrey Compton.

I called him up. He recognized my name and told me that I was on his list of people to get to know. We arranged to meet for dinner at the Golden Nugget.

At first, Jeffrey was less impressive than I expected. He knew quite a lot about some slot clubs, since he played for dollars and I was a quarter player at the time. Also, he researched *all* the slot clubs, while I paid attention only to those in casinos that had games returning over 100%. But I listened in horror as he explained how it was fine with him to play less-than-100% games, as long as he could eat in fine restaurants for free. And I shuddered as he expounded on his system for roulette. I knew there was no such thing as a winning bet at the roulette table (unless you have a coupon), so whatever system he was using had to be flawed. He'd won more than $20,000 at roulette and said, "I don't know

why the system works, but I use it whenever I play." I told him
that it had worked through sheer luck and encouraged him never
to bet on the game again.

For me, the only reason to gamble was to earn an income.
Jeffrey had sold a successful business in Cleveland and was, by
my standards at the time, quite well-to-do. He didn't have to
work. If he lost $10,000 or even $20,000 a year gambling, it was
an annoyance, but not a tragedy. Since my entire bankroll was
$20,000 at the time, we were light-years apart.

Jeffrey told me about growing up in Cleveland. I told him
about my life in Los Angeles. I started to tell him about some of
the slot clubs I knew inside out—the Sahara's, Sam's Town's,
and a few others. Jeffrey was amazed by my insights and suggested we become partners. I'd publish my video poker books
and he'd publish his slot club books and we'd both become rich
and famous.

If I told you I wasn't skeptical at first, my nose would grow.
No one had ever written about slot clubs before and I couldn't
imagine much of a market for this information. Also, my book was
almost ready (I thought) and his was months away. Besides, we'd
just met. Partnering up didn't sound too promising to me.

Then he told me that everyone who'd ever entered into a business relationship with him had been happy about it afterwards.
I looked at him, believed him, and realized that I couldn't say
anything of the kind about myself. I'd had a lot of people work
with me, get mad at me, and want nothing more to do with me.
I'd ended some romantic episodes badly, including marriages. I'd
been fired from more than one job. I figured that if a guy who had
a lot of money could keep his business and personal relationships
intact, it might not be such a bad idea to join forces with him. I
told him it was a possibility down the road. In the meantime, we
should get to know each other a little better.

Jeffrey's partnership suggestion wasn't quite as spur of the
moment as it appeared at the time. Several people (Anthony
Curtis and Jean Scott among them) had suggested to him that

his slot club book could benefit from my kind of expertise. He knew Jacks or Better, sort of. He hated Deuces Wild (it annoyed him that, when he worked so hard to get 4-of-a-kind, it paid so little). He couldn't recognize a good schedule for Bonus Poker, Double Bonus Poker, or Double Double Bonus Poker, let alone the hundreds of other games available. If evaluating video poker was going to be part of his book, he needed some help.

Jeffrey's strategy for his book was to personally join every slot club and play enough on his card to understand the basics of each system. That was fine—in theory. But to find out about a club requires play on both video poker and slots, for which the point countdowns are often different. It was appalling to me that he'd actually play slots to get this information, or 8/5 Jacks or Better for that matter, even when it was the best game the casino offered. It was then, and still is, against my *religion* to play any game in which I don't have the advantage. Jeffrey figured that he needed the information, whatever it took to get it, and that royalties from the book would more than make up for the small amount he lost playing negative-expectation games.

Sometimes this worked well for him. Over the years I've received a number of calls from Jeffrey that have gone something like, "I hit a twenty-thousand-dollar royal on a machine I'm embarrassed to tell you I was playing." On the other hand, I rarely hear about his losses, which are inevitable, as playing bad machines is a costly proposition.

Adam Fine of *Casino Player* once asked me how I could let Jeffrey play so many bad games. I told Adam that, for starters, Jeffrey and I aren't partners in gambling. So whatever he does in that respect is his own business. And more important, as long as he has money to loan when I need it, who am I to complain what game it came from?

Today, Jeffrey can play 9/6 Jacks or Better perfectly, for about an hour at a time until he gets bored. He understands the game, but doesn't have the killer instinct to succeed over time. He thinks writing articles and consulting with casinos is a much

---

Loaning Money Back and Forth

Most gamblers run short of cash periodically, including Jeffrey and I, so we've made short-term loans back and forth a few times. Neither of us has ever been close to being tapped, but one time I was in a situation where if I didn't win soon, I'd have to liquidate some mutual funds, which I didn't want to do. Jeffrey lent me some money, I hit a royal the next week, and the "crisis" passed.

In some gambling cultures, such as the backgammon world, money is lent freely. Video poker is quite different and money is held more closely (though deals and partnerships are often made, which, in many cases, are little more than veiled loans). Shirley and I have lent considerable amounts of money to several people, but usually this is extended family or friends from outside the gambling world. My philosophy on the importance of building a bankroll has caused me to "just say no" to most requests for loans and I expect to continue to do so.

These days, loans between Jeffrey and me are for a few weeks or less and we don't worry about interest or collateral. There are very few people I'd lend money to on a handshake, but Jeffrey is one of them.

---

better way to make money. And it is, for him. For me, the opposite is true.

One of the biggest benefits to having Jeffrey as a partner and friend is that, like Shirley, he's great with clients. They tell him what they want. And he tells me how to give it to them. It's an excellent working arrangement.

But there's a price for Jeffrey's friendship. I learned early on that he has an impish side. Since I play video poker all night and sleep during the day, if Jeffrey calls me at an ungodly time (like 11 a.m.), he'll often be amused that I'm groggy.

Jeffrey: "*Casino Player* has decided to fire you and let Dan Paymar write your column instead."

Me: "Okay. Now let me go back to sleep."

Jeffrey: "Shirley and I have decided that it's time to tell you that we're having an affair."

Me: "I always knew you were a friend I could count on. Anything else?"

Jeffrey: "The Golden Nugget has installed full-pay Double Bonus and will be paying triple points all month."

Me: "Okay, Jeffrey. I'm awake now. Why did you really call me?"

Over the past six years, Jeffrey and I have both changed our opinions on gambling somewhat. He now understands more about video poker than all but the top professionals, although he still doesn't want to be a player. And I can see that there are a lot of intelligent reasons to gamble other than to make money.

Jeffrey was 39 years old when he sold a fairly large business back in Cleveland, "retired," and moved to Las Vegas. He told me that running a business is so much work that he was glad to be rid of it. Then we founded Compton Dancer Consulting (more about this later) and he just kept taking on more and more projects until now he's running a good-sized business again. Jeffrey works far more than I do. I'm in the enviable position of being *required* to gamble 20 hours a week as part of my job. I'm responsible for my wins and losses from gambling and Jeffrey and I split the income from the business. What a juicy racket!

The reason we set it up this way is that a lot of hands-on experience is necessary to be able to write well about gambling. The reason I can write knowledgeably about what happens to players in high-limit slot salons, for example, is that I've been there and done that. No other high-limit video poker player is writing today about his experiences. So I have to play a lot. I like this arrangement.

Writing My Reports

When I began playing video poker, the available literature was sparse. Stanford Wong's *Professional Video Poker* was the first

A Revealing Look at Jeffrey Compton

In 1999, Jeffrey e-mailed this letter concerning his birthday to 500 of his "closest friends." Knowing full well that at least 497 of those people had no intention of giving him a present, Jeffrey wrote:

1999 Policies and Procedures
for Jeffrey Compton's Birthday

My birthday is Tuesday, January 19. All gifts and cards should be delivered by that time. Please be aware that Monday, January 18, is a holiday celebrating something or other and thus there is no mail.

1) All gifts will be judged for taste, value, and appropriateness, with a maximum score of 100 points awarded. Late gifts will always be accepted, but judged down accordingly. Gifts receiving an overall score of 70 will be acknowledged by note. Gifts falling below that score may be acknowledged the next time I see you.

2) Birthday-greeting phone calls made before 8 a.m. (PST) should be left on the voice mail.

3) Cards referring to my age (or my weight) will be deemed inappropriate.

4) A gift of cash, especially a large one, will not be deemed inappropriate. Please use a personal check, so I can write "thank you" on the endorsement and save time.

Thank you,
Jeffrey Compton

Most of us got a chuckle out of it, but someone posted it on some bulletin boards with the suggestion that people send Jeffrey an e-mail telling him what they thought about his letter. He received in excess of 1,000 replies—some cute, some profane. Although I wasn't responsible for any of those e-mails being sent to Jeffrey, I thought it was a good example of the punishment fitting the crime.

book I bought. As one of Wong's monthly blackjack scouts, I knew and respected him, and the book is fine if you want to stick to 8/5 or 6/5 Jacks or Better progressives. I learned the strategies, but found that there were many more lucrative games to be found. And as often happens, Wong's book was so successful that many players began practicing what he preached, so those particular opportunities became fewer and farther between.

Lenny Frome wrote a couple of books containing approximate strategies for a variety of video poker games. They provided an adequate starting place, but I wanted to make a living playing this game and his books were nowhere near accurate enough for that.

Dan Paymar self-published his *Video Poker Precision Play*, with a new edition appearing on a frequent basis. By the time I came along, he was on his eighth edition. Though this book contained a lot of useful information, it had many errors. For six months or so, I worked with Paymar to improve his book and help with his newsletter, and then we went our separate ways. Today, Dan Paymar's *Video Poker Optimum Play*, which is actually the 11th edition of his earlier book slightly expanded, is currently the best book on how to play video poker on the market. I hope to write my own book on "how to play" soon. But until I do or someone else comes out with a better one, Paymar's book, though flawed in places, should be studied by anyone who wants to learn the ins and outs of playing video poker.

When I mention Paymar's "flaws," I'm speaking from a professional perspective. In Jacks or Better, for instance, on hands such as A♥K♥T♥5♥J♠, holding AKT5 is worth 3.7¢ more than holding AKT when playing dollars. Paymar doesn't include this play, arguing that learning such fine points is a waste of time and energy for most players. He might be right—for most players. But I was interested in being a player who could extract every last tenth of a cent out of a hand, and his strategy simply didn't do that.

Since there was no acceptable strategy I could buy, I had to create my own. When I was starting, the best computer programs were *Stanford Wong Video Poker* and Wong's *VP Exact*. Not long after I learned about Panamint's *Video Poker Tutor*, which was a better product than both of Wong's put together. This was a few years before I became associated with *WinPoker*—a much better product yet. As the technology continues to improve, so do these software products. Today, the top product on the market is *Video Poker for Winners!*.

I created strategies for the games I played: Deuces Wild and Jacks or Better to start with, and later Double Bonus and Joker Poker. I started with an amalgam of Frome's and Paymar's strategies and played hands on my computer until I came across one that the computer told me to play differently. I recorded the hand, and when I got enough of them, I combined them to create a better strategy. Then I played thousands more hands until I came across one my own strategy didn't play correctly, then perfected it again. The strategies that I eventually published in my reports came about after hundreds of hours of playing on the computer and waiting for anomalies to show up. In today's computer-world, that isn't necessary. Very strong strategies can be obtained almost instantly from various programs that have strategy-creation components. While these programs produce strategies that are nearly identical, I strongly recommend *Video Poker for Winners!*, which offers what I consider to be a superior user-friendly interface (along with other valuable features, and a real-world interface featuring the all the latest games, that are unique to this software).

My strategies were not devised in a vacuum, of course. Someone told me about a hand in Deuces Wild, 2A♥J♥T♠7♦, where it's correct to hold 2AJ. This is an exception to the normal rule that "straight interference" dictates that you hold only the deuce (you'd hold the 2AJ if there were no Ks, Qs, or Ts in the other two cards). I might not have found that hand by myself, as it comes around only about every 26,000 hands or so and is easy to miss. Another friend showed me that my original rule for differentiating between playing a suited QJ or QT versus a 4-card inside straight in Deuces was not quite accurate. Someone else turned me on to the difference between A♥K♣Q♦T♦8♦ and A♥J♣Q♦T♦8♦ in Jacks or Better. Finally, the strategies were nearer to being perfect than any that had been previously published.

The toughest part of producing the reports was the discussion of "penalty cards." A penalty card is a card that is thrown away that affects the value of the remaining cards. A simple example is found in full pay Deuces Wild, where from Q♥J♥T♥8♥4♠, the correct play is QJT, but from Q♥J♥T♥8♥K♠, the correct play is QJT8. The K is a straight penalty: It makes the AKQJT and the KQJT9 straight more difficult, because there are now only three Ks in the deck rather than the original four. Up until that point, penalty cards had been largely avoided by authors, so I had to figure it out myself and invent some new terminology. Fortunately, I got much of it right, though a few years later when Liam W. Daily and I were creating strategy cards together, Daily discovered (and taught me) a whole lot more about penalty cards.

I also wrote a number of articles about dealing with hosts, getting comps, defining bankroll parameters, and a variety of other subjects, but I didn't have access to a magazine that might publish them. So I combined it all—strategies, penalty cards, and articles—into a manuscript called *Video Poker for Winners!* and submitted it to Anthony Curtis, the publisher at Huntington Press.

Curtis desperately wanted to publish a good video poker book. He read my draft and thought, initially, that we could both make money with it. He agreed to publish it. Anthony began the editing with the Deuces Wild chapter, but he kept getting bogged down. Finally, he gave up.

In fairness, Anthony's specialty is publishing accurate gambling information for the masses. My proposed book was specialized information for people who wanted to be professional players. He couldn't water down the information enough to give the book a mass appeal without destroying its essence. Ultimately, he came to the conclusion that the small market for the book didn't justify the big effort. So sorry.

Still, I was devastated. I'd counted on having the best book on the market and now I had no publisher. I could shop it around to other publishers, but I believed then (and still do now) that having a successful gambler, as Anthony had been, as the publisher for a how-to gambling book would be a big plus. Anthony understood the importance of things that few other publishers could.

I moped around for a few weeks. Then Jeffrey Compton suggested that together he and I break the book into three reports and self-publish them. Had he not spoken up at that time, I would likely have never published anything, possibly giving up writing altogether. Jeffrey stepping forward when things looked bleak was the single most important factor in my deciding to become business partners with him.

To this day, *Bob Dancer's Reports* on Jacks or Better, Double Bonus, and Deuces Wild remain the source of the most concentrated information about these games. You can get appropriate strategies from several sources, but if you want the "how come," these reports are your best bet. (Actually, an improved version of these reports is now available, but first I must tell you more about Liam W. Daily. Which I will, very shortly.)

Ironically, Anthony Curtis' Huntington Press has sold more of the reports, and later, my software programs, than every other sales outlet put together. HP later published the strategy cards produced by Liam W. Daily and myself (and they've published this book), so it all worked out in the end.

Consulting for the Casinos

One aspect of the services Jeffrey Compton and I offer at Compton Dancer Consulting is, naturally enough, consulting with casinos. Many gamblers wonder how I can give useful advice to players, while at the same time advising the casinos. They feel I should pick one side or the other.

Let me explain how I feel about it.

Casinos and players must both survive for either to survive. If no one ever won at the casinos, the players would stop coming. And if the players won all the time, the casinos would go out of business. Players want to learn how to play better, so I tell them what I know. Casinos want to offer promotions in order to increase business without getting killed by professionals, so I share my knowledge with them, too.

Many players take an "us versus them" attitude with casinos. The players are the "good guys" and the casinos are the "bad guys." I don't see it that way. If casinos don't make money from the weaker players, there won't be any money to pay the stronger players. I see no inconsistency between teaching casinos how to make money off the former, while teaching players how to join the ranks of the latter. The better players still win and so do the casinos. It's a stable relationship.

Jeffrey's specialty is to assist casinos in developing effective slot clubs that attract profitable business to the casino by giving a good deal to the players. The better players can take advantage of the slot clubs and prosper. Less proficient players lose enough to support both the better players and the casinos' business.

Casinos are not churches. They are in business to make money. And for casinos to make money, players must lose money (or spend money for other things in a casino). Winning players have to understand this. Sometimes players get angry when a casino removes machines or reduces benefits. Go ahead and get angry if that makes you feel better. But it's a fact of life and it will continue to happen. But for every opportunity taken away, another one pops up.

There are things Jeffrey and I do not do. Casinos have asked us to identify proficient players and tell them which players are team members. Although we get accused of it regularly, we've never done this and never will. It's true that I know most of the top pros in Las Vegas and indeed I'm one of them; still, casinos will have to identify these players in other ways. It frequently happens that a casino makes a change and Jeffrey and I are accused of master-minding it. The truth is, it usually has nothing to do with us.

Liam W. Daily—Master Strategist

As mentioned earlier, Liam W. Daily and I met at a video poker machine and became friends. I soon realized that he's likely the most intelligent man I've ever met. I showed him my reports and he read them. "These are good," he told me, "but your strategies could be better."

"Really?" I was sure that they were 100% accurate. "How can they get better than that?"

"They're accurate enough," he agreed, "but there are many ways to present the same information in a simpler fashion that retains every bit of the accuracy. May I show you?"

"Well, hell yes!"

This was great. Liam worked out six or eight different ways to present each strategy. Every week he e-mailed me another funda-mental change—and each was better than the one he'd sent me the week before. He was always willing to go back and redo something that was already excellent, because in his mind, A-plus-plus-level excellence was better than mere A-plus level. Even if no one was better than B-level, Liam was always searching for ways to make it A-plus-plus-plus. He was incredible. In addition to being brighter than anyone else, he worked harder than anyone else, too.

Liam suggested that together we create a set of video poker strategy cards. I agreed immediately, although neither one of us had any idea what we were getting into. We went with Hunting-ton Press for the cards. They took a long time to finalize—both Anthony Curtis and Liam are even bigger perfectionists than I am (I've come to believe that perfectionism is less a quality and more a disease)—but all in all, the time spent was worth it. When we were done, we had a product that was head and shoulders above anything else on the market. My name comes before Liam's on the cards, but in fairness, he was responsible for 80% or more of the work. I've tried several times to change our 50-50 split on the sale of the cards, but Liam has always declined.

In mid-2002 (after the text of this book was initially written, but before it had completely wended its way through the editorial process), Liam and I decided to create some reports together—using the innovations first published on our strategy cards. The information from the original *Bob Dancer's Reports* is retained, but it's presented in a much more user-friendly fashion. In addition, we've learned a lot more about the games in the past six years, so there's well over twice as much information in the *Dancer-Daily Winner's Guides* than was included in the originals. If you have any realistic desire to be able to beat the casinos at video poker, you must first master the games, which is what the *Winner's Guides* are designed to help you do.

For almost two years, Liam was a behind-the-scenes contributor to my writing. His contributions were invaluable; many theoretical articles I published in 1999 and 2000 were born of ideas generated by him. Thanks to Liam, I know a lot more about bankroll requirements and penalty cards and I've shared this information in a large body of articles. The entire video poker community has benefited from Liam W. Daily's insights.

Sadly, Liam and I had a falling out over a big project he wanted addressed immediately, while I was completely occupied by a promotion at the MGM Grand. Not only did our friendship suffer, but he also gave up theorizing about video poker—for awhile. Fortunately, we found a way to patch up our relationship and we're involved in some projects together again. I hope our collaboration on the *Winner's Guides* is an indication that Liam's contributions to video poker theory will continue.

Dean Zamzow—An Important Ally

Using a computer to practice and learn on is critical for video poker success. Although it's possible to become a decent player without such help, it's extremely difficult. Tutoring software can do several things, but the most important things they do include:

1) Calculating how much a game with a particular pay schedule is worth. In other words, if you play a specified game perfectly, the software can tell you if it will pay back 85%, 98%, 102%, or whatever.

2) Telling you the optimal way to play any particular five cards.

3) Generating a strategy for playing any pay schedule.

4) Allowing you to practice until the cows come home, all the while correcting you every time you make a mistake.

A computer program is useful for many additional tasks, but these above are the primary benefits for most players.

Around 1990, Stanford Wong created *VP Exact*, a program that did nothing other than perform function number one in the list. If you plugged in the values for 9/6 Jacks or Better, the program would take six hours or so to come up with the number 99.5439%. Though that was the extent of its capabilities, way back in the dark ages of video poker analysis, this was *very* useful information.

Wong put out another computer program that performed functions two and four above. It was called *Stanford Wong Video Poker* (the earliest version was called *Video Poker Analyzer*). It had a few severe limitations (for example, flushes and straights in Deuces Wild could be programmed only to return the same amount), but you could practice on it and it would tutor you. Wong's programs were the best available when he created them, but he didn't keep them updated and subsequent software rendered them obsolete.

Programmer Gary Catlin created *Video Poker Tutor* around 1993 or 1994. *VPT* combined functions one, two, and four above in a much slicker package than Wong's and took only 20 minutes to provide the same 99.5439% figure that Wong's program crunched in six hours. (Ultimately, the speed of both was dictated by the muscle and free space inside your computer. But no matter what computer resources you had, *VPT* was quite a bit faster.)

VPT was an excellent product for its time. I used it to prepare my reports, was content in recommending it, and briefly sold copies to students who came to my early video poker classes. But it would require significant upgrades to compete today. For example, it runs on DOS (Disk Operating System—used on most computers before Microsoft Windows). It also doesn't allow for "kickers." When this program was created, games such as Double Double Bonus—which pays more for four aces with a 2, 3, or 4 kicker than for four aces with any other card—had yet to be introduced. Presumably, this would have been an easy enhancement to add, but it never was.

Around 1996, Dean Zamzow, a gifted Windows programmer, created *WinPoker U* as a Windows-based computer trainer. Like *VPT*, *WPU* combined functions one, two, and four from the list. The first version of *WPU* had a lot of bells and whistles that *VPT* didn't, primarily because Dean was creating the program for his wife Sara, who was bedridden much of the time. Sara would say things like, "Wouldn't it be nice if you knew what the next card was after the draw was over, so you'd know that if you drew one more card you could have had the royal flush?" And Dean would add this capability to *WPU*.

Both Zamzow and Catlin were excellent programmers, but neither was successful at getting his program widely sold. An expert video poker player and game designer who calls himself TomSki saw and liked *WPU* and knew that if Zamzow could get some help with marketing, it might really take off. TomSki figured that I might be able to help with this, so he encouraged Dean and me to get together.

When I first saw *WPU*, I was impressed with the way it all hung together, including several additional features it incorporated (such as handling kickers). Still, for serious players, I held *VPT* in higher regard in several respects. I made a list of some 15 ways that *WPU* could be improved, and Dean, Sara, Shirley, and I had lunch at the Golden Nugget to discuss the matter.

Dean told me that most of the items on my wish list were relatively easy to add. And I told him that this would easily make

WPU the best video poker software on the market. From Dean's perspective, what I brought to the table was the best-regarded name among video poker writers, plus a lot of free ad space in the monthly magazine *Casino Player* and the weekly tabloid *Gaming Today*. At the time I was writing columns for each and rather than getting paid, I traded for ad space. Since all I had for sale was my reports, I knew I could use the ads more profitably if I had more products to sell.

So hooking up had benefits for all of us. Dean would presumably sell a lot more copies and I would earn more for my writing. I suggested the name "Bob Dancer Presents WinPoker" on a spur-of-the-moment whim and the Zamzows agreed. (We've all taken considerable heat for this choice of names; more on that later.)

One considerable advantage of *BDPW* over *WPU* had nothing to do with my wish list. TomSki had shared with Dean a way to speed up the calculation of returns. TomSki's technique was powerful, streamlining the process about twenty-fold. If it took 20 minutes to figure out how much a game was worth before the enhancement, it took only a minute to get the information after. It was a *huge* improvement.

So *BDPW* 5.0 came out in August 1998 and I began to promote it. Huntington Press took out big ads in *Casino Player* and *Strictly Slots* and sold thousands of copies. The Zamzows were now making considerably more money off the software than they were before, even though they were paying Compton Dancer a cut and selling the product at a discount to resellers.

Over time, Jeffrey and I learned we could count on the Zamzows to provide sufficient supplies of product and, more important, to correct any defects that were discovered. The Zamzows learned that they could count on us to keep promoting the product and to forward their proceeds in a timely manner.

Things weren't perfect, however. For reasons I've never fully understood, many players decided they had a problem with the "Bob Dancer Presents" part of the name. More than one detractor felt that since I hadn't done any of the programming for the product, my name shouldn't have been on it. Another wrote articles and posted messages on bulletin boards referring to the product as "Zamzow's WinPoker," or sometimes "Zamzow's BDP WinPoker." It got to the point where I told Dean that if he wanted to reconsider the name, we could talk. Dean, to his credit, stood by me and declined.

Dean and Sara told everyone, "Hey! The name works for all of us. We're happy with the way Dancer is holding up his side of the deal. And it's really none of your business what we call it anyway, so let it be." Eventually, Dean had to explain that *BDPW* accounted for a relatively small percentage of Jeffrey's and my income, but a large part of his. So the longer people kept up antics about the name of the product, the more they were actually hurting the Zamzows.

In October 1999, *BDPW* version 6.0 came to market. It added several games to the program and a variety of advanced features, including an error log. We offered a $15 discount to owners of *BDPW* 5.0 on the upgrade and this version sold well too.

Around this time, TomSki created a program called *Video Poker Strategy Master*, which could generate a decent-enough strategy for almost any pay schedule almost instantly. Finally, there was a program that could perform number three on the list of what a computer program should do. And it was the one thing that *BDPW* didn't do.

TomSki wasn't much for marketing, either. Jeffrey and I told him that if we could merge *BDPW* and *VPSM* into one product, we would be able to help promote it. For a variety of reasons, the planned merger between *BDPW* and *VPSM* never came about. While we intended to create a *BDPW 7.0*, that didn't happen. Instead, I threw my efforts behind the new *Video Poker for Winners!*, which is now the industry standard.

Looking back, it was a huge benefit for me to be associated with the Zamzows and *WinPoker*. It was a quality product that was annually chosen "Best Computer Software" in *Casino Player's* "Best of Gaming," as well as in other surveys.

Teaching Video Poker

If I listed the favorite parts of my life right now, teaching classes a few hours a week would be right up near the top. I enjoy seeing a bunch of strangers grapple with such things as why, in Jacks or Better, you hold an unsuited KQJ, but throw the A away from AQJ. When I give them the explanation and it makes sense to them, I get a charge out of seeing their eyes light up. People who've seen me in my normal mode in the casino, then watch me up in front of a class, frequently remark how I come alive with a microphone in my hand.

I started teaching video poker in late 1996 at the Fiesta in North Las Vegas, the self-proclaimed "Royal Flush Capital of the World." At the time, this casino had what were arguably the loosest video poker machines on the planet. And argue they did! The Santa Fe, the Reserve, and others all competed to be known as the casino that was truly the loosest. And each casino defined "looseness" in a way that would make it the winner. The players, for the most part, didn't care one way or the other. They were just glad for the competition, which assured loose machines all over town. It was a good time to be a video poker player.

Fiesta management believed that classes were better at *bringing* players into the casino than they were at actually *teaching* them how to play. They felt that even if the players picked up a few new ideas, they would still play, the casino would still have an edge, and everyone would be happy.

When I began, I taught Jacks or Better, Deuces Wild, and Double Bonus. Roughly 200 people attended each session during the first series of classes. But after awhile, attendance settled down to about 40 per class. After all, how often can you expect someone to learn the same thing?

When Shirley quit her job and moved to Las Vegas in October 1997 (we got married two months later), she started helping me teach the classes. She was wonderful at it. She has a sparkling personality, could remember people's names from week to week, and helped me better relate to and interact with the students.

Teaching Dad

I once tried to teach my father to play Deuces Wild. It was a disaster.

For example, I explained that when you're dealt a straight flush with three deuces, it's far better to keep the deuces by themselves and throw away the other two cards. In the standard game for quarters, a straight flush is worth 45 coins ($11.25), while three deuces are worth about 75 coins ($18.75). Keeping the straight flush would be an error costing $7.50 on a game that returns less than $6 per hour when played perfectly.

Dad couldn't do this. "A bird in the hand is worth two in the bush," he opined. "If it was good enough for Ben Franklin, it's good enough for me."

"Old Ben was never a successful video poker player," I responded.

"Nonetheless," Dad persisted, "you can't go broke if you always take a profit. And if God hadn't wanted me to keep the straight flush, He wouldn't have dealt me a straight flush to begin with."

As long as Dad spouted platitudes, I had no useful response. He wasn't really serious, of course; just having fun arguing. If Dad really wanted to get good at this game, I'd take whatever time was required to teach him. But I suspect pigs will fly before he—like so many other casual players—will choose to do what it takes to become an expert video poker player.

Initially, Shirley wasn't proficient at video poker. So she'd take the classes along with the students. At the end of a Double Bonus class, for example, when I asked the class to vote whether they should go for the 5s or the straight from 5♥5♠6♦7♣8♥, she would often raise her hand on the wrong choice. (In this game you should hold 5678, but in Jacks or Better, which Shirley knew fairly well, the 55 is better.)

Many students who took their cue from Shirley also voted wrongly. They figured that Shirley must know, so if she raised her hand, so did many of the others! On the drive to class every week, Shirley would promise herself that this time she wouldn't raise her hand at all. She would just run the projector and not participate. But when the time came, she'd get caught up in the class and forget her promise. When the class had to decide between the kings and the spades in Deuces Wild on K♥K♠Q♠T♠5♦, up came her hand for the kings. Wrong again. She'd laugh and curse

---

Waiting for the Progressive ...

For years the Fiesta had dollar 10/7 Double Bonus with five progressives—they were attached to the royal, straight flush, aces, quads paying $400, and quads paying $250. This was an excellent game and, had it been closer to my home, I would have played it a lot. But since it was 25 miles away, I played it sparingly on days I was teaching.

One day the straight flush was at $480 when it was hit. It immediately reset to $250, which had the effect of lowering the value of the game by about a half-percent. The other progressives were high enough, though, that it was still a good deal. Pedro, a low-level pro sitting immediately on my left, was dealt a straight flush before the meter had even risen to $251, so he sat there and thought about what he should do.

If he held the straight flush immediately and pressed the draw button, Pedro would win $251, which was the amount everyone got if the progressive was anywhere between $250 and $251. But if he waited a half-hour or so, the progressive would likely rise to $260 or more. So Pedro covered the hand, stacked cups on the chair to prevent anyone else from sitting down, moved over one seat, and continued playing.

I left about 15 minutes later to teach my class and he still hadn't cashed his straight flush. When I saw him afterward, he told me he'd played the other machine for about two hours and cashed out his straight flush for $275.

There was minimal risk to Pedro's tactic early on. If someone else hit a straight flush before he cashed out, the progressive would merely reset to $250 and he'd be in the same situation

herself simultaneously and it was so cute. It warmed my heart, and the students smiled in empathy. By now, she's assisted in each of the classes 50 or more times and knows the material well enough that she no longer makes these types of mistakes.

I have a series of jokes I use regularly in the classes, such as "What's the difference between praying in church and praying in a casino?" Answer: "When you pray in a casino you *really re-*

... to Catch Up

as if he'd cashed it immediately. But at $275, there was risk. By waiting now, he risked someone else hitting the hand and the progressive starting over at $250. It would take at least another few hours to climb that high again.

What's the best price at which to cash out? That's an interesting question and depends on a lot of factors—including how much time you have to spend in the casino.

Normally, these types of "clever" plays rip off the casino and have no direct effect on other players. This one was just the opposite. It had no effect at all on the Fiesta. The Fiesta already owed $250 for the straight flush and would continue adding .1% of all money bet into the straight flush progressive. (It was a .5% progressive at the time. This means that .5% of all the money played was directed to the progressives, with the half-percent split evenly among the five jackpots.) The other players, though, weren't receiving full value as they played. The extra $24 that Pedro collected came directly out of the pocket of the player who got the next straight flush. Since no one knew who would get that straight flush, each of the other players on the progressive, unbeknownst to them, was theoretically receiving a little less than the amount that the progressive numbers actually indicated.

Was Pedro acting immorally here? Not to my way of thinking. Progressives are a multi-player tug-of-war and players are always looking for a way to get the edge. This time Pedro was successful. Rather than condemn Pedro for his actions, I acknowledge that his actions taught me another useful strategy. *Muchas gracias*, Pedro.

ally mean it!" Corny though it is, it still gets a chuckle. Shirley, bless her heart, has heard that one more than 200 times and still manages to smile.

My classes improved immensely when the Dancer-Daily strategy cards were published. The cards have four different strategy levels on them, from beginner to advanced, so I began teaching Level 2 ("Recreational") in the beginner classes and Level 3 ("Basic") in the advanced classes. The terminology became consistent from week to week and players learned more effectively.

Through the years I've also taught at the now-demolished Continental (which was rebuilt and became Terrible's), the Reserve (now the Fiesta Henderson), Arizona Charlie's (both East and West), the Flamingo Laughlin, Caesars Atlantic City, the Regent Las Vegas (which has had more than six names—no telling what it will be called when you read this), the Palms, the Castaways, and occasionally at conventions of various sorts. We published my teaching schedule in publications such as the *Las Vegas Advisor*, *Casino Player*, *Strictly Slots*, and at several Web locations, and the classes have generally been well-attended. If I'm teaching now, my current class schedule will be found on www.bobdancer.com.

I taught for 11 weeks in early 2001 at Arizona Charlie's West. This casino has always had loose video poker, but the building itself is a dark smoky barn that appeals to a less affluent crowd. To ensure good attendance, the marketing director decided to offer a free buffet lunch to anyone who came to the class.

Those classes were absolutely packed. Obviously, the free lunch buffet was a bigger attraction than I was. People living close to the edge have to find ways to eat, and in a contest between listening to me talk about Deuces Wild or listening to the priest over at St. Vincent's preach a sermon, I was the winner!

The big benefit of the classes was that it inspired many people to study the games. The general public's level of video poker knowledge is unquestionably higher now than it was when I started. The combination of video poker books, reports, software, strategy cards, Web sites, newsletters, and my classes has raised the bar considerably in the past several years.

The fact that players know more about video poker these days is a good-news bad-news situation. Casinos can't offer a lot of extremely loose video poker to a knowledgeable player base, but many casinos continue to offer at least some games where the knowledgeable player has a slight advantage.

Video poker is difficult enough that there will always be players who are unwilling to study and, hence, will make a lot of mistakes. For example, 10/7 Double Bonus is very difficult to master. So even though it returns over 100% with perfect play, casinos make money on it, which means they can continue to offer it. This is wonderful news for the dedicated player. Perhaps the games aren't as loose as they were a few years ago, but video poker is still beatable. The dance goes on.

Part Four

My Million-Dollar Six Months

Note: "Michael" and "Richard" are names I use to represent a number of different MGM executives. Sometimes I intentionally switch the names. I'm not trying to blame or embarrass any specific executive with regard to the events described here.

The Dancers at the MGM Grand

From September 1, 2000, through March 15, 2001, the video poker gods smiled down on Shirley and me. We cleared $1 million in cash winnings (including cashback), mostly from the MGM Grand, but the Venetian and a few other casinos chipped in nicely, thank you very much. We also collected more than one automobile, two computers, a home entertainment center, and in excess of four million American Airlines frequent-flyer miles. We lived for four weeks-plus in the MGM Mansion, truly heaven on Earth, and another month at the MGM Penthouse—also a form of heaven and the nicest place we've ever stayed in our lives, with the exception of the Mansion.

The story that follows has two parts. The first is the happy part (for us), which describes how we rode a fantastic wave of favorable circumstances and good fortune to achieve a goal that was painstakingly pursued over the period of time portrayed in the earlier sections of this book. The second part is more matter-of-fact and not so happy. It's the story of the fallout that ensued as a result of our win. I've included it because it was every bit a part of the experience as the winning. Gambling for a living is difficult for many reasons that I've already told you about. But because of the nature of gambling, a winner must create a loser (or losers), and there's always a price to pay.

Cash-wise, we were stuck for the year 2000 going into September, even though I'd been dealt a $100,000 royal on a $25 machine in February and dealt a $60,000 royal on a $5 Triple Play machine in August. Both of these jackpots were hit at the MGM, but we were still behind there.

But something special was going on at the MGM. In addition to some decent games and a good cashback rate, several juicy promotions were running concurrently. What's more, premium players, those who played enough to earn 100,000 points monthly (i.e., $500,000 coin-in for slots or $800,000 coin-in for video poker), received an extra 40% on cashback. Add in comps and special events, and it made for an extremely strong game. And there was one more thing. For several months, the cashback on the $5 Triple Play machines (and a few others) was extra-generous. These video poker machines were awarding slot points at the slot-player rate (.625%) rather than the video poker-player rate (.39%). With the high-roller accelerator, these particular high-limit machines were paying an incredible .875% cashback. It was amazing. Adding everything together and multiplying by the high dollar amounts it was possible to run through the machines created the largest relatively long-lasting advantage I've ever heard about, let alone experienced.

Shirley's White-Knuckle Ride

We get a lot of casino mail. Shirley and I belong to 80 or so slot clubs, usually with separate accounts, and we average more than 150 pieces of casino mail per month. I at least look at all of it—but not always carefully. For example, if I know we have no plans to be in Mississippi, I don't spend time salivating over who's appearing at the Bluesville Showroom at the Horseshoe in Tunica.

At many casinos where we've played modestly, we'll get 2-for-1 buffet offers and such, which get trashed quickly. While these coupons are worthwhile to some people, we have comps for more food than we can physically consume, so even paying half-price is way too much. Conversely, we play heavily at a few other casinos and read their mailers closely. We'd arrange our playing calendar based on taking advantage of the best deals.

We might not care if we played at the Mirage on the second or third weekend of any particular month. But if we learned through a mailer that they were giving away $100,000 to 400 invited guests on the third weekend, that's when we'd play.

On Thanksgiving weekend 1999, I got a letter from the MGM Grand. I was surprised. At that time, I'd never once found a reason to play there. I wasn't even a member of its Director's Club. But apparently, MGM was trolling for new customers and I ended up with an invitation for double points between November 28 and December 23.

Oh my. In round numbers, Director's Club points paid video poker players .39% cashback, plus American Airlines miles worth around .12%. With the double points, this added up to .90% cashback, because with the Internet, airline miles can be bought and sold. They didn't say so in the letter, but points put on my card in the first week got an extra .2% or so worth of merchandise credit from the casino's Holiday Gift Shoppe promotion.

The best base game at MGM was $25 9/6 Jacks. Shirley and I had a large enough *financial* bankroll to play this game. What Shirley didn't have was enough *psychological* bankroll for these stakes. Over a weekend a few months before, we'd lost $35,000 on such a game somewhere else and Shirley didn't like it. She trusts me with these financial decisions (sort of) and she believes that my video poker expertise is sufficient to do well in the long run (mostly). But sometimes she finds that it's a white-knuckle ride. And you have to be in the right mood to appreciate a white-knuckle ride.

So, to take advantage of this promotion and to keep my

wife happy, I sought out some financial partners. I asked Jeffrey Compton and Liam W. Daily if they would like to invest. I figured if each man took 20% of the action, that would leave plenty for me and take the edge off Shirley's anxieties.

Jeffrey decided to pass. "If we had to share a big loss, the emotional upheaval could affect our friendship. And I think you're insane for willingly facing regular twenty-grand-per-day losses. Besides, the last time we were partners it cost me three thousand! But good luck all the same."

Liam passed too. But he did so not for emotional, but for mathematical, reasons. "You realize, of course, that assuming you play one cycle of forty-thousand hands over the next month and if you calculate the cashback at point-nine percent, you have a twenty-five-percent chance of being down sixty-one thousand or more and one chance in nine of being down a hundred thousand *or more*, with a very bumpy ride along the way. Are you sure your bankroll and Shirley's temperament can handle this?"

So it was Shirley and me.

I put on my salesman's cap. Arguing finances wasn't going to work, so I argued amenities. "I'll bet they'll give us Barbra Streisand tickets. And the Eagles will be in town. And Tina Turner is opening for Elton John. If we play big, they'll give us tickets to all of them. And the restaurants. Of the top twenty restaurants in town, three or four of them are at the MGM. And we can try them all! What do you say?"

"Can you guarantee me we'll hit a royal and come out all right?" she wanted to know.

"No to the first part, but yes to the second. We may or may not hit a royal. We could end up losing more than a royal. But I *do* guarantee you that our future is fine one way or the other."

"Okay, but I'm *not* happy about this."

"Thank you, Shirley. Let's go out and hit a royal flush!"

We began our play on the last two days of November. One day we lost $13,375 and the other we were down another $7,500. Shirley complained, "We had such a good result in November!

Losing twenty grand just ruins our score. You've had your fun. Let's quit now."

"No, no. It was a good opportunity two days ago and it still is. We'll hit them hard in December."

By December 4, when the Holiday Gift Shoppe bonus ended, we were down another $16,000, but we had $11,000 in cashback coming. We got some gifts with a retail value of $3,000 or so, but we were in for about $25,000. And the downhill streak continued. After the Holiday Gift Shoppe was over, we lost another $12,000 two days in a row. Then things turned around a bit—we won $4,000, $8,000, and $9,000 over the next three days.

"We're starting to play better!" I kidded.

"Maybe our losing sessions are now a thing of the past!" Shirley hoped.

Actually, we both knew better. We'd played every hand computer perfect. Some days the 4-of-a-kinds and straight flushes came and some days they didn't. We didn't know what the future held, but we did know that it would include huge ups and downs. We lost another $26,000 and took a break for a few days because of other commitments. Everything considered, we were down almost $40,000 at this point.

On December 16, I returned to the MGM and hit a $100,000 royal flush at about 3 in the morning. A friend was passing by and asked how many $100,000 jackpots I'd hit lifetime. "You mean including this one?"

"Yes."

"You mean also including larger ones?"

"Yes."

"Well, including this one and all larger ones I've had exactly one."

"Well, if you don't include this one how many have you had?"

"I'm sorry. There's a limit to the amount of personal information I'm willing to divulge at any one time."

He got the message.

I paid off $20,000 in markers and got a check for $80,000. Then I took some pictures and played some more. I cashed out for $21,000 at the Director's Club, got another check, and went home. I strategically placed the two checks and the pictures where Shirley would discover them when she came home in a few hours from a short trip to California, then went to bed. Suffice it to say that Shirley comes with sound effects and the minute she got home, everyone in our zip code knew that *something* had happened.

"Okay. Let's quit now," Shirley said. "We're way ahead of the game. You're probably not going to hit another royal in the next week. *Please* don't give it all back."

"No, Shirley. It was a good promotion yesterday and it still is. Today's score doesn't matter. Even when it's a big one. And ask yourself, wouldn't you like to tell people that we hit *two* hundred granders in the same week."

"Of course I would."

"Well, you'll never have that chance if we stop playing after we hit the first one."

"Damn you and your logic!"

There's Luxury, and There's *Luxury*

The MGM has its high-roller act down cold and by this time, we'd become part of it. We got all the show tickets we could use. We also knew all the hosts and other slot personnel on all shifts. Since my picture is in the *Las Vegas Review-Journal* every Friday accompanying the "Player's Edge" column that Jeffrey Compton and I co-write, everyone knew I was "Bob Dancer," even though the name on my driver's license says something different. Several of the workers in the high-limit slot area were even planning to come to my next class at the Fiesta. And casino executives were well aware of my expertise, yet didn't shy away from my action or give me the slightest indication that they resented my "taking advantage" of the double-point offer. Very classy.

Two days following the royal, our main host, Mary, told us about the Mansion. "You really should stay there for a few days," she said. "Every suite is actually a villa and many have their own swimming pools. There are only twenty-nine villas, but more than a hundred employees make sure that your every whim is satisfied."

This sounded good. "We're going to be playing here five more days. We'll be playing six hours or so a day on the twenty-five-dollar machines. Can we stay in the Mansion for all five days?"

Mary checked with her boss, then said yes. "We'll even pick up two one-hour massages for Shirley, if you like." (This was a welcome touch. Playing for big stakes is *very* stressful for Shirley.) "All you pay for is phone calls, tips, and dirty movies!" This was the week before Christmas, the slowest time of the year for casinos. Whether our amount of play would qualify for the Mansion during normal times, I don't know. But it was plenty during this week.

Shirley and I are used to high-roller suites. But the Mansion was far beyond our experience. A separate hotel actually, it's reserved for high rollers only. I don't think you can rent these villas, but if you could, they would probably run in the $3,000-per-day range for a small one like we had. The larger ones (reputed to be 15,000 square feet)? Who knows?

Ours was around 2,500 square feet. We had a living room, bedroom, kitchen, closets, and bathrooms——all oversized. The bathroom alone was bigger than my first apartment. It had a hot tub, huge shower/steam room, heated floors, towel warmer, two TVs, plus several built-in conveniences. No actual toilets, of course. There were two separate rooms to handle that, one of which also had a bidet.

Every day we got four sets of BVLGARI toiletries. (That looks like a typo, but it's not. High-class Italians sometimes use Roman letters.) However many five-piece toiletry sets found their way into our suitcases or were given to friends who came by at our invitation, another four sets were provided the next day. "They're wonderful. Take them home with you," the maids urged. We did.

Although we would have preferred a king-size bed, the only suitable villa available had two queens. Life is tough, but we coped. Each queen was outfitted with Egyptian linen, down comforters, and seven pillows per bed. Every piece of furniture was one of a kind, tasteful, and expensive. A dozen different coffee-table books graced five or six exquisite tables, along with four or five old leather-bound books, published in French or German.

Our balcony overlooked a five-acre covered atrium, complete with fountains and full-time gardeners. In other areas of the Mansion there was a dining room, several interesting bars, a game room with pool tables and grand pianos, a huge screening room, and a spa. At least one concierge was on duty at all times, along with butlers, maids, security personnel, and others. We threw a cocktail party on our last night and a uniformed butler was there to do our bidding until we released him.

Everything was free—as long as we played the agreed-upon amount. And play we did. The first two days after the royal we weathered big fluctuations, but ended up slightly plus. Then we lost more than $26,000 in about five excruciatingly painful hours.

"Let's go home!" cried Shirley. "We don't need this luxury!"

"It's still a very good play," I replied. "You have to expect the swings. Hitting a royal doesn't mean you should quit and neither does having a losing day or two." The next day we collected $12,000 in slot club cash and promptly lost it, plus another $7,000. Shirley was not a happy camper.

The day after that, though, things began to get better. I was dealt a QJT98 straight flush (worth $6,250). About an hour later I got a KQJT9 straight flush. A floorman remarked, "Queen high and then king high. The royal, which is actually an ace high straight flush, must be coming next. Any fool can see that!" Outwardly, I couldn't have agreed more. But anyone who would assume that this "trend" *really* meant the royal was right around the corner was being very foolish indeed.

The last two days resulted in plus scores and we played so much that we earned another $11,000 in cashback. All told, our five-day stay in the Mansion ended up costing us about $10,000. It could have been much worse, of course. Then again, we could have hit another royal and been major-league winners. Still, spending $2,000 per day for the Mansion was a reasonable price for an exceptional experience.

Then again, if you'd asked us up front to pay $2,000 per day to stay there, we would have passed. Being pampered is nice, but $10,000 for a whole week of it is more than we would have chosen to spend.

For the entire month of play, we did very well. And we earned more than a half-million frequent-flyer miles. I wanted to sell them, while Shirley wanted to plan a nice trip or two. "If I have to suffer when we lose," she argued, "at least make it so I get a nice reward when we come out ahead." That's an argument I let her win.

Still the Best Deal in Town

Sometime during our pre-Christmas 1999 play with double points, a player told me about a "75% premium" for big players. This turned out to be a 40% premium, but I didn't realize it at the time. A 75% premium would have amounted to a .68% slot club, and the best elsewhere was a .67% rate at the Mirage and the Golden Nugget (which were not part of the same corporation as the MGM at the time). With the air miles and the Holiday Gift Shoppe, this *had* to be the best play in town.

In early January, Shirley and I decided to play at the premium level and see what happened. She was no more optimistic about our chances in January than she was at Thanksgiving, but the fact that we had an extra $60,000 cushion (and that I'd promised that if we earned enough for a car, it would be hers) was enough to soothe some of her fears. We set some stop-loss figures and plowed forward.

In January we lost about $20,000. We'd discovered that the premium-player cashback was actually .54% rather than .68%, but we felt the bonuses more than made up for it and we kept going. (Plus, the Mirage had lowered its cashback to .33% on the first of the year, which eliminated some of the competition.) In early February we lost another $15,000. Then, one evening during a Valentine's Day special giveaway, I was dealt a $100,000 royal flush. There was no skill involved whatsoever. All I had to do was be there at the right time to watch the machine deal the lovely hand and lock up. We'd hit another $100,000 royal two months earlier. Extrapolating, we figured we would get six of them a year. We figured wrong.

For the next few months, we lost. By June or so, we were even for the year, but not including the value of the air miles or the Holiday Gift Shoppe credit. Plus, we figured we had $20,000 or so worth of automobile for Shirley at this point. It hardly was a wasted year, but we'd given back the $75,000 we were ahead after the dealt royal. We knew that if we didn't get another royal soon, we'd be in the hole. It didn't have to be dealt. We were willing to draw a card or two … or even three if we had to.

In June the MGM added some $5 Triple Play 9/6 Jacks. These machines weren't new to the casino, but the previous best game on them was 8/5 Jacks, so they'd been avoided by everyone knowledgeable. Many players had been requesting more 9/6 Jacks machines in lower denominations. Those that were already there were $25 or $100 machines, and that was simply too expensive for most. Even $5 Triple Play was too rich for many players, but for those who liked to play video poker in the MGM Grand high-limit room, this pay schedule on these two machines was very welcome.

Switching from the $25 single-play machine to $5 Triple Play was a simple choice. The big quarter machines were old and clunky, spilled at 48 coins, and had huge swings. The $5 Triple Plays were much newer, didn't jam nearly as often, and had much smaller swings. Even though we were betting only $75 rather than the $125 it took to fully load one of the older machines, we could actually get more dollars per hour through the $5 machines than the $25 machines.

The return on these machines was less than the $5 10/7 Double Bonus Triple Play machines we played with the Dailys at the Orleans, but this was a machine/slot club combination that would last for months (we hoped), while the Orleans promotion was a one-month-only situation. The biggest difference, though, is that we'd now had considerable success at higher stakes. These machines still had to be treated with a great deal of respect, but these stakes were no longer terrifying.

Then, sometime around July 1, I made a remarkable discovery. Something was out of whack with the tabulation of my cashback. The way the system worked, when you put your card in, it took about 10 seconds to say "Card Accepted. Welcome Bob Dancer to the MGM Grand. You have 16,275 points."

To find out how many points were earned per play, you had to play one hand, then check to see how much the accrued points had changed. On the $5 Triple Play machines, one hand requires a $75 bet, which adds 15 points if it takes $5 to earn a point or 9.375 points if it takes $8 to earn one. After playing the hand, you had to remove and reinsert the card. Then in 10 seconds, you read what it said. If it said, "Card Accepted. Welcome Bob Dancer to the MGM Grand. You have 16,290 points," you knew you'd earned 15 points; hence, the machine was paying at the higher rate. If, instead, it gave you 16,284 or 16,285 points, you knew you'd received either 9 or 10 points and were earning at the regular video poker rate.

This was tedious and most players never bothered to do it. Whatever rate the machine paid was presumed to be the correct one.

The machine periodically updated the total: "You have 17,260 points" or whatever. I noticed one night that every time the machine displayed my points, the last digit was either a 4 or a 9. This was strange. Since I was supposed to be getting 9.375 points per play, the last digit should have varied. It could only be a constant 4 or 9 if I were accumulating points at a rate of 5 or 15 or 25 or some other number that ends in 5.

When I noticed this, I checked more closely. If I was getting only 5 points per play (one point per $15 coin-in), you can bet

---

Being a Bad Winner is More Fun ...

I was playing a $5 9/6 Jacks of Better Triple Play at the MGM Grand, while Liam and Katherine Daily were playing a $5 8/5 Bonus Poker progressive with the meter at $28,000 and climbing. Their game was worth 100% by itself, and adding in the cashback and other extras made this as high a return as $5 games offer in Las Vegas, worth about $100 per hour.

Back at my 9/6 game, I was dealt a dream hand: K♥Q♥J♥T♥9♣. A dealt straight. I quickly discarded the 9, as a four-card royal is worth far more than a made straight. Also, since it was on Triple Play, I had a 1-in-16.35 chance to get one royal flush (worth $20,000), a 1-in-752 chance of getting two royals (worth $40,000), and an in-your-dreams 1-in-103,823 chance of getting all three royals (worth $60,000).

I pressed the right buttons and drew. On the bottom line I got the A♥. A royal flush! On the middle line I got an A♥. Another royal flush! On the top line, I got the 9♣. The straight I'd thrown away! It added up to a $40,100 payoff on a $75 bet. An excellent result.

These moments don't come along very often. And 20 feet away from me were 10 people feverishly chasing a progressive. I knew nine of the 10 players. So I started to think about how to announce my good fortune to them.

The truth of the matter was, except for Liam and Katherine, the others cared only about whether *they* hit a royal. So if I ruffled a few feathers with my announcement, no big deal.

I went over to Katherine and said (loudly enough for the others to hear), "Damned nine of clubs! I would've had a nice hit except for that card!"

I'd have reported it. This would be equivalent to .21% for regular players or .29% for premium players, which was not enough to make playing this game acceptable. But when I learned that I was receiving 15 points, I was willing to be quiet about it. I told Shirley and Liam. No one else.

In July, Shirley spent three weeks in Africa. She and a few

... than Being a Good Loser

Katherine looked at me funny. Not getting the card you want is a *very* common experience in video poker. And I'm not one to complain about bad beats. So what was this about?

I continued, "I was dealt the king of hearts through the ten of hearts and on the top line only drew the nine of clubs. It was just awful!"

Liam, a clever guy at riddles, figured out what I was saying. "By any chance did you get the ace of hearts on the other two lines?"

"Sure. But the nine of clubs is such a lousy card. When you run bad, you run bad!"

Someone else chimed in. "You just hit two royals and you're complaining?" He looked at the guy to his left and said, "Do you want to kill him or should I?"

Liam and Katherine congratulated me. A few others smiled at the way I announced it. Some mumbled under their breath. And a couple not so silently cursed me. They were losing heavily and weren't in the mood for anyone else's good fortune.

One guy I didn't know came by while I was waiting to be paid. He said he was losing and wondered if I would consider "leaving" him a loan. I told him, "Yes. I'll be happy to leave you alone. Now please leave me alone!" Sophomoric, but I felt so witty!

Being a bad winner is a lot more fun than being a good loser!

(The progressive was hit at $34,000, and not by Katherine and Liam, who lost $12,000 going after it. They knew the risks going in. They could afford it. And next time maybe they'll be the ones on top.)

ladies from her church went to help set up an orphanage for AIDS-stricken children. I was very proud of her for doing this and simultaneously frightened for both of us. I knew she'd wear gloves, a mask, and probably other protective gear. I knew she'd be as careful as possible. But I also knew that accidents happen and that making a mistake in that environment could be fatal. I wasn't ready to lose her and I was aware that if she became infected, my days were likely numbered, too. This was a very uncomfortable time for me.

Shirley being out of town, however, gave me a tailor-made excuse to "live" at the MGM. The real reason I was there was because of the higher-than-normal return on the machines, but I told the casino workers that with Shirley out of town, I was at loose ends and didn't know what else to do with myself.

Despite the higher-than-average slot club rate and one beautiful hand consisting of $60,000 worth of hearts—my second dealt royal of the year—I lost over the summer. Not a lot, but by the end of August we were slightly behind.

Playing On

The reason these video poker machines paid out at the slot rate instead of the normal video poker rate is not completely known, though I think it had something to do with the fact that there used to be slot machines at these locations. When they switched to video poker, someone neglected to convert the rate.

Whatever the reason, they were awarding points at the slot-player's rate of one point per $5 coin-in, rather than the video poker rate of one point per $8 coin-in. The normal video poker-player cashback rate was .39%, and now I was getting the slot-player rate of .625%. Better yet, the high-roller premium was also applied to the higher rate, taking it up to .875%. How much was this worth? We were getting .33% extra and we were putting about $30,000 per hour through these machines. So the error was worth an extra $100 per hour played.

Crunching Cashback

Perhaps you're wondering just how I calculate these numbers. If $75 in play equals 15 points accrued in a slot club, then each point costs $5 to earn. Since it takes 32 points to redeem for $1 in cashback, you have to play 32 hands of $5 to earn that dollar. The equation is 32 x $5 = $160, which means it takes $160 in coin-in to earn the $1 cashback rebate. To get the percentage that this adds to the overall return rate, divide the payoff (1) by the required action (160): 1/160 = .00625 = .625%. To figure the added value of the high-roller premium, multiply the rate by 40% (.00625 x .4 = .0025) and add that to the base rate: .00625 + .0025 = .00875 = .875%.

While the numbers differ for every casino, the way to figure it remains the same. It's wise to do these calculations. Not because you're likely to run into the type of bonanza I did, but because mistakes happen and if you don't notice, you can get burned. Many video poker players at the MGM didn't even know that it took 32 points to earn one dollar in cashback. Why not? Because MGM's slot club literature referenced a cashback rate of $1.25 for every 40 points ($1.75 for premium players). This is tricky math for some. The equivalence of $1.25 per 40 points and $1 per 32 points is not obvious to a considerable number of people. A lot of premium players swore they were earning a 75% premium because they were paid in units of $1.75. The true cashback rate (.54%) was not bad by any means, but it wasn't as good as some players believed.

As I've mentioned, up until September we were stuck for the year (including cashback), even though by then we'd logged more than 200 hours on the machines returning the extra $100-per-hour cashback and several hundred hours on machines with the normal small advantage. Being stuck at this point was unlucky, but not unusually so. Video poker swings can be long and large, and I was experiencing one firsthand. Between February and September I'd lost more than $100,000, despite always playing machines where I had the advantage. Shirley was in full mumble mode. She's a wonderful winner, but a lousy loser. You can't make a living being even a little stuck for the year. Thanks to writing and teaching, I enjoy a larger non-gambling income than most full-time gamblers, though those things are time-consuming.

We were also building our two additional "bank accounts": the Holiday Gift Shoppe points and the American Airlines miles, which were being tacked on in addition to cashback. Holiday Gift Shoppe points accumulated all year long, but were cashable only in the week following Thanksgiving. American Airline miles were awarded at the rate of one mile per every two slot club points. Since both accounts were based on points, they also accumulated faster when you earned at the slot rate rather than the video poker rate. Considering the value of these accounts, we really weren't stuck at all when we started our run. We were slightly ahead.

Part of the problem in 2000 was that we didn't understand how much the Holiday Gift Shoppe points were worth. When we actually got to cash them, we found they were worth more than we thought. In 2001, we could better evaluate this promotion, so we devoted much more playing time in 2001 than we did in 2000.

I Can Do it ...

I was playing a $25 machine at the MGM Grand. Josh, an acquaintance, was playing the $25 machine to my left.

At the time, the $25 machines held only 47 credits (before spilling coins), so there were several thousand dollars of coins in his tray. He was going to rack them before he left, but saw no reason to keep them racked as he went along.

A woman came up to his left and told him he was making a big mess. She said she would help him straighten it out. (We later speculated that she was a prostitute. Don't know for sure and weren't about to find out.) She reached into his tray, picked up a handful of coins, and started to put the coins in a rack. Josh immediately grabbed her wrist and told her to drop the coins.

NSU Deuces at the MGM

For six months or so mid-to-late 2000, the MGM had $2 and $5 NSU Deuces Wild at the Cabaret Bar. This game returns 99.73% with perfect play. The next best $5 game at the MGM was 8/5 Bonus Poker with a progressive. The meter reset at $20,000 and at that level the game was worth 99.16%. At a progressive amount of $25,500 or so, it returned more than the NSU Deuces. At progressive amounts less than that, the NSU game was better.

The NSU machines returned considerably more than the typical MGM games, so it was widely assumed that management put them there by mistake. This game had made brief appearances at both the Mirage and Bellagio, but was quickly removed for being unprofitable, and these casinos had only a .33% slot club. With the MGM's .39%, plus air miles, plus Holiday Gift Shoppe points, we were surprised to see it at all and amazed that it lasted as long as it did.

The game I had been playing at the MGM was 9/6 Jacks and since this returned only 99.54%, it would seem a no-brainer that

---

... Myself

When she did, he stood up, pushed her back about 10 feet, and told her not to come any closer.

It took about 10 seconds for a host to come up to see if there was a problem. "This lady was just leaving," Josh replied. Within another 10 seconds, two security guards were escorting her out of the area.

Casino employees are the allies of the players, especially in well-run high-limit salons like the one at the MGM. If someone makes you uncomfortable, don't hesitate to raise your voice and call for security. It's far better to call for security when it's unneeded than to be distracted by a tight dress and find out later that the "helpful" lady was primarily interested in helping herself.

I would switch to the 99.73% game. But I didn't (for the most part). Why not? I could get only $15,000 per hour through the NSU game, while I could get $60,000 through playing Jacks or Better when I had two side-by-side Triple Play machines (playing the second while waiting for a hand pay on the first). And if I could get the $10 Five Play machine with a $5 Triple Play machine next to it, I could often put through $90,000 per hour. Here's how the math worked:

Normal cashback	.39%
Extra premium cash	.15%
Air miles	.06%
Holiday Gift Shoppe	.22%
Total:	.82%

Adding .82% to 99.73% results in a 100.55% payback. And multiplying this by $15,000 yields an $82 hourly expected profit. Not bad. Adding .82% to 99.54% comes to a lesser 100.36%. But multiplying this by $60,000 to $90,000 in play works out to a per-hour return between $215 and $320. Playing Jacks was much better. And by this time, I'd had enough success with the bigger machines that playing them caused me no anxiety.

I did play the NSU game on occasion—when, for example, the Triple Play machines were unavailable. And even if the Triple Play machines were available, sometimes I played NSU because Liam W. Daily and I had recently worked out the strategy for our strategy-card series. But regardless of how much you work on strategies at your computer, you can't really know the game until you use those strategies at the machines. A lot of changes to the strategy cards were derived from actual play. Those changes would be considered minor unless you were driven to produce *extremely* accurate strategies that were a significant improvement over those of anyone else. And we were.

Another reason I played the NSU game was because it's so much more *fun*. Deuces Wild is a *much* more interesting game than Jacks or Better. In fact, Jacks or Better is downright boring for most people. The main reason I play it is that it's the most profitable game at my stakes of choice in my casinos of choice. But sometimes I get Jacks or Better'd out and want a different game. Although I almost always play the game with the highest return, I can occasionally justify switching to a game that pays less—as long as it's still significantly positive.

The thrill of Deuces derives from both the every-eight-hours four-deuces mini-jackpot (worth $5,000 on this game) and the fact that the four wild cards in the deck produce a lot of different possible hands on every draw. In Deuces Wild, if you start with two or three deuces, you have no idea what you'll wind up with. Could be a straight, flush, 3-of-a-kind, 4-of-a-kind, straight flush, 5-of-a-kind, wild royal, or four deuces. None of these hands is bad, though clearly some are better than others. Most players who play multiple games well will tell you that if the return were the same, Deuces would be their game of choice.

One night in September 2000, the NSU game was accidentally installed on a new $5 Triple Play machine. A slot technician had been instructed to install the same games on this Triple Play machine that were on the others in the casino. But the new machine was a slightly different generation and the order of the schedules on the chip confused the tech. He merely counted the number of pay schedules down from the top (and installed the corresponding number)—he didn't pay attention to the actual returns on the games.

It was an easy mistake to make—and a big surprise for me to find NSU on a Triple Play. How do you find such a manna-from-heaven pay schedule? You look! The Triple Play machines at the MGM always had very tight (in the 96% range) schedules for all games other than Jacks or Better. We checked the existing machines only about once every twenty times that we played, but since this was a new machine, we checked *every* pay schedule.

The Deuces game usually found on the $5 Triple Play machines at the MGM returned only 97%. Anyone playing a

97% game on these machines would lose well over $1,000 per hour. And that's *if* they were playing perfectly, which they surely wouldn't be, because anyone knowledgeable enough to play the game well would also be knowledgeable enough to run, not walk, away from such a pay schedule.

If you think the NSU game surprised me, you should have seen the staff! Bob Dancer playing Deuces on that machine set off warning bells galore. At least five floorpeople or supervisors came by and asked me why I was suddenly playing Deuces Wild when I'd been playing Jacks or Better 30 hours a week for 10 months. They suspected there was a good reason for the switch.

But none of them was knowledgeable enough to recognize that this Deuces game wasn't the same as the others. I told them that since Shirley's mother and sister were visiting and their favorite game was Deuces, I thought I'd change for awhile to make it easier on them. The employees nodded and went away, but I suspect they didn't buy this lame explanation. About five hours after I started playing, a vice president came by and watched for a long time, then disappeared.

From what happened, I suspect that the veep ordered the slot supervisor to let us play for as long as we wanted, but to shut down the machine as soon as we left and change the pay schedule to match the other Triple Plays. The casino could have saved a few hundred dollars in equity by kicking us off the machine then and there, but that might have generated considerable ill will, which wasn't the style of this classy place.

I was relieved they didn't remove the game immediately, but I was pretty sure the game would be gone the next day. Therefore I played (with my two "assistants") for as long as I could. Since we were playing only one machine, we probably got $30,000 per hour through it. But this game returned $50 or so extra per hour than Jacks or Better, and as long as I could play alertly, I would continue. I ended up a few thousand dollars ahead.

At about this same time, the MGM re-opened its newly remodeled former high-limit slot area with a number of good machines. They had dollar NSU Deuces in both the Triple Play and Five Play. These games were a huge improvement over the usual fare the MGM offered at the dollar level—likely the loosest dollar games at any quality resort on the Strip—and they became very popular among the knowledgeable. No one knew why the MGM offered such loose (for a Strip property) machines, but looking a gift horse in the mouth is not something video poker professionals do. Some players lived on these machines until they were removed a year later.

Meanwhile, the $5 NSU Deuces at the Cabaret Bar disappeared about this time. The pay schedules on those machines were never explicitly changed. Instead, the entire bar was removed as the Cabaret Theater was converted into a showroom suitable for the *La Femme* topless review. When the bar was reinstalled three months later after the completion of the showroom, NSU Deuces were not on the menu.

Double Holiday Gift Shoppe Points

Eventually, I settled on the estimation that Holiday Gift Shoppe points were worth .22% based on video poker machine coin-in and .35% based on slot machine coin-in. But I couldn't know for sure until the HGS event itself. Richard, the MGM executive in charge of the HGS event, wouldn't give us a straight answer regarding how much the points were worth.

I don't blame him for hedging; I'm sure there were lots of behind-the-scenes things happening regarding the pricing of items. But we had *millions* of points, so it made many thousands of dollars difference to us what the rate would be.

Also, the intelligent player calculates these rates differently than the casino executive. The executive looks at how many HGS points are on the books, how much the estimated breakage will be (points earned but not redeemed), and how much the total budget for the promotion is. The intelligent player looks at how much the points add to the particular game he's playing.

For example, let's assume that 50 HGS points equals $1 retail and it costs $8 to earn an HGS point. That means it takes $400 in coin-in to earn $1 in retail value, so $1/$400 = .25%. If it takes 60 HGS points to earn a dollar, then it's $1/($8 x 60) =.21%. When you're playing $60,000 through the machine per hour, the difference equates to $24 per hour.

Anyway, in September and October of 2000, the MGM awarded double HGS points, as I recall. We didn't know what a point was worth, but we were now collecting them twice as fast. Based on a rough approximation (that turned out to be low) in which I assumed the points were worth .167%, I figured that September was worth $50 per hour more than August if I could only get one $5 Triple Play machine, and closer to $75 more if I could get on the Five Play machine that was available during this period.

You could buy lots of things with the HGS points, including cars. Shirley wanted a new top-of-the-line Chrysler Town and Country Limited minivan. One of the ladies at the Compton Dancer office who had recently gone through a divorce also needed a new car. Her credit was messed up, so we decided we'd get her a car and carry the paper. And Shirley's mother needed a new car. We told her we'd get her one with a "mother-in-law" discount and she could delay paying us until she sold her house. Three cars require a lot of points, so we got busy.

I'd been playing about 20 hours a week. Between Shirley and me, we upped that to around 50 hours weekly. After this increase, the machines started to respond. In September we hit seven or eight $20,000 royal flushes. Royals definitely come faster on a Triple Play machine, but that was still a lot. In October we hit more than 20 royals, some of them for $40,000, but now we were playing Five Play, and royals, of course, come faster on Five Play than they do on Triple Play.

Some of our friends weren't doing as well. We'd play over a weekend, hit two royals, and end up $25,000 or so ahead, while our friends would play about the same amount and lose $30,000.

This happened during at least four weekends, including two in a row, and it was very awkward. Seeing people you care about lose a considerable amount of money takes a lot of the pleasure out of your winning. They would put on a stiff upper lip and tell us not to worry about it, but we knew it was bothering the hell out of them. More than once they were on the verge of giving up video poker permanently. And it wasn't as though Shirley and I were playing well while our friends were playing badly. We were playing pretty close to the same skill-wise. It's just that the royals showed up on our machines and stayed away from theirs.

Something else was puzzling. For the entire year of 2000, Shirley hit two $20,000 royals (and nothing larger)—and she hit them both in one day (in December). During that same time period, I hit more than 70 royals for at least $20,000 apiece. I played four or five times as much as she did, but I was definitely "over-royaled" and Shirley was "under-royaled." There was no difference in the skill level, because until late October 2000, I approved *every* hand that Shirley played, so I know we played exactly the same.

Shirley probably lost $150,000 that year. This wasn't a serious problem for us (although she didn't like it), as I earned considerably more than that. Still, it's a good indication of the magnitude of the swings on these machines, which can eat up bankrolls. You have to survive every one. If one of them busts you, you're back to playing quarter Deuces Wild with virtually no hope of ever playing in the big leagues again.

During this time in late 2000, MGM had only two $5 Triple Play machines. The casino was fully aware that both were busy all the time. Other people played them a lot during the day and Shirley and I played them during graveyard. The staff promised to install more and we encouraged them to do so. We told them that the cars we needed to get for Shirley's mother and our recently divorced employee would be earned faster during double-HGS days, which was why we were playing so much. All of this was absolutely true, but it was also smoke and mirrors.

The truth was that we figured the $5 Triple Play machines

during this period were worth $150 or so per hour—including full retail value for the HGS. The MGM Grand had put together too many generous promotions all at once. We knew it and they didn't—at least not yet. Meanwhile, I talked about assisting Shirley's mother and helping the girl at the office and the staff ate it up. Several of the female employees said that they wished they'd had friends like Shirley and me after *their* divorces. We were using the same technique I'd perfected back at the Tropicana while qualifying for the Bahamas, and used again in explaining why I was playing so much when Shirley was in Africa. I gave the casino employees a rational reason for my behavior and they not only bought it, they appreciated my candor. The underlying dollars-and-cents reason, of course, went undisclosed.

Yet *another* promotion came around during the double-HGS-point days. It was a drawing for which tickets were earned based on play. So now players were pounding the machines for double points *and* drawing tickets. It made for one crowded high-limit slot salon. The floorpeople were running around madly trying to take care of everyone. The staff did the best they could, but service suffered because of the volume.

The service may have deteriorated a bit during this time, but it wasn't as bad as it was going to be in a few weeks. Why? Because while this new promotion was good, the one they ran next was *very* good. Every casino groups its customers into categories of Marginal, So-So, Good, and Wonderful. Each has its own unique criteria for inclusion in each category, but most consider how much a player plays per visit, how often he visits, and what kind of machines he plays. Some also consider how much a player has won or lost.

The first promotion was for people with a Good rating (or higher). The second was for people with a Wonderful rating. The amounts given away were something like $30,000 shared among 300 Good players in the first event and $100,000 shared among 200 Wonderful players in the second.

The disparity realistically portrays the difference in the way a

Shirley's Mother Comes to Town

Shirley's mother, Virginia, lives in Northern Arizona, gets to Las Vegas about once a month, and likes to play video poker. One weekend, the three of us played $5 9/6 Jacks or Better Triple Play at the MGM Grand. Though the MGM had only two of these machines, we all played together (with one always sitting out). These $75-per-hand machines quickly generated all the comps we needed (and during this time, playing accurately and having fun was more important than playing the maximum amount of hands).

The first night, we didn't do so well, losing $9,000 in three hours. Afterward, Virginia asked me why we were playing so heavily. I told her the casino was running the double Holiday Gift Shoppe points promotion.

"So how much gift credit did you earn?" she asked.

"We played almost a hundred thousand through the machine," I told her. "Normally that would give us two hundred dollars in credit, but today we earned four hundred."

"Let me get this straight. You earned an extra two hundred dollars in merchandise credit and it cost you nine thousand in cash to get it? And you think that's a good deal? I must be missing something."

I explained that losing the $9,000 was totally irrelevant (assuming it didn't seriously jeopardize my gambling bankroll, which it didn't). If I played several hundred thousand hands over the year, which I did, and I played very close to perfectly, which I do, then the return on the game will wind up being reasonably close to 99.54%. So the slot club benefits put the payback over 100%. Some days I'll hit more than one $20,000 royal. Others I'll lose $15,000 or so. No big deal either way.

Virginia accepts that I'm an expert, but she still took what I said with a grain of salt. Understandable. After all, "playing only when you have the advantage" is largely just a buzz-phrase to her. So far she doesn't have any experience with being a long-term winner and doubts that she could ever learn enough to become one. But she does listen and attempt to apply the lessons taught. And she's improving.

casino treats its players in the different categories. The Good players get invited to a giveaway worth $100 per person ($30,000/300 = $100), while the Wonderful players get invited to one worth $500 per person ($100,000/200 = $500). The players worth more to the casino get more and the players worth less get less. Still, both groups represent valuable customers in the eyes of the casinos. After all, many of the Good customers of today will become the Wonderful customers of tomorrow if they feel well-treated.

I Should Have ...

The band at the dance party was called the Dumkopfs, a bunch of 60-year-old smart alecks who play some mean polka music. Shirley and I danced together, doing elaborate variations on the simple dance. At the end of the set, there was as much applause for us as there was for the band.

One of the party events was a polka contest and mine was the first name called. Everyone screamed foul. They had just seen Shirley and me shine and now some poor couple had to compete against us. Rather like David and Goliath—or so they portrayed it.

There was a kicker, however. I couldn't dance with Shirley. Instead, I had to dance with one of the slot hosts. As I got up from the table, Shirley strongly suggested that I pick Allan to be my dance partner.

Although I didn't seriously consider it at the time, it was actually a savvy suggestion. Allan is a fine dancer, well-practiced and enthusiastic. Would he have danced with me? I'm not sure. I didn't ask. I suspect yes. (Especially if the other hosts egged him on.) Most of the crowd would have loved watching two old-enough-to-know-better guys dancing with each other and trying to figure out who was going to twirl whom. However, I assumed a few people would be offended, so I picked Mary instead.

I'd danced with Mary a few times at earlier parties. She's not nearly as good as Shirley (who is?), but she does all right and she's our slot host and, hey, I had a lock on this contest anyway.

The next contestant was a lady who hadn't been to one of these parties before and didn't know how well the hosts danced.

Ordinarily, Shirley and I would pass on a $100-per-person event as not being worth our time, but we signed up for this one: We were already playing 50 hours a week at a game I believed was the best in town even without a special promotion. All we had to do "extra" for this event was show up at the party. And since they promised to have a dance floor, there was no decision—even if it was going to be a polka band.

The Good customers play a lot over an invitational weekend.

... Picked Allan!

She picked her host, Ramil, a popular 30ish Filipino. Ramil was willing, but they don't do many polkas in the Philippines and he didn't have a clue how to go about it. So I showed him. (I could afford to be generous; I was going to win by a mile!) Left two three, right two three, left two three, right two three. His partner told him not to worry. "I'm from Poland," she said. "Just hang on and I'll lead!"

The last contestant, a lady who had been to MGM parties before, knew who could dance and immediately picked Allan.

Mary and I went first. Starting off well enough doing the basics, I decided that Mary could handle a little twirl. Big mistake. She added a couple of extra little steps during the twirl and we never recovered, winding up on different beats for the rest of the dance. Oh well, maybe no one noticed.

Ramil and his partner did well, considering that it was his first polka and they did just the basic step over and over. Technically, Mary and I were ahead on the dancing, but Ramil took top honors in the good-sport category.

Now it was time for Allan and his partner. He did something clever: He let her keep doing the basic pattern and *he* did the twirls. When it came time for the voting, Allan and partner were way out in front and Ramil and partner edged out Mary and me. Oh well. So much for being a lock.

I did take some teasing. "Do you mind if we call you Bob 'Third-Place' Dancer now?" But how much worse would the teasing have been if I'd taken Shirley's suggestion and picked Allan?

That's what makes them Good. But the Wonderful customers might play five times as much, both in terms of stakes and hours. So during the first weekend, consisting of mostly Good players, the high-limit room was full, but not that full. When the Wonderful players came two weeks later, the room was *full*.

These were two of the first big events after the MGM opened its big new elegant high-limit slot salon. Thus the first event became a stress test, while the second event created a serious stress test. All in all, MGM management handled problems well: They went around asking many players (and *all* the biggest players) how the events could be improved. They took notes and promised to make changes in the future. In my opinion, other casinos would do well to emulate this strategy. Whenever there's a problem (and there's *always* at least one), customers should be allowed to be involved in the solution. The customers feel heard and tend to forgive the casino for any immediate inconvenience.

By the time of these promotions, all of the video poker machines that were generating slot club points at the slot machine rate had been discovered and corrected. Three days before the Wonderful promotion, however, they installed a machine where you could play $5 or $10 on either Triple Play or Five Play—and it had been set to pay at the slot machine rate. Fantastic! This meant that premium players received an extra .33% in cashback. Plus the double HGS promotion added .25% worth of retail value. And the air miles accumulated significantly faster, too.

I recognized right away that playing this machine at the $10 denomination wasn't a good idea during the promotion. In Jacks or Better, a 4-of-a-kind pays 125 coins, which is $625 on a $5 machine. But on a $10 machine, a quad pays $1,250, generating a hand-pay because of the tax form. We play enough to get several million dollars worth of W-2Gs each year, so a few more hand-pays wasn't an issue. But I expected the high-limit slot room to be in stress mode again and it might take 10 minutes or more for every hand-pay.

Since 4-of-a-kinds show up on a Five Play machine every 10

minutes or so, adding a 10-minute wait to each of these wasn't conducive to getting a lot of money through the machine. This was a case where playing $5 Five Play would generate more than twice as much action as $10 Five Play.

We also had to decide between $5 Triple Play and $5 Five Play. Both lock up on dealt quads, any straight flush, and at times when you start with trips and convert at least two hands to quads. You're more likely to convert trips twice when you have five pops at it rather than three, but I figured this would happen only a few times all weekend. So the Five Play was the better bet.

There was another potential problem. At least two very good players were well-known for their ability to play for 30 hours straight during a good promotion. These players might or might not eventually check the point countdowns on this machine. At least one of them was aware of the earlier extra-point bonanza (and participated in the casino's unintentional giveaway). If I had to bet, I'd bet on him to check. And if he discovered that this machine was issuing points for $5 rather than $8 per, Shirley and I might never get on it again.

We considered forming a temporary team. Unlike most teams, this wouldn't include any sharing of wins and losses; it would merely guarantee that we'd get seats. I decided to ask "John" and "Larry," who also played these machines a lot, to share time with us.

Points could be earned toward the promotion from Friday at noon up to Saturday night's drawing. I arrived at 11:30 p.m. Thursday, figuring I'd bump into John and Larry before they left. (Their usual pattern was to play for several hours and go home about midnight.) When I got there, Larry was playing alone. He told me that John would be taking over the machine at midnight and that the two of them were planning to hold the machine all weekend by themselves. Uh oh. So much for my plan. John was in charge, so I had to wait until he got there before I could discuss anything.

John came in at 11:55 and agreed to listen to what I had

to say. Players who participate in a lot of promotions around town tend to maintain civil relations and try to accommodate each other, if possible, without giving up too much. Whoever has arrived first this time might be second to arrive next time, and taking a hard line today can and will come back to haunt you later.

I started off by acknowledging that John and Larry had "squatter's rights." I was stating the obvious, but I wanted John

---

The Price ...

At one of the MGM parties, Shirley and I sat with George and Kathy—frequent visitors to the MGM's high-limit room. George played $100 Double Diamond slots until he decided that Jacks or Better was a smarter choice. He'd purchased *WinPoker* and my Jacks or Better report a few months earlier and studied them for an hour or two before this trip.

He asked me to sit by him while he was playing and evaluate his performance. I told him I'd be glad to do so and that my hourly rate for such tasks was $200, with a two-hour minimum. Unless he was serious, I didn't want to waste my time. George flinched a bit at the rate, but agreed.

After the session, we went to their suite and talked. George had held a low pair over a 4-card flush, never held a 3-card straight flush of any sort, held all high cards suited or not (such as A♥K♥J♠), and on a hand such as KK553, kept the kings only. Kathy played for about a half-hour while I watched and was equally bad. I guestimated they were each giving the casino 2% more than they had to.

"How much is that in real money?" he wanted to know.

I asked him how many points they accumulated in a weekend and we figured that between the two of them, George and Kathy played almost $2 million through the machine every trip. And they came to Las Vegas every month.

"In round numbers, you're losing an extra half-million dollars a year, because you don't take the time to learn to play the game." George was amazed. He knew he lost a lot, but figured to know that I had no plans to muscle him out. Then I asked him why he and Larry were locking up the machine so early. He told me he wanted tickets for the promotion and was worried that the same two guys I was worried about would take over the machines indefinitely. I realized then that he didn't know about the higher point structure.

I told him that I wanted the extra play that Five Play offered over Triple Play, because I was trying to get cars for Shirley,

---

... of Ignorance

it was because he was unlucky. "I want to personally thank you for this," I continued. "It's because of people like you that the MGM can offer games from which I can prosper."

Kathy all but ordered me from their room. She felt my rudeness was uncalled for. Perhaps she was right.

George, however, took my words as a wake-up call. Two months later he asked to buy another two hours of my time. I watched him play. In two hours I saw him play every hand perfectly—except one. From K♥T♥9♠6♦3♥, he held KT rather than just the K. Holding K rather than KT is a rare play involving two separate penalty cards. This was a mistake costing about 20¢ on the $25 machine he was playing. He'd played approximately $100,000 through the machine and his only mistake was worth 20¢. The fact that this was the only mistake he made in two hours was truly remarkable. Less than one player in 100 can play so mistake-free.

"Congratulations," I told him. "You just saved yourself a quarter of a million dollars a year. And if Kathy learns to play as well, you'll save another quarter mil. How much did you have to study?"

He told me he'd spent 50 hours practicing in the past two months. "It wasn't fun, but I decided that half a million a year constituted serious money. So I decided it was worth it."

I reminded him that he should still practice a few hours before each trip or the information gleaned from that 50 hours of study wouldn't stay completely with him. Meanwhile, Kathy still thinks I'm rude.

Shirley's mom, and the girl at the office. I admitted that points for the promotion weren't as high a priority for me and that if we could have the Five Play machine for the next 12 hours until the promotion started, then he and Larry could have the machine when they really wanted it. Shirley and I could earn an extra "tire or two" for her mom's car over the next 12 hours and we'd stick to the Triple Play machines during the promotion.

This gave him what he wanted most: plenty of hours during the promo. Besides, he wasn't that eager to play 12-hour shifts. He would if he had to, but if he could find a way to get the machines when he wanted without the 12-hour shifts, that was much better for him. In addition, he had a deal with me that he knew would have to be reciprocated someday. This had some real, though at the time unknown, value. So it was goodnight, good luck, and we'll see you at noon tomorrow.

An extra tire or two, did I say? On my second-choice machine, the $5 Triple Play, we could put $30,000 per hour through. That was worth $125 per hour in HGS credit. The cashback on this machine was maybe $25 per hour more than the expected loss on the play (because 9/6 Jacks returns less than 100%). This was how I arrived at the $150 per hour estimate cited earlier. On my first choice, this $5 Five Play that paid at the reel slot rate, we could play probably $45,000 through per hour. With the higher point structure, this was worth $300 per hour in HGS credit. Plus cashback at the higher level was about $150-per-hour more than the expected loss. All told, I was looking at a $450-per-hour game (and don't forget the air miles). The difference between the two machines was very big.

The good news was that I had the machine I wanted for the next 12 hours. The bad news was that I'd been up much of Thursday doing other things and didn't feel capable of playing alertly for 12 hours straight. What to do? Shirley was available and willing to help, but up to this point, she hadn't played video poker without me being there. Ever. She still made an occasional mistake, but we had such a huge overlay, thanks to all the promotions and the extra-generous slot points, that we would still be the favorite by a large amount. So Shirley played from midnight to three while I went upstairs to sleep. Then I played from three until nine while she slept. I was still alert when Shirley came back at nine, so she sat down at a Triple Play while I stayed on the Five Play. I tried very hard not to watch her play and succeeded, for the most part. She was delighted to be trusted to play on her own. This was a *lot* more fun for her.

So the four of us locked up the Five Play machine until the giveaway party Saturday night. The timing of all this was a bit inconvenient for me. I'd recently written an article for *Casino Player* where I expressed the opinion that teams were bad for video poker. My argument was that teams kept good players on the machines, thereby precluding the casinos from making money off the weaker players. In this case, three out of the four players on the machine were probably weaker on average than the two guys we were knowingly keeping off. (I'm likely in the same league ability-wise as the other two, but Shirley, John, and Larry are not.)

Several members of the largest video poker team in Las Vegas were also present at the event. One came over and asked me point blank, "Are you against teams only when you're not on them? Seems a bit hypocritical, don't you think?" She had a point, but I couldn't tell her what was different about this situation without disclosing a lot more than I wanted to. (I certainly didn't want this team to get hold of the machine. They had eight or more players to rotate in and out.) So I just smiled weakly and let her think whatever she wanted. Some months later, after the machines were set to pay out points at the correct rate, I explained to her what I'd been doing and why.

On Saturday night, we had a lot of tickets in the barrel (though not as many as John and Larry), but none of us got called. Not a surprise, really. The prizes were awarded to only five people out of 200 of us. We wanted to win the $50,000 first prize, of course, but these events are a numbers game. If you enter enough of them, occasionally you get the big prize. Usually, though, you get nothing.

With all five people already chosen for the giveaway prizes, we left to get back to the machine. One of the guys who could play for long periods at a time came by and told me that he couldn't figure out why we were locking up that machine, but he was going to be in the Mansion for the next four days and would check it out when we took a break.

This told me that if we wanted to continue to earn money on this machine, we had to continue to keep it locked up. The only way to do this was to let John and Larry in on the secret about the extra point rate. Once I did, they were only too happy to agree to shifts where we would all get a turn. Eventually, we told a few other people, as well—there was no way I could survive 12-hour shifts seven days a week, along with everything else I was doing.

And, of course, whenever the staff would ask why we were playing so much, we gave them the same old song and dance—cars for Shirley, Shirley's mom, and the girl at the office.

Taking the Occasional Potshot

"Taking a potshot" means entering into a high-risk venture that has a small likelihood of success, but if it does succeed, it yields great benefits. Gambling potshots that come to mind include buying lottery tickets and playing Megabucks. Investment-wise, these particular potshots are the pits. Not only is the likelihood of success infinitesimal, but also a large percentage of your bet is taken off the top by the organizers. If you want to spend a few bucks on a dream, fine. But playing lotteries or Megabucks isn't what I would call intelligent or responsible gambling.

Consider the following situation instead. Assume you're a quarter Deuces Wild player and have a gambling bankroll of $4,000. You play the game essentially perfectly. You come to play today with $500 in your pocket, knowing from experience that losing half a royal during one session is not out of the question. On the way to your normal Deuces game, you pass a dollar 9/6 Jacks or Better progressive with the meter at $8,000, and (wonder of wonders) a seat is open.

You know that about $5,000 is the breakeven point for this game, so $8,000 gives you about a 1.5% edge (plus slot club benefits). This opportunity is more lucrative than you're used to, so you sit down while you figure out whether or not to invest (if you don't sit down immediately, the seat may be taken by another opportunity-seeker).

At dollars, $500 can go quickly; a bankroll of $4,000 is nowhere near enough to play a game like this on a regular basis. But this may be a case where the term "responsible potshot" isn't an oxymoron.

I believe the general principles for selecting these responsible potshots should be as follows:

• You're unquestionably the favorite and by a reasonably large amount. Being under-financed for any game puts you in a vulnerable position. Don't compound the problem by playing a game where you're the underdog to boot. And if you're not sure whether you have the edge or the house does, it's a safe assumption that it's the house and that this isn't the right time to take the potshot. So you need to know the magnitude of your advantage and, of course, how to play the game.

• You've set a firm loss limit and will stick to it. In this example, the $500 in your pocket would be the limit. If you lose that, you quit. Some people are better at this than others and you probably know whether or not you tend to keep promises to yourself. If there's a possibility that you could go on tilt and head for the ATM after the $500 limit is reached, you should *never* take a potshot.

• Your loss limit is a relatively small percentage of your total bankroll. In our example, $500 is one-eighth of a $4,000 bankroll. That's a little high, but probably acceptable. Remember, if this play goes bad, you'll have to recoup your investment by earning $6 an hour or so playing quarter Deuces Wild or, horror of horrors, going out and getting a real job. Your bankroll can be destroyed at dollars much faster than it can be recouped at quarters.

• You can handle a loss psychologically. Are you a second-guesser? Will you be happy if the potshot succeeds, but devastated if it fails? What about your spouse? Explaining to someone who wasn't there how you just lost an amount that took the two of you three years to accumulate isn't a comfortable conversation. Discussing your strategy for this kind of thing in advance is definitely a good idea.

In my family, Shirley's the second-guesser and I'm the philosophical one. As a practical matter, when we're playing stakes that make her uncomfortable, she expresses herself fully, loudly, and frequently, but usually goes along with my recommendation. She knows how successful I've been and believes that I won't put our savings in serious jeopardy.

• Your chance for success is reasonable. Needing to hit a royal is a longshot, but an acceptable one at video poker. On every hand, the odds of hitting a royal are 40,000-to-1 or so against you, but you play several thousand hands in the course of such a play. If you need to be *dealt* a royal (650,000-to-1) or perhaps a sequential royal (2.4 million-to-1) to succeed, this is not the time for a potshot. For chances that slim, you need to be well-financed, because there's a high probability that this venture will fail.

• This potshot is a rare event for you. If you're taking potshots regularly, then they're no longer potshots. You're regularly investing at the higher level and need the bankroll to support that play. If you don't have this bankroll, you're risking bankruptcy. Living close to the edge bankroll-wise repeatedly is a prescription for disaster.

Think of it as a form of Russian roulette with a gun with one live round and 99 blanks. It's probably safe (relatively) to do it once. With a fresh spin, it's probably safe to do it twice. But somewhere along the way, keep doing this and you'll end up dead. The particular event that killed you will be something unlucky, but putting yourself repeatedly in a position that demands good luck is not a smart move.

• You're not so worried about losing the money that you play less than optimally. For example, consider someone used to playing for quarters. He's now on a dollar 10/7 Double Bonus machine, taking advantage of a high progressive, and is dealt aces full—A♣A♥A♦3♠3♥. Keeping the full house is worth an even $50. Keeping the aces and going for the quad is worth $50.57 on average, but turns into $15 nearly 90% of the time. For someone used to quarter jackpots, a guaranteed $50 looks pretty sweet and is too big to throw away. But if this describes you, you shouldn't be taking potshots.

If all of these criteria are present, then the potshot you're considering is probably a reasonable risk. Every gambler I know who's been in this business for awhile has taken potshots on occasion. For many of us, successes at these gambles have generated a significant part of our bankroll. We're the lucky ones. Others have ended up bankrupt.

For me, my Bally's adventure was a potshot. My adventures at the Desert Inn and the Frontier would have been potshots had I not partnered with Arnie. I ended the partnership early in both cases because of early success and probably inched into the "irresponsible-potshot" category. Fortunately for me, I prevailed in all of these cases. Let me tell you now about a potshot of mine that didn't succeed.

Big-Time Potshots

On November 1, 2000, the double HGS points ended. We were still playing a lot of hours. The biggest machine continued to award points at the slot machine rate. Also, we could play considerably faster than before, now that hand-pays were handled quickly (because fewer players were around) and I could move over to a vacant $5 Triple Play machine while waiting to be paid.

And then one day, the machine stopped paying points at the higher rate. No employee talked to me about this. No one asked me, "Did you know?" I assume what happened is that the person who discovered the error decided it was best not to report it. Maybe it was the same tech who'd made the error to begin with and he didn't want to announce that it had cost the casino more than $200,000.

We kept playing. We still felt it was the best play in town. By hammering the $10 Five Play machine and using the $5 Triple Play machine as a backup while waiting for a hand-pay, I could get $90,000 per hour through the machines. That was $200 per hour worth of HGS, even at single points, and we had a $100 cash advantage on the machine, plus the air miles.

Also, quitting immediately after they'd fixed the machine would have made it obvious that we'd intentionally taken advantage of the wrong rate. We didn't want to make this point crystal clear to the casino. It was okay if they wondered. But they weren't likely to take action against us if they weren't sure. So we kept quiet and played.

One weekend in November, we hit five $20,000 royals in two days! We gave much of it back, but were still up $70,000. Potshot time! I talked it over with Shirley, who agreed that we could take a $40,000 potshot on the $100 machine.

A $100 machine! This bad boy can eat you before breakfast. We knew that we'd probably lose. But then again maybe we'd get lucky and make a big killing. At this level, every 4-of-a-kind pays $12,500, straight flushes pay $25,000, and the royal returns a whopping $400,000—big numbers indeed. We were on a pretty nice run that weekend and figured, what the heck, maybe our luck would hold.

It took less than three hours to lose the entire $40,000. We did hit a quad early and were up for a short time, but after that it was a steep downhill slide. The only thing that kept us from losing faster was that there were a lot of hand-pays and the machine spilled at 12 credits.

Shirley grumbled that we would have been better off keeping the $40,000. The fact that we earned more than $5,000 in cashback and HGS credit didn't cheer her up. I wasn't thrilled with the loss, of course, but it didn't bother me that much. I felt the potshot was responsible and adhered to the "rules":

• I was unquestionably the favorite in the game.

• I had a definite loss limit that I would stick to; no ifs, ands, or buts.

• The amount of the loss limit was small in proportion to our total bankroll.

• And an additional rule not mentioned in the previous listing: I was a winner by more than the potshot immediately prior to taking it.

(The last rule is more psychological than anything else. The ups and downs of gambling don't get me real excited, as long as the bottom line comes out okay. Shirley, on the other hand, hates to go home a loser. My life works better when she's happy, so risking a portion of recent profits is less of a problem for her than if we'd lost recently.)

Let me present this another way. Let's say we had a bankroll of $500,000 when we took this potshot. Does it really matter if the previous week we had $450,000 (meaning we had just won $50,000) or $550,000 (meaning we had just lost)? I don't think so. Whether you've won or lost recently has no bearing on the mathematics of the potshot. But Shirley thinks otherwise and this isn't worth fighting over. A friend of mine espouses the maxim: A happy wife makes for a happy life! I concur.

Bonanza at the Holiday Gift Shoppe

The Holiday Gift Shoppe itself lasted for a week, anytime during which you could cash your points for merchandise. A number of players (both good and bad) used this as an excuse to schedule another trip to Vegas. Of course, this is part of what made it a good deal from the MGM's point of view. So just before this week-long event where higher-than-average crowds were expected, they put in another $5/$10 Triple Play/Five Play machine. Incredibly, the machine was set to accumulate points at the slot machine rate. Here we go again!

Strange things were going on at the MGM. Making a mistake once is understandable; mistakes happen all the time. They made the same mistake a second time and it took a month to discover and fix it. Now they were doing it a third time (and it would take another month to be discovered). The MGM easily

---

An Impossible-to ...

When you hit a hand-pay jackpot, some casinos "salt" the machine by betting the first five coins (using their money) on the next hand. For low-stakes games, this is a nice touch and not a significant amount of money to either the casino or the player. After all, an extra five coins every time you hit a royal doesn't add up very quickly.

But on high-stakes machines, it can add up fast due to frequent "jackpots" at or above the $1,200 W-2G limit. On a $10 Jacks or Better machine, for example, this policy adds a quarter of a percent for the player, who's earning an extra five coins ($50) for every 4-of-a-kind, straight flush, and royal.

On one occasion, Sunset Station put in a $100 machine with a horrible pay schedule—it might have been 7/5 Jacks or Better. This game returns 96.15%, which means it costs about $19 to play *one hand*. But if you throw in a generous salting policy, this game gets real good real fast. Due to this policy at Sunset Station, players were getting an extra $500 for every 3-of-a-kind, straight, flush, full house, 4-of-a-kind, straight flush, or royal flush, making it one of the most lucrative games ever—a 107%+ return worth more than $35 per hand. If you could get 30 or more hands an hour (the low number is due to the frequent hand-pays), the hourly return exceeded $1,000!

Three professional players discovered the game and recognized the opportunity. To finance the $500-per-hand play, each chipped in $5,000 for the first try.

paid out more than an extra half-million dollars because of this recurring mistake. Although some unwitting players accidentally received some of the benefit of the casino's unintentional largesse, probably more than 75% went to a relatively few players, including me, who set out to systematically exploit the situation.

Was it unfair of us to exploit these mistakes? I'm sure many people would say yes. But I say, emphatically, *no.* When I'm in a casino, I'm trying to bring home the bacon. It's not my job to

---

... Lose-on Machine

One of the players sat down and started to play—and the machine turned cold. He played 10 hands, made a high pair twice and two pair once, and was down $3,000. He invested $500 more and his dealt low pair turned into 3-of-a-kind. This is normally worth $1,500, but when the casino put in five coins to start the new hand, it was actually worth $2,000.

When the player was paid, the floorman who inserted the five coins into the machine commented that a $500 bonus "seemed like an awful lot." The machine continued to eat money, but eventually the player made a straight. This is a $2,000 payoff—plus the $500 bonus. This time the floorman muttered a little louder. The player tipped him generously, hoping to keep the muttering under wraps. Apparently, though, the floorman made a phone call, because on the fourth hand-pay, the casino shut down the machine. The player received the $500 bonus the first three times. On the fourth jackpot, he received his normal $1,500 for the 3-of-a-kind and was told the machine was out of service.

All told, playing an impossible-to-lose-on machine, the group lost $3,000. They made no flushes or higher in the 40-or-so hands they played. Oh well. It happens. Had the casino kept the machine going, the players certainly would have won big. But the casino wised up in time and the players lost. Losing a grand apiece wasn't terrible, but when you compare the result to the expectation, the disappointment was.

tell the casino what machines to put on the floor, or what slot club system to run, or even not to leave buckets of dollar tokens lying around for the taking. The casino hires a lot of people to protect what it has and concoct ways to get more. Casinos are not churches, where everyone is on the same side. The casino sets out games on which it has the advantage and invites you to come in and try your luck. If you win, you get to keep the money. If you don't, which is usually the case, you leave your money behind.

Put another way, let's say you and I are playing poker. You've figured out that when I look upwards in a certain way, I'm bluffing. That's when you should bet the farm against me. Is it unfair for you to exploit what you've figured out? Most people would say, "Of course not." Winning poker players seek out these types of tells and attempt to exploit them. What we were doing at the MGM is no different. If I'd paid a slot technician to change the point structure, that would be a serious crime and, when caught, I'd likely learn about prison firsthand. But nothing of the sort happened. The slot techs, or whoever, made the mistakes, then discovered and fixed them, with no help from me either way.

I was surprised MGM management didn't discover that something was amiss throughout December. The Holiday Gift Shoppe ended on December 3 that year and HGS points were not awarded again until January 1. Players still got cashback and airline miles, but when you take .22% off of someone's return, usually he goes away. But we stayed and kept hammering. All through December we showed up 30 or so hours a week and ran large sums through the new machine.

We could no longer say we were working on cars for Shirley, Shirley's mom, and the girl at the office. That was over. All we could say now was that we really liked playing at the MGM and staying in the Mansion. This was the stone-cold truth, no doubt about it. But you'd think they would have figured out that something else was going on.

The First Forty Days and Forty Nights of 2001

At the start of 2001, I figured that if we played hard enough, there was no reason we couldn't earn at least a quarter-million dollars worth of HGS retail credit during the year. I also anticipated that we'd easily earn a $100,000 cash profit (coming from an expected loss of about $200,000 counterbalanced by cashback of $300,000) at the same time, not to mention a few million miles on American Airlines. If we did well during the promotions, some of which were very strong, we could make a lot more. And if the casino added new machines at the slot rate, these numbers would go up further. I believed these predictions were conservative, though they did depend on the MGM not changing its point structure, machines, or its stance toward our welcome.

Any casino that offers a situation where a knowledgeable player can realistically predict such success has a major problem. Shirley and I had done very well the previous year, but the casino didn't know *how* well, because on top of everything else, there was also a problem with their player-tracking system.

The system showed that Shirley and I had *lost* more than a half-million dollars in 2000. My bank account says that we were winners that year, but the fact that casino management didn't know this was good news as far as I was concerned. It was fine with me if management believed that I *talked* a good game and *wrote* about a good game, but, in fact, was a losing player. As long as they believed that, Shirley and I would be welcome forever.

How can a casino make such a big blunder? I don't know. Obviously, this casino is doing a lot of things correctly, as it's a highly profitable operation. But the slot management team seemed to be asleep at the wheel during this period. So many players were able to take advantage of so many mistakes that we began to think of the MGM as Santa Claus personified. Every day was Christmas! Shirley and I were among the few who were ultimately punished for our success, but we were by no means the only ones clever enough to figure out the blunders there.

So we continued to play from 20 to 30 hours a week solidly into

February. Shirley and I each averaged running more than $1 million through the machines at the MGM each and every week.

And the royals kept pouring in. By mid-February we'd hit twelve $20,000 royals, six $40,000 royals, plus two bigger ones that I'll tell you about soon. Not all at the MGM—the Venetian donated a few of these—but regardless of where we played, they just kept coming. I was somewhat overroyaled, and this year

---

The Road to ...

I have a friend, "Joe," who visits Las Vegas a couple times a year. Once, while Joe was watching us play, Shirley hit a $20,000 royal. The royal wasn't that unusual for us, but to Joe, a diesel mechanic, it looked like manna from heaven.

In addition, that night we were staying in a villa at the MGM Grand Mansion. Needless to say, Joe was amazed by the combo of a $20,000 royal and the Mansion.

The next day, Joe announced that he'd decided to become a professional gambler. Everything he'd seen the night before seemed like a pretty good way to live. And since I was used to teaching and had figured out how to do all of this, I could easily show him how.

"Okay, let's start at the beginning," I said. "How much money do you have that you can afford to gamble with?"

"None, really, although I did bring two hundred for this trip. I hope I don't lose it, though, because I really can't afford to."

I told him that he needed a reality check. Of the many skills necessary to be successful at gambling, two of the most basic are *obtaining* and *keeping* a bankroll. As long as I'd known him, Joe had demonstrated neither. He made a middling living and spent money as fast as it came in.

"Tell you what," I said. "If you can come up with a bankroll of ten thousand dollars in the next year, I'll teach you how to gamble successfully." If he was serious, getting the money together wouldn't be that difficult. If he wasn't, he would never succeed as a professional gambler anyway.

"How can I save that much money?"

Ruling out illegal methods, there are only two ways to do it:

Shirley was *way* overroyaled.

We weren't playing because of this success. We never assumed the royals would keep coming at this higher-than-average rate. Whether we've had more or fewer royals than average in the past has no bearing whatsoever on how many royals we will hit in the future. We were playing because of the numbers I've detailed—the cashback, HGS points, and air miles, plus all the comps.

... Becoming a Pro

Earn more or spend less. To earn more, he needed more hours on the job, a better job, or a second job. For a healthy 40-year-old with no family, working two jobs was manageable.

Spending less? People can adapt to having and spending *more* money almost instantly. Unfortunately, it's difficult for most people to learn to spend *less* money. We talked over the possibilities.

"Okay," he promised. "I can do all that. But do I really have to wait a year to start? What can I do *now*?"

"The best thing to do with your two hundred dollars," I replied, "is to keep it in your pocket. Until you know more, there's no intelligent bet you can make. This way, when you get home, your bankroll-accumulation program will have a two-hundred-dollar head start.

"Secondly, start studying. With a bankroll of ten grand, the games you'll play are Deuces Wild and 10/7 Double Bonus. Plan on spending fifty hours or so learning each game. It might not take you that long, but it takes many people considerably longer. And it doesn't take money to study. By the time you have the bankroll, you'll be well on your way to knowing what to do.

"You'll still have a lot to learn once you know how to play each hand, but until you obtain that basic knowledge and the minimum buy-in, you're dead in the water. Good luck. I'm rooting for you."

Joe was serious. It's taken him longer than a year, but he's still working at accumulating that $10,000 bankroll. And when he does, I'll be around to help him with all the information he needs.

Our Biggest Night Ever

February 12, 2001, was the night of the Espies at the MGM Grand Garden Arena. We had eight tickets to die for: Second-row seats in the second section. We kept two seats for ourselves and distributed the rest to business associates—one casino general manager, one publisher, and one video poker game designer—and their guests. We like to be able to entertain our friends and associates lavishly, albeit totally comped. Our faces were on television more than a dozen times. At the last minute, Shirley's son and fiancée came to town and we were able to obtain less glamorous tickets for them, too.

The Espies are the Academy Awards of sports, sponsored by ESPN. We'd seen Tiger Woods and Jack Nicklaus in the Mansion and dozens of football, basketball, and track and field notables on the casino floor. Trust me. Some of these guys are *big*. I read the sports pages enough that I recognized most of them. Sitting right up close with these superstar athletes is pretty awesome.

At the end of the show, we invited our guests to see our villa. One of the best parts of staying at the Mansion is showing it to others. Shirley never tires of giving tour after tour. And almost everyone who sees it says something like, "I can't believe a place this elegant and serene and peaceful exists right in the middle of Las Vegas. Incredible!"

After the tour, we decided to go down and play. We were quite a bit ahead that weekend and decided to take a $20,000 potshot on the big machines. I played the $25 machine. Shirley played the $100 machine, but from my vantage point I could see her every move. Shirley had now graduated to playing unsupervised on the 9/6 machines, but on the $100 machine, we both felt it right to have two pairs of eyes looking at every hand. These are stakes that make us nervous. Excited, to be sure, but nervous as well.

One of the couples with us at the Espies had hung around to watch. They play quarters and dollars themselves and it was exciting for them to watch someone play for these stakes.

We started with $4,000 in $25 coins and $6,000 in $100 coins. I watched Shirley play until her machine locked up, which happened every 3-of-a-kind ($1,500) or higher. While waiting for her to be paid (which usually only took a few minutes), I played the $25 machine and Shirley chatted with "Don" and "Donna" about the Espies, the Mansion, and about their impending trip to Hawaii.

About 15 minutes into this session, I hit a $100,000 royal flush. I sat quietly while Shirley, Don, and Donna chatted merrily away. I was wondering how long it would take any of them to notice.

It took almost 20 seconds. Donna noticed first and gasped. When Shirley figured out what had happened, she screamed. Don had seen a few $4,000 royal flushes before, but never anything bigger. He was thrilled for us.

Since the amounts of all hand-pay jackpots register in the cage area, the attendants came rushing out. Six-figure payoffs don't happen every day. Two floorpeople came over to shake my hand, while another kept calling, "Misdeal! Misdeal! Mistake! Mistake!" This was just her sense of humor. Shirley and I played there so often that we were essentially family to all of the employees. This "misdeal" noise was akin to teasing a favorite older brother. They were genuinely happy for us.

The rules at the MGM stipulate that a "chip check" be conducted before jackpots of $100,000 or higher can be paid. This means that slot technicians do some analysis to verify that the machine hasn't been tampered with. No problem. I'd wait until lions levitate for 100 G's. Besides, I was supervising Shirley on the $100 machine.

Actually, there turned out to be a problem. The machines were so new that they couldn't find whatever equipment it took to perform the chip check. So they had to phone whichever vice president was on call that night, who made the decision to go ahead and pay us. All the machines had been checked the previous weekend. Plus Shirley and I were well-known customers. So they gave us a check for $100,000 and reset the machine.

"So you're going to keep playing?" Don asked me.

"Sure. Why not?"

"Well," he said, "I thought the goal of gambling was to hit the big one. You did. You can't possibly top this. So why not leave?"

"I don't use today's score as any kind of barometer for when to stop. We're playing tonight because it's a good game. Plus, we both took a nap and are probably too excited to go to sleep anyway."

"Obviously, your theory is working. Hope it continues for you," Don responded. "Before we have to go, I want to thank you once more. Going to the Espies was the nicest thing that's happened to me for quite awhile."

"Not for me," I said.

"Really? You'd didn't think the show was great?"

"Of course it was. It's just that it can't be the nicest thing—because winning the hundred grand was nicer."

Don agreed with a smile and they left.

Shirley and I continued playing, taking all of our hand-pays in coin rather than cash. If Shirley hit a flush ($3,000), for example, we'd either take the money in $100 coins or $25 coins, depending on whose supply was lower.

Shirley hit four jacks ($12,500) and our stacks of tokens were quite high. And then the stacks went down to zero. I bought another $10,000 worth of coins and we agreed to quit if this went, "locking up" an $80,000 win. Shirley hit four 4s almost immediately, so we were "smokin' with tokens" again for awhile.

This wasn't a problem. The secure space between the $100 machines could accommodate hundreds of thousands of dollars worth of $100 coins, so we just kept stacking them up and pulling them down as the machines gobbled the tokens. At the end of the session, the staff would help carry them to the cage if necessary and we could sell them back all at once.

Fifteen minutes after Don and Donna left, Shirley started

with J♥T♥Q♥ and two small spades. I know which cards she held, because we have pictures of them—plus the K♥ and A♥ that arrived on the draw. Four hundred big ones! Shirley turned around and looked at me. Eyes open wide. Speechless.

I'd told the staff that if Shirley ever connected on the big royal flush, they'd all need new eardrums, she'd be screaming so loud. Turns out I was wrong. She didn't say a word for the first 15 seconds, then all she managed to whisper was, "Oh my God."

The staff yelled and screamed for us, and we heard "Misdeal! Mistake!" all over again. The same vice president was woken again (he probably hadn't gone back to sleep yet) and in 15 minutes or so we got a check for $400,000.

We just couldn't play much after that. Don was wrong about topping the $100,000 jackpot, but right about stopping. We'd hit the really big one and the evening was complete. My earlier $100,000 jackpot was as big as any previously in my life, but it didn't seem that big anymore. It certainly wasn't small, but in terms of what we were really after, it wasn't big enough to make us say "Wow! This is great!" When we hit the $400,000 a half-hour later, though, that *was* big enough.

We had wondered about whether we would ever hit the $400,000 royal. On that machine, factoring in all the hand pays, it probably takes an average of 200 hours of play to hit a royal. We'd played only 20 hours lifetime on that size machine. When you only play a few hours at a time, it's reasonable to expect that it would take a few years before hitting the royal, if it happened at all.

So we cashed out, left $2,000 in tips for the staff with hugs all around, and headed back to the Mansion. No way either of us could go to sleep, so it was time for a discussion about what to do with the money.

Getting nicer cars wasn't on the agenda. Shirley had a brand new minivan and we'd already earned more than $30,000 in HGS points that I was going to use for a new car in December.

Nor was a nicer house in the cards. Ours was only two years

old when we bought it less than a year before. Shirley had spent hundreds of hours and tens of thousands of dollars fixing it up just the way she wanted it, including an in-home office set-up for me. We owed about $200,000 on the house, so we decided to pay that off.

This wasn't an easy decision. We had an 8% mortgage and the stock market has historically gone up quite a bit more than 8% annually. So paying off the home will likely cost us some money. But it's also a security blanket. If things go badly in the gambling world, at least we'll have the house. This is especially important to Shirley, who may never feel comfortable with the swings. If she feels more secure, it's easier on me too.

We invested the other $300,000 in tax-free municipal bonds. Since most of our assets were in mutual or index funds, we figured that adding real estate and munis would balance our portfolio. We sought professional assistance in managing our assets a year later, but at that time we were on our own.

We knew we'd have a substantial tax liability for this half-million-dollar payday. Since we were already considerably ahead for the year, this $500,000 was fully taxable as ordinary income. Not a pleasant thought, but I could live with it. In fact, give me another half-mil and I'll happily pay taxes on that, too!

Several people asked me how I felt that night. Did I, for example, feel at the top of my game? Or really proud of Shirley? I kept thinking back to the line by Edward O. Thorp, author of *Beat the Dealer.* He wrote: "It isn't so much the money; it never has been. The big part of winning is being able to feel the way David must have felt when he killed Goliath." That night I felt like David.

Knowing the End is Near

The night of the half-million-dollar bonanza was our high point at the MGM. We played for another month and hit several more royals, including a dealt $60,000 royal for Shirley. But we lost more than we won. One of the reasons was that we went back to the $100 machine and tried for a repeat performance. As usual, I took the losses in stride. I knew we had a several-hundred-dollar per-hour edge and it was just a matter of time before we started to win again. As usual, Shirley was annoyed that we were no longer at our high point.

I also knew that $500,000 worth of royals in one night paid out to two people who were already way ahead is the type of information that gets kicked all the way upstairs. And whichever senior vice president learned that this much money had just gone out to us would certainly not be happy about it.

Of course, word got out among most of the professional players that Shirley and I were hammering away long hours and doing extremely well. Enough players had participated in the 2000 Holiday Gift Shoppe that the value of those points was widely understood. So other players decided to get theirs while the getting was good. The percentage of knowledgeable players increased. If we'd been the only ones hitting the 9/6 machines while everyone else toiled away at Double Double Bonus or short-pay Deuces Wild, the MGM would have made more than enough on the other games to pay us. But with so many strong players monopolizing the 9/6 machines, the casino had to be losing money on them.

And it wasn't only the machine losses. The plain fact was that they were giving away too much and had been for a long time. I knew the other shoe had to drop. What I didn't know was the nature of that shoe. Would the casino eliminate the 9/6 machines? Or the HGS? Or the air miles? Would it slash cashback? Would Shirley and I personally get booted?

Rumors were rampant. Several hosts shared information with their favorite customers, warning that "things" were going to "come down soon." Some of these rumors turned out to be realities. Others didn't. But they were contradictory, so we had no idea what would actually happen.

I figured this impending reaction would take place even if

we quit playing, so we might as well extract as much as we could before the game ended. We continued to play, but meanwhile I tried to hold off the inevitable by doing a special feature on the Holiday Gift Shoppe at the MGM Grand and Grazie Points at the Venetian for *Strictly Slots*.

I'll never know how much extra consideration I got because I was a writer. I was elected "Favorite Gaming Personality" in the 2001 "Best of Gaming" voting in *Casino Player* primarily on the popularity of the Bob and Shirley articles I wrote, and about half of them took place at the MGM. The readers liked the articles. The MGM staff liked the articles. Maybe it bought me an extra month or two.

It's easy to imagine that MGM management cut me some slack due to the publicity. I was allowed to win some, as long as it wasn't too much. "Too much," of course, was never clearly defined. And then, all of a sudden, it was an extra half-million. I'm speculating here, but perhaps management felt betrayed—as though my hitting the half-million violated our "understanding." If the executives did take this as a personal affront, it might explain many of their actions afterwards, including taking it out on the magazines I wrote for. There may be another explanation, but this is the one that seems most likely to me.

Facing the Inevitable

When Richard asked to have a talk with me (and Shirley) on March 15, I strongly suspected that I was about to hear the details of the second shoe dropping. Shirley had an appointment of some kind, so it was just Richard, Mary (our host, whom we both like, but who reports to Richard), and me.

I was told that two things were going to happen to *all* video poker players: first, no more premium status, and second, no more Holiday Gift Shoppe points.

As far as I was concerned, this was a reasonable thing for the MGM to do, although I suspected they'd find it still wasn't enough. After all, they continued to offer a .39% cash club with air miles at .10%, while their competition was offering a .33% cash club with no air miles. I wasn't happy with what I was told—I would have preferred that the gravy train keep rolling—but it made sense to me.

Richard presented the situation as though he were the messenger of a decision that had been made quite a few levels above him, so there was absolutely nothing for me to gain by arguing with him. He couldn't do anything about it and my future involvement with the MGM could be damaged by whatever I might say. I told Richard that I understood and would publish the information in the *Las Vegas Review-Journal*, in the Friday "Player's Edge" column.

That weekend the Venetian was sponsoring a promotion. There was considerable overlap between MGM and Venetian players, so I shared the MGM information with a few fellow pros. I wasn't angry. A casino cutting benefits is major news and since these benefits constitute part of the "salary" of players, it was like letting everyone know that they were facing a huge pay cut.

The news spread like wildfire. Almost immediately, a lot of players went back to the MGM and screamed about their benefits being cut without notice.

Now, curiously, MGM had two problems: one, a lot of irate video poker players; and two, a bizarre predicament that arose because it turned out that Richard had misled me. He'd told me that the new rules applied to *all* video poker players, when, in fact, they applied to only six. Whether he chose to give me the incorrect information on his own or on directions from above, I have no way of knowing. But whoever formulated the disinformation policy had no understanding of the extent of the grapevine among players. Within a day of our discussion, the MGM was deluged with angry players. Worse, the whole inaccurate story was about to be published in the newspaper (in good faith on my part—I had no idea I'd been fed a falsehood) and they didn't want that to happen.

Three days later I was called in to meet with Michael (a higher vice president than Richard) and Richard. Michael initiated the discussion by telling me he wanted to "clear up any misunderstandings."

I asked point blank, "Why did Richard lie to me?"

Michael hemmed and hawed, trying to sell me a story about how Richard and the other MGM staff were very fond of Shirley and me and didn't want to offend us, so he told the "white lie" to protect my sensitivities.

The look on my face told Michael I wasn't buying any of it. Michael invited Richard to join the discussion, but Richard wanted no part of it. "You're doing fine, Michael," he said and otherwise sat silently.

I asked who the other four players were. They refused to tell me, so as not to compromise their privacy. I responded, "What makes you think that the names Al, Bea, Charlie, and Dan are a secret? I just wanted to get a good idea of what 'clearing up misunderstandings' means to you. I've provided this casino with a lot of favorable publicity and I thought I at least deserved the truth." To say Michael and Richard were uncomfortable at the way this meeting was progressing would be an understatement.

It might sound strange that I refer to the vice presidents as Richard and Michael rather than Mr. Smith and Mr. Jones. But the truth is that Shirley and I had spent so much time around the MGM for 18 months, we were truly this familiar with these men and others in the casino's employ. There was a genuine affection. This was an awkward situation that we had to handle together, but for the most part it was handled amicably. Both knew I'd likely tell this story in print. Richard said that as long as the coverage was balanced, he wouldn't object to me writing about it. I told him that I had no intention of trashing the MGM and that I hoped that the restrictions could be lifted someday.

I also informed them politely that restricting six players wouldn't solve their problem. I didn't go into details; I wasn't in a very charitable mood at the time. But if a casino is giving away far too much, imposing relatively minor restrictions on players that make up a small percentage of the dollar action in the high-limit slot area won't go very far toward remedying the problem.

The reason I say the restrictions were "relatively minor" is that the MGM was still playable for me. We still had a small advantage with the .39% cashback and the air miles. We could also go to the promotions and earn comps. It wasn't as good as it had been, but it was still better than anyplace else on the Strip, other than the Venetian.

Dozens of other players who played every bit as well as we did were still getting the full complement of benefits. Still, these restrictions caused shock waves to ripple through the video poker community. We had our defenders, to be sure, while other people didn't give a hoot. But a lot of players were trying to figure out how this affected them. Should they back off and play less? Should they play harder, getting all they could before it was completely over? Were more restrictions on the horizon? It was even rumored that I would "name names" of other pros so I could get reinstated. (Never happened. Never will.)

All this, naturally, made MGM management uncomfortable. They wanted their customers to focus on the fun and excitement, rather than ask their hosts embarrassing questions about impending policy. Several players just stayed away.

I knew that restricting six players wouldn't give the MGM the results it wanted. That was something akin to sending a Band-Aid to do a tourniquet's job. On May 1, the MGM increased the video poker requirement to earn points of any sort from $8 to $10—a 25% across-the-board cut of cashback, HGS points, and airline miles. It was *still* more generous than average for the Strip, but considerably less than before. Had they implemented this reduction originally, instead of restricting Shirley and me, it would have cut our expected dollars per hour by $200 or so—sufficient to diminish our ardor significantly.

We could have continued playing after either the restrictions or the 25% cutback, but not both. When I tallied things up, I found that the casino would have an advantage on every bet we made, which was an intolerable playing condition for us. Ninety-nine percent-plus of all players accept the fact that the casino has the edge and if you want to gamble, you just have to live with it. We don't accept that. If we can't find a profitable opportunity in a casino, we don't play. Period.

I did write about my experience and the MGM's reaction in *Strictly Slots* magazine. The article I wrote was indeed balanced, at least in my opinion. It told the story that you've read here, and general managers from two different casinos called Jeffrey Compton and me to compliment us on how well the article presented the actual problems facing the casinos. Part of that article discussed what I considered an important sub-plot of this story: the fact that casinos could, and obviously now would, bar video poker players, much as they have barred skilled blackjack players for years. I wrote:

> *Whenever players are "backed off," especially high-profile players, rumors are rampant. Soon after the "short list" came out, there was talk of a "medium list" of fifteen or so other players that the MGM was considering taking action against. Now a lot of players are uneasy. Should they stay away? Should they play slot machines as "cover"? Will they also be penalized if they hit royals? Nobody knows.*

I don't know if Michael had a personal problem with it, but upper management at the MGM Grand had a cow. They went so far as to cancel advertising in *Strictly Slots* and other publications I wrote for. For these magazines, whose viability depends on casino advertising, it was a huge, totally unexpected, hit. A casino certainly has a right to choose where and how much to advertise, but I feel punishing *Strictly Slots* was unfair. This magazine had published six or eight Bob and Shirley stories, each of which presented the MGM in a positive light. The casino received substantial extra business because of these articles. The article about restricting players was neither inflammatory nor accusatory. With so many stories about Shirley and me playing at the MGM, it was necessary, I felt, to explain why these stories wouldn't be appearing anymore. I concluded the article as follows:

> *Players ask me if I am angry with the MGM for doing this. I think "disappointed" expresses it better. We liked playing there. A lot. We have very warm feelings for a number of the employees there. And we love the Mansion. I never had any agreement with the MGM that my writing about them would make me "bullet proof" in any respect, but I figured I was in a special-enough category that I would never be restricted. As it turned out I was wrong. But it was a very nice run and I'm sorry it is over.*

In June 2002, the airline frequent-flyer miles ended. The Holiday Gift Shoppe program survived, sort of, and is said to be continuing at least through 2003. In 2002, after I had stopped playing at the MGM, HGS points were devalued by about 40%. A lot of players had played all year long with a good-faith understanding regarding the value of HGS points, only to face a multi-thousand-dollar negative surprise. One player I know was told the rate he could trade the points in for a new car was being adjusted downward because he was an "advantage player." What will these points be worth in 2003 and beyond? I haven't a clue.

In fall 2002, the MGM Director's Club was merged into the MGM Mirage Player's Club. Early indications are that this will not be good for the knowledgeable player. The Mirage has stopped allowing known skilled players to attend many of its special events. (This has been the policy at Treasure Island for a number of years, and when the vice president responsible for this policy was transferred to the Mirage, he brought the policy with him.) More of the same is expected at the Golden Nugget when it joins the MGM Mirage Players Club. This is an unfortunate development for the player community.

The Venetian Dances to its Own Drummer

The Venetian may be the second-most elegant resort in Las Vegas, behind Bellagio. And that's quite an accomplishment. Even tenth place in Las Vegas is very nice. Second place is truly magnificent.

Unlike most Vegas pleasure palaces, the Venetian is pri-marily a resort (with a convention center, shopping mall, superb dining, and gorgeous artwork) that also happens to have a casino attached. Most other megaresorts are casinos first and have hotels, restaurants, and other amenities intended to support the casino. This isn't just semantics; it's a completely differently philosophy.

If you try to get a food or room comp at the Venetian, you'll find that it takes considerably more play than it would at any other casino. If you attend one of its special events, be prepared for the rules to change (usually to the detriment of the players) by the time you arrive. This has happened at the Venetian more often than at any casino I've ever been at. The closer I look at this operation, the more I believe that management views its casino as an underperforming nuisance.

When the Venetian opened, it had a large number of 9/6 Jacks or Better machines in denominations from 50¢ to $100, with a .50% cash slot club. This put them right near the top of places to play video poker, especially if you valued elegance and liked eating in five-star restaurants. Quarter and dollar players could get a better financial deal at the locals casinos, but let's face it, the rooms, food, and other amenities at the Gold Coast or Santa Fe Station are simply not in the same league as those at the best megaresorts on the Strip.

So when the Venetian opened its doors, many players came to roost. In the first couple of months, three players hit $100,000 royal flushes on $25 machines. Not a big surprise. Just like lower-denomination machines with the same schedules, these machines will yield a royal every 40,000 hands or so and whoever is sitting there at the time will reap the benefit. But the Venetian promptly eliminated the slot club privileges of all three players!

I was not affected directly by this, but I sought an audience with Venetian executives to let them know that this was a bad idea. As a video poker writer, I felt it was my duty to speak up. I met with three executives. One was the general manager, one was in charge of slot operations, and the third was in charge of slot marketing. I told them that restricting players was a short-sighted policy. If a $100,000 jackpot was going to cause them that much anxiety, then they should remove all $25-and-higher machines. Earning the reputation of "hit a royal at the Venetian and get barred" wouldn't do them any good.

They listened to what I said. Three months later, at least two of the players were welcomed back, although a lot had happened in the interim (including at least one of the players protesting to Gaming Control). I can't say whether my efforts had anything to do with their reinstatement or not. One of the previously restricted players hit two $100,000 royals in the first hour or so on his first trip back. He was never forgiven for this. When the Venetian restricted dozens of players a year later (including Shirley and me), this player got re-restricted.

Assume someone plays 200,000 hands at 9/6 Jacks or Better. Since a royal flush occurs once in 40,000 hands, he will hit five royals on average. But there's only a 17.5% chance of hitting *exactly* five royals. There's also a 1.8% chance of hitting 10 royals and a 0.6% chance of hitting zero royals.

This isn't real complicated. The effect is similar to a bell-shaped curve. Many players would hit four or five royals with this much play. A few would hit more than that. A few would hit none at all. This is the everyday mathematics of video poker.

Based on their actions, however, I have to assume that the Venetian management made the following assumption: The player who hit 10 royals over this time period is a more formidable opponent than the player who hit zero royals. This is ludicrous.

The player who hit zero royals might be an even better player than the one who hit 10 royals. They couldn't know. A sample of 200,000 hands is much too small to make that determination accurately. In the next 200,000 hands, the player who hit zero royals before has just as good a chance to hit 10 royals as the other player. *When* royals occur is largely luck and the guy who got the most last month may or may not be the guy who gets the most this month.

My personal fate was sealed at the Venetian when I was playing $5 Five Play and was dealt a $100,000 royal flush. As you know, being dealt a royal requires no skill whatsoever. It's merely being in the right place at the right time. In my seven years of play, I've had eight dealt royals, which is more a statement of how many hands I've played than anything else. I'd been moderately ahead before and this put me *way* ahead—which was unforgivable at this casino.

Shirley was a modest loser at the Venetian until one night she collected three $20,000 royals playing a $5 Five Play. First, she was dealt A♣K♣J♣T♣5♥. She held the clubs (of course!) and the Q♣ came out twice. Players on these machines often get one or more of these 4-to-the-royal hands per session. Each time you start from this position, you have an 89.7% chance of getting zero royals, a 9.8% chance of getting exactly one royal, a 0.4% chance of getting two royals, and almost no chance of getting three, four, or five. This time, the 0.4% chance came in.

A half-hour later she got another royal in clubs. She was playing the way she always does. But this night the royals came out—again, unforgivable at the Venetian.

The restrictions at the Venetian were threefold. First, the cashback rate was reduced by a third, from .43% to .29%. (They had already reduced the return since opening. Not so unusual. Many casinos adjust their slot clubs periodically.) Second, we could no longer earn Grazie Points. Similar to the HGS points at the MGM, Grazie Points at the Venetian were worth about .12% of coin-in. And third, there were no more invitations to special events. "But if you still wish to play here, you're welcome to do so," we were assured. Yeah, right.

Venetian management told me that well over a dozen players

had been similarly restricted. But not all players received the same treatment. Some were no longer invited to special events, but were otherwise unrestricted. The player who made the egregious mistake of hitting three $100,000 royals had all cashback, comp, and invitation privileges revoked. But he, too, was welcome to continue to play. Although this sounds like a heavier penalty than what Shirley and I received and was clearly intended to be, both restrictions had the identical result: They dissuaded us from ever playing at this casino as long as the restrictions were in effect.

Winnings at the Venetian contributed about $180,000 or so to our million-dollar six months. Most of it was my dealt royal and Shirley's three-royals-in-one-night bonanza. Since this took place, the Venetian slot club has been lowered more and most of the 9/6 Jacks machines have been removed. As of this writing, it remains a barely acceptable place to play—as long as you don't wear out your welcome.

And be extra careful of those special events. In spring 2002, several Venetian employees were accused of rigging a drawing in favor of an Oriental high roller in an invitational giveaway—somewhat ironic given the actions and policies described above. Gaming Control got involved and at least a few of the Venetian's high-level employees were fired. When I asked several high-limit players if they were surprised that the Venetian rigged drawings, every one of them said that they weren't surprised at all.

Let's Be Fair

As of this writing in mid-2002, the MGM is still the best place in Las Vegas to play high-stakes video poker—assuming you're not on the restricted list. Most of its employees are excellent and the casino remains world-class for amenities. Because of our success there, today Shirley and I enjoy a standard of living that is far beyond what we ever did previously.

Let's look at the mistakes that MGM made.

Paying the wrong amount of slot club benefits on the highest-stakes machines was an error that had big-time consequences and at least one slot-department vice president is no longer there.

The MGM offered more promotions and slot club benefits (all at once) than was prudent. This is largely a problem of casino executives not understanding the mathematics of video poker. Casinos tend to look at averages, as in: "The average house hold percentage is 6% and this new promotion gives the players an extra .2%. This is not such a big deal."

Intelligent players, on the other hand, look at how the promotions affect individual games, as in: "I'm currently playing a game worth 100.1% including all the bells and whistles. If they give me .2% more, it effectively triples my return. This is wonderful."

Intelligent players don't even go near the games that account for the average house hold. They play only the highest-returning games in the house. Being confused on this point is not unique to MGM management. People inventing new promotions are often right-brained and creative, while the best video poker players often are left-brained nerds.

When the MGM got burned, they restricted the people they felt caused the problem. This is a natural reaction, perhaps. My view is that their own ineptitude caused the problem. They felt otherwise. That's understandable.

When the restrictions came down, at least one MGM executive didn't level with me. That, again, is not so hard to understand. The restrictions were enforced in reaction to the casino taking a hit. The vice presidents I dealt with couldn't know at that time whether or not they would also end up being dismissed in the fallout. They were under a considerable amount of stress and sometimes things said under those conditions are not well thought-out. The majority of my dealings with both Michael and Richard were professional and appropriate. I bear them no ill will.

There was a reason that we played at the MGM and the Venetian: Their games were better than every place else. The reason I don't write Bob-and-Shirley stories about playing at

Caesars Palace, for example, is because it doesn't have profitable games, so we don't go there. Had my success story taken place a few years earlier, likely there would be stories from Caesars Palace and more stories from the Mirage and Treasure Island. These casinos had a very beatable game in the late 1990s. But I didn't have a sufficient bankroll then, so my biggest adventure took place elsewhere. Who's to say where the best adventures will lie in the years to come?

Yes, Shirley and I are enjoying the results of this wild ride. For Shirley, one of the best things about it was getting to know the people at the MGM. For our money, the MGM and the Golden Nugget have the friendliest staffs in town. But for me, the best part was the ride itself. I enjoy the battle. Figuring out how to wage the war—not knowing how it'll all turn out—then going out and executing that battle plan is very exciting. This particular war is over for us. You could say we won it. Certainly, winning is a good thing, but I miss the war.

Finally, Shirley's and my overriding emotion is one of gratitude toward both MGM and the Venetian. They presented us with an opportunity of a lifetime. We have no regrets. Garth Brooks sings a song called "The Dance," about the pain of a loved one dying balanced by the joy of being with the loved one earlier. In many ways it parallels what Shirley and I went through. Using the metaphor of a dance, Brooks wonders if he would have gone through with the dance had he known how much it would hurt when it was over. In the song, Brooks concludes that he'd gladly take the pain, because to give up the pain would mean he'd have had to give up the dance, and the dance was too wonderful for that.

That's the way it is for us. We're not in pain, but we're disappointed it's over. And we had an absolutely wonderful dance.

Part Five

Winning is a Process, Not an Event

Shirley's and my million-dollar six months are over. It would greatly surprise us both if we ever have such a run of good fortune again. I'm frequently asked how much of the win was luck and how much was skill.

I can't give you exact percentages on that. Every royal is lucky. Big royals are luckier. Discovering lucrative casino mistakes also requires a large amount of luck. If you look at the specific events of those six months, yes, a lot of luck was involved. But if you look at the pattern of winning year after year, there must have been a lot of skill there, too.

When people refer to "luck," they're usually citing specific events, such as, "Hitting three royals on the same day was very lucky." I don't believe that winning is a single event. I believe it's a process made up of zillions of events. Whatever those three royals paid will all be squandered back—unless you have a winning process to back them up. I'm so confident of this that I'm willing to bet a large amount of money that I'll be a gambling winner in at least four out of the next five years—starting from whenever the first bet is made. And I further believe that no sensible person would bet against me on this.

The reason I am so confident is that I understand the winning process—and always play within this understanding. In fact, anyone who understands the process and proceeds accordingly will also win at gambling. I'll go over that process here, which will also serve as a review and a summation of the book.

• Obtain a bankroll and keep it. This is critical. You have to be willing to do anything legal to get money, then hoard it once you have it. There will always be pressure on you to spend what you have. Many feel that since you can't take money with you when you die, you might as well spend it while you're living. I agree with this. However, since you don't know how long you will live, you must keep a sufficient bankroll for as long as you intend to play. I intend to play as long as I'm mentally capable, which probably means I'll die with my bankroll intact.

• Learn the games as if your life depended on it. Your bankroll is not as important as your life, but the player whose goal is to learn the game perfectly does a lot better than the player whose goal is to learn the game "well enough."

• Practice on a computer. This is actually a corollary of the previous paragraph, because you can't learn the games perfectly without using a computer. People who tell me that they're computer illiterate and too old to learn how to use one are simultaneously telling me that they are too old to learn how to win at video poker.

• Learn to evaluate slot clubs and promotions. Do most of your playing during double points and other promotions. Many casinos have numerous promotions going on at once. Some (like half-price margaritas on Tuesday nights) will not fit in with winning, but many will.

• Know at least three or four different games well. Your primary games will be determined by what exists at the casinos you frequent. But when a good situation arises, you have to be ready to jump on it. If a particularly juicy promotion is good only for Double Bonus and you don't know that game, the promotion is useless to you.

• Never play any game where the house has the advantage, unless you recognize the play as strictly recreational and keep it in moderation. People pay to go bowling or to the movies, for example, so spending a few dollars to enjoy a few hours of nickel slots can be viewed in the same light. But playing slots or craps for significant stakes (however that's defined for you), or for extended periods of time, will destroy a bankroll.

• Understand the swings of the games. Know that you'll have more losing sessions than winning sessions. Either learn to deal with this or take on another hobby.

• Bet within your bankroll. My three-to-five-royals rule of thumb is crude, but serves well enough as an easy-to-remember guideline. If you're over-betting your bankroll, set a firm stop-loss restriction beforehand and stick to it.

• Never play while intoxicated, overly tired, angry, or otherwise not at your best. The machines are always playing their best game. It's a nip and tuck contest when you're at your best. When you're not, you'll take the worst of it.

• Review the strategies regularly. Even if you knew a strategy perfectly three months ago, the likelihood is that you've forgotten some of the obscure cases unless you've gone over them recently.

• Read. Most casino locations have a local publication with coupons and information of various sorts. Many locations have columnists with useful information. In Las Vegas as I write this, the best two sources are Jeffrey Compton and myself in the Friday "Neon" section of the *Las Vegas Review-Journal* (reprinted at www. reviewjournal.com) and Jean Scott in her weekly "Frugal Fridays" column at www.lasvegasadvisor.com.

I write columns in *Strictly Slots, Casino Player, Gambling Times, Jackpot!, Southern California Gaming Guide,* and online at www.casino gaming.com. Skip Hughes has *Video Poker Player* and he also presents good information in his monthly contributions to the *Las Vegas Advisor.* Other knowledgeable writers continue to show up.

• Participate in, or at least monitor occasionally, Internet video poker chat groups and mail lists. The oldest is vp-mail (the Skip Hughes Group), but it's only available to subscribers to Skip's www.vphomepage.com service. There's currently a quality free group at vpfree@yahoogroups.com. Others may arise.

• Set aside a few hours every trip to scout. Casinos change all the time. To find the really good opportunities, you have to go looking. If everyone on the Web is talking about a certain play, it might be good, but it's not great or probably won't last long. (When the word gets out, it's standing-room-only at the casino. Casinos will notice and address the situation, usually by diminishing the promotion.) The really great plays are kept quiet by those who discover them.

• Maintain your health. Playing long hours is grueling. Do what it takes in order to be able to survive it.

• Evaluate whether you're keeping your edge. There are people who could play a winning game a year ago, but can't today. Whether you're ahead or behind over the past six months is an important statistic. If you're behind, it might be that you've been unlucky, but it's more likely that you aren't playing a winning game. The edge you have playing video poker is, at best, very small. Since casinos keep making adjustments to increase their profits, you have to be making adjustments, too, or you'll be left behind.

• When you find a good situation, play it for as long as you can. There is always a chance of "killing the golden goose" by over-playing a good situation, but that risk is usually minimal unless you're playing for very large stakes.

• Enjoy yourself. Very few of us have managed to make a good living doing what we most enjoy. But it's possible to do and a worthy goal to pursue. If video poker ever becomes drudgery to you, I strongly advise you to find something else to do with the rest of your life.

Index of Additions

The expanded explanations that appear in boxes throughout this book fall into three categories: Technical, Strategic, and General. Technical additions contain mathematical and statistical information relative to video poker. Strategic additions discuss playing and related psychological strategies that can be applied to enhance results. General additions are predominantly anecdotal in nature, though they convey valuable lessons and insight.

Bob Dancer and Liam W. Daily's
Video Poker Strategy Cards

These are the best video poker strategy cards ever developed. Four strategy levels take you from beginner to advanced, all on one six-panel tri-fold pocket-sized card. The "Beginner" strategies alone will improve almost anyone's play, while those who graduate to the "Advanced" strategies will be playing virtually as accurately as a computer. Carry the cards in your shirt pocket and check 'em when you need 'em.

Double Bonus	Double Double Bonus	8/5 Bonus Poker
$6.95	$6.95	$6.95
Jacks or Better	Joker Wild Kings or Better	Joker Wild 2-Pair
$6.95	$6.95	$6.95
Full Pay Deuces Wild	NSU Deuces Wild	Pick 'Em Poker
$6.95	$6.95	$6.95

Carry these cards with you into the casinos and refer to them while you play. Never misplay a video poker hand again!

BUY THE SET AND SAVE!
All nine cards for only $50

To order, call 1-800-244-2224
or log on to www.ShopLVA.com

Want More Bob Dancer?
How About His New How-to-Book!

As you no doubt know by now, after reading his *Million Dollar Video Poker*, Bob Dancer is the world's number-one video poker expert and teacher. Now, after years of creating the industry standards in video poker reports, strategy cards, and software, Dancer has written the quint-essential beginner's guide on the game.

Video Poker for the Intelligent Beginner is a how-to-win blueprint for players seeking the fast track to the upper levels of this beatable game. First, you'll master the techniques for finding and identifying the highest-returning games; then you'll learn how to generate, understand, and implement the computer-perfect strategies that yield the ultimate goal: monetary profit!

Additionally, *Video Poker for the Intelligent Beginner* imparts Dancer's professional insight regarding the game's many nuances and related considerations—including in-depth coverage of slot clubs, casino promotions, progressives, team play, scouting, and tournaments. PLUS, this is the first book to explain in detail how Dancer's powerful *Video Poker for Winners!* software can be employed to solve previously unanswered questions about bankroll needs, promotions analysis, and profit potential.

There's no need to say it again, but we will. Bob Dancer is the best. Now you can know what he knows about the most exploitable gambling game of them all.

Plus, *Video Poker for the Intelligent Beginner* is the perfect companion to the bestselling software, *Video Poker for Winners.*

To order, call 1-800-244-2224
or log on to www.ShopLVA.com

Visit
LasVegasAdvisor.com
for all the latest on
gambling and Las Vegas

Free features include:

- Articles and ongoing updates on gambling.

- Tournament listings and articles.

- Up-to-the-minute Las Vegas gambling promotion announcements.

- Question of the Day—In-depth answers to gambling and Las Vegas related queries.

- Active message boards with discussions on blackjack, sports betting, poker, and more!

Become a *Las Vegas Advisor* Member and get our exclusive coupons and members-only discounts.